The Ryder Cup

The Ryder Cup

AN ILLUSTRATED HISTORY

Dale Concannon

Aurum

First published in Great Britain
2001 by Aurum Press Ltd
25 Bedford Avenue, London WC1B 3AT
www.aurumpress.co.uk

This illustrated edition first published 2006

A catalogue record for this book is available from the British Library.

ISBN 1 84513 171 1

10 9 8 7 6 5 4 3 2 1

2010 2009 2008 2007 2006

Project managed by Anne McDowall
Text design by Ashley Western
Layout designed by Rich Carr
Colour reproduction by Classicscan, Singapore
Printed and bound by MKT Print, Slovenia

Contents

	Introduction	6
1	Humble Beginnings: The Origins of the Ryder Cup	10
2	First Blood to Uncle Sam – *1927*	16
3	Britain Hits Back Twice – *1929–33*	22
4	An Unwelcome Break – *1935–37*	34
5	The Hogan Era – *1947–51*	42
6	False Dawn – *1953*	54
7	Swings and Roundabouts – *1955–57*	60
8	A Non Contest – *1959–63*	70
9	America Brings Out the Big Guns – *1965–67*	84
10	Pushed to the Limit – *1969–75*	94
11	Changing Times – *1977–81*	108
12	Enter Tony Jacklin – *1983–89*	120
13	The War on the Shore – *1991*	142
14	Building Bridges – *1993*	148
15	From Oak Hill to Choke Hill for the USA – *1995*	162
16	Seve Reigns in Spain – *1997*	170
17	The Battle of Brookline – *1999*	178
18	Strange Gets the Belfry Blues – *2002*	186
19	Europe Slays the Monster at Oakland Hills – *2004*	194
	Records	204
	Index	219
	Acknowledgments	224

Introduction

BY DALE CONCANNON

From humble beginnings, the Ryder Cup has evolved into one of the great sporting occasions of the modern era. Played since the bygone days of hickory shafts and woollen plus-fours, these dramatic head-to-head encounters between the best golfers of Europe and the United States have captured the imagination of sport lovers everywhere. Producing some of the most memorable moments in the history of golf, the Ryder Cup is unsurpassed for drama and excitement.

My own first memory of the Ryder Cup dates back to a fresh September day in 1977. Barely out of short trousers, I had made my way up to Royal Lytham and St Annes to watch Britain's best do battle with the might USA. It was my first experience of big-time golf. I had been to a few professional tournaments before, but nothing like this. It seemed wherever I turned there was some golfing superstar to be found either practising, playing or just walking around. Within minutes of arriving, I had counted six famous faces! There were Lanny Wadkins, Hale Irwin and Tony Jacklin on the putting green; Lou Graham was with his wife on the clubhouse steps; US Open champion Jerry McGee was talking to a journalist, while Brian Barnes stood nearby, banging his pipe on the heel of his golf shoes.

For five wonderful days I wandered around opened-mouthed, collecting memories as I went. In between the foursome and fourball matches I would head off to the practice putting green, hoping to catch a close-up glimpse of Nicklaus or Watson. Then came the obligatory pilgrimage to the practice ground one last time before leaving. There I would lean up against a picket fence and watch some of the greatest golfers in the world smash drive after drive into the leaden sky. What better way to end the day than this, I thought.

Like most youngsters, confirming a sighting with an autograph was the main priority. Earlier in the week my total was seven. By Saturday it had risen to twelve, but still no 'Tom Watson'. Then came a moment that has remained with me ever since. Having watched Watson and Hubert Green defeat Barnes and Horton by 5 and 4, my elusive prey set off for the clubhouse with his caddie, Alfie Fyles, trailing a few paces behind. (Back then players were expected to make their own way back, unlike today where a chauffeur-driven golf cart would be waiting for them.) Fleet of foot, I caught up with the great man, offered him a pen and asked for his signature. Smiling, he duly signed my book before asking me where I was from and what handicap I played off. I told him and, before I knew it, we were strolling unhindered for twenty minutes or so. On reaching the clubhouse he gestured towards his caddie for a golf ball and a few tees, which he handed over as a gift. Afterwards I had to keep reminding myself that this was the number one golfer in the world, the man who had vanquished the 'Golden Bear' in the Open Championship at Turnberry just two months earlier.

Some years later I had the opportunity to interview Tom Watson about his life and career and reminded him of the incident. He smiled indulgently, checked his watch and politely asked if the interview was over. So much for nostalgia, I thought. That said, this is just one of a number of memories the Ryder Cup inspires in me. As someone who writes about the game for a living, I have been fortunate to attend many Ryder Cup matches over the past two decades or more. So when I started putting together material for this book, I did not intend merely to assemble a dry collection of historical facts and figures. For me, the Ryder Cup is about passion and pride, and with each match surpassing the last in drama, excitement and, in some cases, controversy, this is a story I have long wanted to write. I hope it is also a story you will want to read.

1

Humble Beginnings: The Origins of the Ryder Cup

Today we have the Ryder Cup, though it might just as easily have been known as the Ross Cup, the Hartnett Cup or even the Sylvanus P. Jermain Cup.

The idea to stage an international challenge match between teams of professional golfers from Britain and the United States was not a new one. While details are sketchy, the man credited with the original concept was Ohio businessman S.P. Jermain. Instrumental in inviting English professionals Harry Vardon and Edward Ray to compete in the 1920 US Open at his home club of Inverness, he believed that an international match between these two great golfing nations should be encouraged. Aware of this, Walter Ross, President of the Nickel Plate Railroad Company in Cleveland, even offered to pay for a trophy.

That same year, American golf star Walter Hagen put his considerable weight behind the idea and was enthusiastically backed by James Harnett, circulation manager of *Golf Illustrated* magazine in New York. Looking to increase his readership figures, he began raising the necessary funds to send a representative American side over to Britain, but came up short of his target despite a blaze of publicity. Consequently a meeting was hastily convened with the United States Professional Golfers' Association on 15 December, at

which it was proposed that Harnett be advanced the money he needed.

Then came the problem about who would play. With few American-born players of any real quality, it was decided that British professionals working in the United States should be eligible to play for their newly adopted country. Unfortunately, this was like a red rag to a bull for retiring PGA president John Mackie. Believing it was little more than a gimmick dreamt up by immigrant British pros looking to get a 'free' trip home, he opposed the idea at every turn. Despite his vocal opposition, the motion was eventually passed, but with one proviso: foreign-born professionals who wanted to play for the American side had to have lived in the United States for no less than five years and intended to become US citizens.

With each player offered $1000 to cover expenses, the match was given the green light; and while the Ryder Cup itself was still seven years' distant, the idea behind what has become the most eagerly contested team event in world golf had been born.

Scheduled for 6 June 1921, the match was to be played over the recently opened Kings Course at Gleneagles in Perthshire, Scotland. Having arrived in Southampton a week earlier, the American team made their way to Glasgow by sleeper train. With the magnificent hotel still under construction, accommodation was surprisingly crude, consisting of five railway carriages moved into the sidings at the railway station near Auchtermuchty, and players were forced to fetch and carry their own water for much of the week. The 'international challenge match' was run in conjunction with a much larger tournament known as the Glasgow Herald 1000 Guineas – a grand affair with a huge prize fund on offer – and the promoters had little difficulty in attracting the top names in British golf, including six-time Open Champion Harry Vardon.

Along with his old rivals James Braid and J.H. Taylor, Vardon was scheduled to play in the ten-man British team along with Ted Ray, Abe Mitchell, Josh Taylor, James Ockendon, James Sherlock, Arthur Havers and George Duncan. (In truth, without Vardon's participation it was possible the match might not have happened at all.) Coming just three weeks after a team of American amateurs had defeated their British counterparts 9–3 at Royal Liverpool, it was hoped that the match would restore national pride; sadly, enthusiasm for it was fairly limited.

The match was played the day after the 1000 Guineas tournament and the crowds that had flocked to see the in-form Duncan pick up the first prize of £160 had virtually disappeared by the time the international challenge got underway. The press and public alike had a point in considering it little more than an elaborate exhibition match. Apart from Walter Hagen – who still had to make his mark in Britain despite being a two-time US Open winner – the American team hardly sparkled with talent. Captained by Emmett French and including unknown players such as Clarence Hackney and 'Wild Bill' Mehlhorn, the nearest it came to 'star' players were Scottish exiles Jock Hutchison and Fred McLeod. Therefore it came as no surprise when the outspoken professional Andrew Kirkaldy predicted a complete whitewash. 'It will be too one-sided', he said. 'The Americans haven't a chance.'

As always, the sage of St Andrews was proved right. Great Britain trounced the Americans 9–3 with three matches halved. After the match, commemorative gold medals were presented to all the players courtesy of the *Glasgow Herald*, but no one suggested that it become a regular event. Or, if they did, no one listened. (Interestingly, the US ambassador had driven up to

Above: A rare photograph of the British team that faced America in the international challenge match at Gleneagles in 1921. The line-up included legendary champions Harry Vardon (back row, second from left) and J.H. Taylor (sitting, centre), both of whom were considered too old to play by the time the inaugural Ryder Cup match was played at Worcester six years later.

Scotland after being invited to make the presentation. Anticipating an American victory, he then beat a hasty retreat back to London on hearing that his team had lost!)

Quite simply, the experiment had failed. Considering it little more than a crude exhibition match, crowds were sparse and the atmosphere muted. The teams hardly socialized and even the course at Gleneagles came in for some criticism for its ragged fairways and unkempt greens. 'The sand used in the bunkers is of the wrong type', said *The Times* golf correspondent, Bernard Darwin, 'being far too gritty and full of shells'.

Despite the carping criticism the contest attracted from the press, Hagen never quite gave up on the idea, and when the opportunity arose again six years later to play in another Britain versus America match, he gladly accepted. It would also be the first time that he would encounter a seed merchant from St Albans called Sam Ryder.

Samuel A. Ryder was a successful businessman who made his fortune selling packets of seeds through the post for a penny. Born in March 1858, the son of a Manchester corn merchant, Ryder left the family firm at a young age and moved south to St Albans, 30 miles north of London. Along with his younger brother,

Above: Samuel Ryder (right) and Abe Mitchell at Verulum Golf Club in 1926. The St Albans seed merchant employed Mitchell as his personal tutor when it was suggested that he take up golf for his health and the pair remained close friends for many years. The figure of Abe Mitchell still adorns the lid of the trophy played for by Europe and the USA.

of 1909 to come to his mansion six days a week to give him lessons (a deeply religious man, he never played golf on the Sabbath). Playing off an unofficial handicap of 6, he felt sufficiently confident to join nearby Verulum a year later. Twelve months after that he was elected Club Captain, a post he was to hold in 1926 and 1927.

In 1923, Ryder took his interest in golf one stage further when his Heath and Heather Company sponsored a professional tournament, held at Verulum –the first of seven events that he and his brother James would sponsor between 1923 and 1925. He stunned everyone by paying all competitors an appearance fee of £5, with £50 going to the winner. Attracting such star names as Harry Vardon, James Braid, George Duncan and Sandy Herd, the tournament was eventually won by Arthur Havers, fresh from his Open victory at Troon. Havers' prize was only £25 less than he got for winning the most famous title in golf!

One of the professionals competing in the event was Englishman Abe Mitchell. A shy, courteous man, Mitchell supplemented his relatively meagre existence as club pro at North Foreland Golf Club with exhibition matches and the occasional tournament. The two men became friends, and in December 1925, Ryder offered Mitchell a three-year contract at the princely sum of £500 per year to become his personal tutor. Adding £250 to cover his tournament expenses, Ryder hoped that by freeing him from any club responsibilities Mitchell would be able to concentrate on winning the Open. Sadly, he was never to realize this dream and he is known as the best British golfer never to win it.

Mitchell was also instrumental in sparking Ryder's interest in the professional game over the coming years. By the mid-1920s, the golden era of Vardon, Braid and Taylor was over, but dashing young professionals like George Duncan had emerged and British golf was increasingly buoyant in the face of strong American opposition. The Open Championship had proved an intriguing battleground, as British and American professionals attempted to get the upper hand. With Hagen winning twice, in 1922 and 1924, 'home' players had hit back, with victories for Duncan in 1920 and Arthur Havers in 1923. Not surprisingly, clubhouse talk often revolved around who was the stronger golfing nation. The first opportunity to find the answer came at Wentworth in 1926. Not surprisingly, Samuel Ryder would be involved.

James, he formed the Heath and Heather Seed Company in 1898 before branching out into Ryder and Son. A tall slender man, who hid a mischievous smile beneath a bushy moustache, Ryder was a tireless worker. A pillar of the local community in later life, he not only maintained close ties with his own business but also served as Town Mayor, Justice of the Peace and church deacon. Indeed, it was following advice from his church minister, the Reverend Francis Wheeler, that he reluctantly took up golf at the relatively advanced age of fifty.

Suffering from ill health, Ryder was forced to give up his first love of cricket and decided to play golf in preference to bowls. Never one who did things by halves, he hired local club pro John Hill in the spring

1926 The 'Lost' Ryder Cup

WENTWORTH GOLF CLUB, SURREY, ENGLAND

4–5 JUNE

Although the history books show that the Ryder Cup began in 1927 in Worcester, Massachusetts, some people allege that it actually began one year earlier at Wentworth. So what is the truth?

The story goes that an informal match was played between British and American professionals in June 1926. It was a fairly relaxed affair, in which the home team dusted off their opponents by 13½–1½, then retired to the clubhouse for champagne and sandwiches. Little more than an interested spectator, Ryder was said to have marvelled at the camaraderie shown by the players before announcing 'we must do this again!' Agreeing to provide a trophy, he commissioned London silversmiths Mappin and Web to make a golden chalice adorned with the figure of Abe Mitchell. A year later, the two teams got together in Worcester, Massachusetts, to play for Sam Ryder's Cup – and the biennial match was born.

The truth, however, is a little different and a lot more complex.

With entries to the 1926 Open at Royal Lytham and St Annes oversubscribed, the Royal and Ancient decided to hold three regional pre-qualifying events at Sunningdale in Surrey, St Anne's Old in Lancashire and Western Gailes in Glasgow. Announcing their decision at the end of 1925, it meant that Sunningdale had been chosen to host the dozen or so American players – including the great Bobby Jones – that were expected to arrive in Southampton a week earlier. Ultimately, it was this decision that would prove the trigger for the *first* Ryder Cup match.

Early in 1926 an invitation had gone out asking if a representative team of American professionals wanted to take part in an international match against their British counterparts at nearby Wentworth. Never one to turn down a challenge, Hagen had accepted on behalf of his countrymen and the match was set for Friday 4 and Saturday 5 June.

Above: A successful businessman, Samuel Ryder was among the first to recognize the commercial benefits of sponsoring golf tournaments and exhibition matches in the early 1920s. Unwilling to travel to America, he nevertheless attended every British leg of the biennial match up until his death in 1936.

It is unlikely that the British PGA officially endorsed the invitation to the match, which was no doubt seen as a gentle warm-up to the serious business of Open qualification. It is more likely that it was a marketing exercise for the Heath and Heather Company – Sam Ryder was involved from the start. Writing in the *Daily Telegraph* in 1925, George Greenwood noted that the

Ryder brothers were 'two keen golfers and enthusiastic sportsmen who originated the idea of an annual match between American and British golfers of front rank'.

Then on 26 April 1926 it was announced in the press that 'Mr S. Ryder, of St Albans, has presented a trophy for annual competition between teams of British and American professionals. The first match for the trophy is to take place at Wentworth on June 4th and 5th.'

From this we can conclude that Sam and James Ryder had already seen the possibility of a Britain versus United States match *every* year prior to the Open. Described in *Golf Monthly* in May 1926 as a 'Walker Cup for professionals', the original venue was going to be Wentworth *and* St George's Hill. Why this was changed is unknown, but accessibility from 'the Metropolis' was a high priority and the tree-lined Weybridge Course was notoriously difficult to get to. In the end, Wentworth was probably chosen for no other reason than its close proximity to the Open qualifying tournament at Sunningdale.

Above: Rival captains Walter Hagen (left) and Edward Ray at the beginning of the 'lost' Ryder Cup at Wentworth in 1926, which was described as 'the Walker Cup for professionals'. The General Strike that year ruined the travel plans of many of the American players and other nationalities were drafted in to play against Great Britain and Ireland. Despite a home victory, it was decided to expunge the result from the record books and that the trophy would be presented the following year at Worcester.

The idea of international challenge matches was nothing new to Sam Ryder. Early in 1926 he had resurrected the old England versus Scotland rivalry by matching the ageing Harry Vardon and J.H. Taylor against Scottish professionals James Braid and Alex Herd. Played at Verulum Golf Club near St Albans, the match was deemed a 'great success', with the English pair running out winners by 10 and 8. Yet, remarkably, none of them was deemed good enough to play in the 'Ryder Cup' at Wentworth just two months later.

That said, the international competition was a big success, with small but enthusiastic crowds following each match, played over the fledgling West Course (opened in 1924). The British team boasted former British Open Champions Ted Ray (1912), George Duncan (1920) and Arthur Havers (1923), along with experienced campaigners Abe Mitchell, Archie Compston, Fred Robson, Ernest Whitcombe, Herbert Jolly, Aubrey Boomer and George Gadd, so it came as little surprise when the home team made the perfect start by winning all five foursomes on the Friday. Then, in the nine singles scheduled for the following day, Duncan destroyed the great Walter Hagen by 6 and 5. Preceded by an 8 and 7 thrashing for Jim Barnes by Abe Mitchell, the match ended in victory for the home team.

So why has this match been struck from the records? The reason is simple, as a report from *Golf Illustrated* dated 11 June 1926 clearly shows. Under the headline, 'The Ryder Cup' it explained that:

> Owing to the uncertainty of the situation following the [General] Strike in which it was not known until a few days ago how many American professionals would be visiting Great Britain, Mr J. Ryder decided to withhold the cup, which he has offered for annual competition between the professionals of Great Britain and America. Under these circumstances the Wentworth Club provided the British Players with gold medals to mark the inauguration of this great international match.

There we have it. The General Strike, which lasted from 3 to 12 May, had ruined the travel plans of the American team, forcing Sam Ryder to come up with an alternative solution. Rather than cancel this inaugural match, the United States team invited a number of non-Americans to make up the numbers. So, along with

Walter Hagen, Bill Mehlhorn, Al Watrous, Cyril Walker and Emmett French, they included the two Scots, Fred McLeod and Tommy Armour, two Englishmen, Jim Barnes and Joe Stain, and one Australian trick-shot artist, Joe Kirkwood! (The players who missed out on the match included illustrious names such as Gene Sarazen, Johnny Farrell, Bobby Cruickshank and Macdonald Smith.)

With that type of eclectic international line-up there was never any chance that the United States PGA would sanction the result when it was approached a short time later about making the Ryder Cup official, and it was expunged from the records forever. The tale about George Duncan casually suggesting to Ryder afterwards that a trophy might be donated is simply untrue. Or, if it did happen that way, as Sam's daughter Joan Ryder-Scarfe said it did, then perhaps he was just confirming that the trophy would be ready for the *next* match.

As reported on Wednesday 2 June 1926, 'The first important match in which they [the American professionals] will take part is a game against a team of British professionals for the *Ryder Cup* at Wentworth next Friday and Saturday.' Proof, if proof were needed, that

Above: Abe Mitchell strikes the opening drive at Wentworth in 1926 with Jim Barnes and Walter Hagen looking on. Obviously well attended, it was hoped that the match between Britain and the USA would bring the two great golfing nations even closer through the spirit of competition.

the Ryder Cup trophy had been put up as a prize by the time the first shot was struck at Wentworth in June 1926. Whether it was ready to be presented or not is another question entirely. Bearing a '1927' hallmark, it is unlikely that old Sam had it ready in time, despite all the pre-match publicity. The cost of the trophy was split between Ryder (£100), *Golf Illustrated* (£100) and the Royal and Ancient Golf Club of St Andrews (£50), and the history books show that the first time it was actually seen in public was when Great Britain took on the United States twelve months later in Worcester, Massachusetts. In the meantime a legal contract was drawn up handing over the running of the new biennial event to the British PGA (Ryder would later give the trophy into the safe keeping of the same organization).

After a faltering start, the Ryder Cup had finally been born.

2

First Blood to Uncle Sam

1927

WORCESTER COUNTRY CLUB, WORCESTER, MASSACHUSETTS, USA

3–4 JUNE

Even with the backing of the Professional Golfers' Association, most of the British pros taking part in the first Ryder Cup match needed permission from their Golf Clubs to take a leave of absence. It could easily have proved a big problem for the professionals involved. As many of them planned to compete in the US Open at Oakmont the week after the Ryder Cup, they would be away for at least five weeks, and in some cases this permission was only reluctantly granted. (Unlike today, players were totally reliant on their Club posts to make a living, and while they considered it an honour to represent their country against the USA, more than half of the team would be forced to rely on the PGA's generosity to supplement their income during the period they would be absent.)

Sadly, the problems did not end there. Getting a British team to America by ocean liner, even in second class, would cost far more than the PGA could afford. Finances had been tight since World War I, and it was left to George Philpot, editor of *Golf Illustrated*, to launch a £3000 appeal to find the money. Realizing the importance of such a match, he sent a subscription list to every golf club in Britain asking for a donation. A dynamic and forceful character, Philpot had no reservations about using the pages of his magazine to enforce the patriotic nature of the appeal in the weeks and months before the match in Worcester in June:

> I want the appeal to be successful because it will give British pros a chance to avenge the defeats which have been administered by American pros while visiting our shores in search of Open Championship honours. I know that, given a fair chance, our fellows can and will bring back the

Cup from America. But they must have a fair chance, which means that adequate money must be found to finance the trip. Can the money be found? The answer rests with the British golfing public.

Considering how low golf professionals were on the social scale, the appeal proved spectacularly unsuccessful, especially as the vast majority of club golfers in Britain were mostly middle or upper class. This meant that, while they were open to appeals of a patriotic nature, professionals were hardly worthy of their consideration. In short, although they were perfectly happy to cheer on their golfing heroes at the Open Championship each year, sending them over to America on an all expenses paid trip was not really on. As one irate reader said in a letter to George Philpot, 'I would no more send a professional player to America to play golf than I would my chimney sweep!'

Philpot remained undaunted but, despite donations from Canada, Australia, Nigeria and, of all places, the United States, the appeal failed to meet its target, even after a substantial gift of £100 from Sam Ryder. Philpot was still £500 shy of the money he needed. The shortfall was made up by Philpot and his magazine., but having been put in this highly embarrassing situation, the frustrated editor had some strong words of condemnation for the British golfing public:

It is disappointing that the indifference or selfishness of the multitude of golfers should have been so marked that what they could have done with ease has been imposed on a small number. Of the 1750 clubs in the British Isles whose co-operation was invited, only 216 have accorded help. It is a deplorable reflection on the attitude of the average golfer towards the game.

In a later edition Philpot commented:

We are reluctant to think that this represents the attitude of a great section of the golfing community towards a matter in which the nation's credit is at stake. When our professionals are undertaking a crusade for the sake of the prestige of British golf, an expedition in the spirit of amateurs, the people of this country might reasonably be

Below: Samuel Ryder (with his dog) is photographed with the British team shortly before they boarded the boat train in London en route to Southampton in May 1927. Sadly for all, Captain Abe Mitchell (second from right) was struck down by appendicitis shortly after this photograph was taken and would not make the trip to the United States. It was a blow from which the visiting team would not recover and they fell to a heavy defeat at the hands of the Americans by 9½ to 2½.

expected to help as a duty. After all, they ought not to pursue the principle of taking everything out of the game and giving as little as possible to it. No doubt it is mainly slackness, the traditional British way of beginning slackly and muddling through, which has caused so many British clubs to allow their imaginations to slumber when it is their active assistance that is needed.

Having financed most of the journey himself, Philpot was appointed team manager in April and administered the 36-hole Ryder Cup trials that took place at Verulum in the second week of May. Once the final line-up had been decided, he prepared to board the boat train from Waterloo to Southampton on 21 May,

accompanied by the eight-man British team. Then disaster struck: just hours before departure Abe Mitchell complained of severe stomach pains and was diagnosed with appendicitis. Losing Mitchell, barely strong enough to make his farewells, so close to the match was a huge blow to British hopes. Team captain and Britain's best player by far, Mitchell had won the *Daily Mail* tournament only two weeks before and now he was forced to stay behind. It was not a good start. 'Let us hope our team can win, but it is the play without the Prince of Denmark', Sam Ryder said afterwards. Prevented from joining the British team on the *SS Aquitania* because of his overwhelming fear of sea crossings, Ryder must have been bitterly disappointed to see his friend lose out in this way.

Now came the problems of appointing a new captain and finding a replacement player for Mitchell. The team already had a reserve in George Gadd but if anything else went wrong, they might not have enough players to finish the match! As things turned out, finding a new captain would prove far easier than finding another professional at such short notice.

Before leaving, Mitchell recommended that the experienced Ted Ray take over as captain, and, after a vote by the players on the train, it was unanimously agreed. At the same meeting, Percy Perrins, Secretary of the British PGA, was called upon to provide a last-minute replacement. After some false starts, he chose the talented young professional Herbert Jolly. He sent off a cable to Foxgrove Golf Club where Jolly was employed and an agreement was finally reached enabling him to play.

Four days later, Jolly travelled over to the United States onboard the *Majestic*. A competent match-play golfer, Jolly was deemed to be the perfect choice to join a team that included Aubrey Boomer, George Duncan, Ted Ray, Charlie Whitcombe, Archie Compston, George Gadd, Fred Robson and Arthur Havers. Despite the hurried arrangements, Herbert Jolly had a relatively easy crossing, which was certainly not the case for his fellow professionals. In what turned out to be a particularly rough passage, the six-day journey left most of them locked in their cabins, unable to keep anything down. If that was not bad enough, they arrived in New York to find the Americans out in force.

At Walter Hagen's instigation, dignitaries from the United States Golf Association, the American PGA and Metropolitan PGA had all gathered on the dockside to welcome the visitors. Somewhat taken aback by the reception, the ashen-faced British team were escorted through the streets of New York accompanied by wailing sirens and screeching tires. This welcome was followed by a veritable whirlwind of civic receptions and society events that left the British professionals, fresh from the austerity of post-war Britain, over-whelmed. As Arthur Havers later recalled:

> Everywhere we went we were submerged by hospitality and kindness. Suddenly we were in a world of luxury and plenty – so different from home. It was something we never expected. Even the clubhouses were luxurious with deep-pile carpets, not like the rundown and shabby club-houses at home.

Taking a few days to shake off the effects of the sea journey, Ted Ray and his men played one or two practice rounds at courses near New York before moving to the tree-lined Worcester Country Club for some more serious practice. Back in Britain, the golfing

Left: Walter Hagen escaping from the sand in his match against Fred Robson and Edward Ray (standing right.) Hagen was part-nering Johnny Golden in this opening game of the Ryder Cup, which was won by the American pair. The most famous golfer in the world at the time, the flamboyant Hagen was accompanied throughout by his liveried chauffeur (centre), who supplied cold drinks and cigarettes whenever his master felt in need of them.

press seemed confident of victory. Speaking in his position as editor for *Golf Monthly*, Harold Hilton, two-time Open Champion, wrote:

> This team is a well-considered blending of experienced skill and rising skill. Every man in it has, at some time or other, exhibited the capacity to achieve the big thing in golf. They look every bit as capable of winning the 'Ryder' Cup – a keen affair in which each country will be represented by eight players – as the British party which so signally triumphed in the experimental event of that character at Wentworth.

While young players such as Aubrey Boomer and Charlie Whitcombe adapted well to the alien conditions, others struggled badly. George Gadd, who had suffered most on the outward sea journey, lost his form completely and was omitted from the team at his own request. With each match played over 36 holes, he was physically not up to it and neither were some of his teammates. Things went from bad to worse when the British were asked on the eve of the match about changing the actual format!

The American PGA had four demands. They wanted all foursome matches to be changed immediately to fourballs, as hitting alternate shots was a game seldom played in the USA. Second, they requested that any match finishing level after 36 holes be continued until a result was achieved. Third, they wanted two points instead of one to be awarded for a fourball victory; and, finally, for both teams to be allowed to substitute a player in the singles on the second day. Infuriated by these 'Johnny-come-lately' requests, George Philpot would concede only the final point about substitutes (mainly because a precedent had already been set in a previous Walker Cup match).

On the opening day of the so-called Ryder Cup, any reservations the Americans had about 'Scotch foursomes' were quickly dispelled after they crushed their British opponents by 3–1. Speaking afterwards, Ted Ray refused to be downhearted. In an interview with *The Worcester Telegram* he blamed his teams' failure on 'the superior putting of the American side', before saying how the result had 'not killed our team spirit'.

In the end, the Great Britain and Ireland team was not up to the task either mentally or in golfing skill. Duncan and Compston were demolished in the opening match by 8 and 6 against Farrell and Turnesa. Ray and Robson held a 3-up lead in the morning round before Hagen and Golden found some form in the afternoon, the British pair finally succumbing by 2 and 1. In another disappointing display, Havers and substitute Jolly lost 3 and 2 to Sarazen and Watrous, while the only British victory came from Boomer and Whitcombe, who overcame Leo Deigel and 'Wild Bill' Mehlhorn by 7 and 6. Coming on top of everything else, it was no wonder that some of the British team expressed their desire to return home the moment the Ryder Cup match was over.

Defeats kept coming for the British team, who were overwhelmed both on and off the course. The singles were a near American whitewash, the only bright spots for a dejected British camp being Duncan's victory over Turnesa and Whitcombe's creditable half with Sarazen. The post-match interviews brought few excuses from the British, except to hint that perhaps the result might have been closer had Abe Mitchell been present. However, manager George Philpot quickly put this in perspective, arguing that 'several Mitchells would have been needed to alter the result'. He was probably right.

After the Brits had lost the match by 9½–2½, questions were asked about the whirlwind reception the team received in New York prior to the match. Sensing Walter Hagen's influence behind it, some of the British team complained about gamesmanship. Philpot protested, and many agreed, that they had been kept up late almost every night, 'like mice on a wheel'. So was it gamesmanship or merely old-fashioned American hospitality? In their defence, the Americans had offered to play the match a week later than was originally scheduled but the British had turned them down because it would interfere with their travel arrangements. And with no money on offer at the Ryder Cup, the players wanted to enter the forthcoming US Open to have a chance of winning at least something. (In the end Archie Compston was the best-placed British player, in seventh place.)

With the first official Ryder Cup proving a bruising experience for the British side, the final word on the matter fell to past British and American Open Champion, Ted Ray. As captain, he commented on how his own experience of playing in America up to this point had been nothing but pleasurable. Regarding the match, he summed up his feelings in a cable to the editor of the *Daily Express*:

Ryder Cup

Our opponents beat us fairly and squarely and almost entirely through their astonishing work on the putting greens, up to which point the British players were equally good. We were very poor by comparison, although quite equal to the recognised two putts per green standard. I consider we can never hope to beat the Americans unless we learn to putt. This lesson should be taken to heart by British golfers.

For those, like George Philpot, who had put so much effort into making the event possible, putting a positive spin on the competition must have been difficult. Writing for his own magazine, he said optimistically, 'If our young players profit by the experience, we can reasonably hope for a happier fate in the next match for the Ryder Cup. It is a soundly established truism that experience is a good teacher and the British professionals have every incentive to make the most of it.'

Above: The victorious USA team at Worcester in 1927. The match was well attended and covered extensively in the American press, but the few reports that found their way into British newspapers and magazines downplayed the loss by blaming the 'alien' conditions the British players had to contend with throughout the week.

Bernard Darwin of *The Times*, one of the only British writers to accompany the team, talked later about the 'fallacious, altogether too good to be true' nature of the British win at Wentworth the year before. The first 'official' Ryder Cup match was now over, with previous victories like the one at Gleneagles in 1921 nothing more than a distant memory. The matches were now truly underway and in two years time the Ryder Cup would see its first match in Britain – at Moortown Golf Club in Leeds. With national pride and professional honour at stake, it was a match everyone looked forward to with great anticipation.

3

Britain Hits Back Twice

1929

MOORTOWN GOLF CLUB, LEEDS, YORKSHIRE, ENGLAND

26–27 APRIL

The first American Ryder Cup team to compete in Britain was a mixed bunch. Sam Ryder had specified certain conditions under which the competition was to be held, which included that all contestants must be native-born citizens of the nation they represented. The Americans, while all 'native-born', included two players of German origin (Watrous and Diegel), two Italians (Sarazen and Turnesa), two Englishmen (Smith and Dudley), one Spaniard (Espinosa), one Hungarian (Golden) and an Irishman (Farrell). Walter Hagen had announced only weeks before the match began that 'foreign-born' players would be considered for future American teams – after all, he argued, they had been permitted to fight in the war.

There had been some changes in the British team since the defeat at Worcester two years earlier. George Duncan was made captain, Abe Mitchell was back, and three bright young professionals, Henry Cotton, Stewart Burns and Ernest Whitcombe, were given their official debuts. With Ray, Havers and Jolly dropped, only Charlie Whitcombe, Fred Robson and Archie Compston remained from the team that had lost the Ryder Cup in America. Of the rest, two were non-residents: Aubrey Boomer, who was club professional at St Cloud in Paris, and Percy Alliss, who was at Wannsee Golf Club, Berlin. In a later amendment to the Ryder Cup rules, both players would have been excluded.

As in the previous encounter between the two sides, the British golfing press was confident of victory. Great hope was placed on the spirited and independent Cotton, especially. Unlike his working-class teammates, Cotton had a public school upbringing and his privileged background had enabled him to play occasional tournaments in the United States and study their techniques. Indeed, Cotton was on tour in America when he received the cable inviting him to play. His long-term association with the Ryder Cup would be sporadic at best: in the future, often acrimonious brushes with the golf authorities would deny him opportunities to represent his nation. But for now, the twenty-two year old was eager to play his best and keen to avenge the 1927 Ryder Cup result.

Despite the thousands of well-heeled, middle-class supporters who turned out to watch the match, lack of financial support was a cause for concern. Compared to the Americans, who had little trouble in raising more than $10,000 for their trip to Britain (mainly through donations from equipment manufacturers and a series of exhibition matches), the British PGA were struggling. Considered little more than a glorified exhibition match, the Ryder Cup had yet to capture the public's imagination and this was reflected in the woeful sum of £806 raised by yet another *Golf Illustrated* appeal. This was barely enough to cover expenses and *Golf Illustrated* was highly critical of the lacklustre response. Frustrated by the lack of organization shown by the PGA, it even proposed that the whole event should be handed over to the Royal and Ancient, declaring that 'if this is not done, the match will either die or develop into a private match with little or no interest'. Ultimately, the money was found once again – via a combination of fawning begging letters and not-so-subtle arm-twisting by George Philpot – but the relationship between the professionals' own organization and the golfing press was becoming increasingly strained. Before the second Ryder Cup had even got underway, the need for a 'home' win to retain interest was becoming vital.

The British team's headquarters were a few miles north of Moortown, at the Majestic Hotel, Harrogate. Unlike Hagen, who wanted to give a game to all his players, British captain George Duncan had decided right away to play only eight of the ten men at his disposal. Diplomatically described as 'short of practice', Stewart Burns, a Scottish professional from Cruden Bay, and Percy Alliss were to be the unlucky ones. Duncan had gone for the men in form, and despite their obvious disappointment, both Burns and Alliss were later credited for the wholehearted support they had given to the team.

American captain Walter Hagen had his own problems to deal with, not least of which was the

Above: The British team that faced the USA at Moortown in 1929. A more youthful side than two years earlier at Worcester, they ran out victors by two clear points after a devastating display in the singles, where they won 5 out of the 8 matches played.

weather. Practice days at Moortown had been miserably cold and wet. The smooth, rhythmic swings of the Americans, honed in the more clement conditions of the United States, were now being battered by the gale force winds of an unpredictable English spring. Shortly after disembarking from the *Mauritania* at Ramsgate, Hagen had lost no time in taking his team to the local steam baths. On 22 April, just a few days before the start of the match, it was reported that the American players were 'undergoing special treatment at the Harrogate Baths'. Hagen, a regular visitor to Britain for the Open Championship, knew well the bad effect that cold weather had on the swing and was determined that his players should at least have some respite.

Another curious problem for Hagen was the British ban on metal shafts. In the United States, steel shafts had been in common use for the past three years, but the Rules Committee of the Royal and Ancient Golf Club of St Andrews had steadfastly refused to legalize them in Britain. Horton Smith, winner of various tournaments on the US Winter Tour, was just one of the American team who was forced to switch from his favoured metal-shafted clubs back to hickory for the Ryder Cup. Long, lonely hours of practice followed, but for Smith (who exactly five years later became the first winner of the US Masters at Augusta) it would mean missing the opening foursomes.

Fortunately for Walter Hagen and his team, the poor weather subsided a little on the first day of the Ryder Cup. Although it was still very cold, the lashing rain of the previous few days had been replaced by a light breeze, prompting one spectator to note, 'The American players looked less pinched and wore fewer sweaters.' In the opening foursome match, Duncan threw his strongest pairing of Archie Compston and Charlie Whitcombe into battle against Johnny Farrell and Joe Turnesa. Farrell, reigning US Open Champion, struggled with his game, as did the others. Followed by an

Below: Posing for the camera (with the match referee) before the opening match at Moortown, (left to right) Charles Whitcombe and Archie Compston for Britain line up alongside Willie Turnesa and Johnny Farrell for America. Their halved game set the tone for the entire Ryder Cup match as both teams struggled to get the upper hand.

enormous gallery, the lead went back and forth until the final hole. With the British pair standing dormie 1-up on the 36th tee, Whitcombe contrived to slice the ball into a gorse bush, forcing Archie Compston to take a penalty drop. To make matters worse, Compston pitched his next shot into a greenside bunker and, despite the Americans struggling themselves, the hole was lost to a four and the game halved.

As in the previous Ryder Cup match in America, the opening foursome results set the pattern for the day. With just four matches being played, bitter disappointment followed for the British camp, particularly for their captain, George Duncan. The most dominant performance for any pairing came from the partnership of Al Espinosa and Leo Diegel. Taking on Aubrey Boomer and Duncan himself in the third match, they played wonderfully to record a 66, finishing 7-up at lunch. Apart from his fine golf game, Diegel was attracting as much attention for his unique putting style, which involved crouching over the ball with his arms splayed out alarmingly in an effort to take any

wrist movement out of the stroke. Diegel was an erratic putter at the best of times, but his joint demolition of the British pair 7 and 6 (and later Abe Mitchell 9 and 8 in the singles) led to a pronounced spell of 'Diegeling' among British golfers.

With Golden and Hagen beating Ernest Whitcombe and Henry Cotton 2-up in a closely fought game, it was left to Abe Mitchell and Fred Robson to restore some pride to the British. Facing the highly respected partnership of Gene Sarazen and Ed Dudley, they were all square at lunch. With Sam Ryder in the gallery, Mitchell, playing in his first match in the event, came out with all guns blazing and managed to secure an early lead, which they never relinquished, winning in the end 2 and 1. The opening day foursome results of 2–1 to the Americans was disappointing but not impossible to come back from. Duncan settled on his order for the singles the next day, and in what was to become one of the most famous matches in Ryder Cup history, found himself up against the flamboyant American captain, Walter Hagen.

The second day at Moortown, like the first, was favoured with reasonable weather. Saturday 27 April was also Cup Final day (Bolton v Portsmouth) and the crowds had had more than a little football crowd feel to them over the two days. Having paid three shillings entrance fee, they were fiercely partisan and thought little of cheering a missed American putt or poorly executed shot. The first game in the singles matched Charlie Whitcombe against the in-form Johnny Farrell. This was followed by the game everybody wanted to see – George Duncan against Walter Hagen.

Since the 1926 match at Wentworth where Duncan had defeated Hagen, the English professional felt he had the measure of the American at match play. Hagen, for his part, considered himself unbeatable and when the news arrived that he had been paired against Duncan, he is quoted as saying to his teammates, 'Well boys, there's a point for our team right there'. Whether true or not, it is thought that George Duncan overheard this comment and he inflicted on the American one of the greatest defeats of his career. Round in 69 in the morning eighteen, a very determined Duncan eventually won by the enormous margin of 10 and 8.

Duncan's historic win over the legendary Hagen was just the inspiration the British team needed. With wins for Charlie Whitcombe (8 and 6 over Farrell), Compston

Above: George Duncan in action against Walter Hagen in the battle of the captains. A fiery personality, the Englishman took huge offence when he overheard the American boasting how certain he was of victory! Barely looking at the American throughout their match, he inflicted one of the largest defeats in Ryder Cup singles history, winning by 10 and 8.

(6 and 4 over Sarazen), Boomer (4 and 3 over Turnesa), Cotton (4 and 3 over Watrous) and a half between Ernest Whitcombe and Al Espinosa in the final match, the British had won five out of the eight singles matches and defeated the Americans 6 to 4. The Ryder Cup was back in Britain.

1931

SCIOTO COUNTRY CLUB, COLUMBUS, OHIO, USA

26–27 JUNE

The third match in the Ryder Cup, the second to be played in the United States, began controversially. Henry Cotton, whose defeat of Al Watrous two years earlier had won the Ryder Cup for Great Britain and Ireland, had been omitted from the team. In a ruling that also applied to Percy Alliss and Aubrey Boomer, it was deemed that all players must not only be natives of, but resident in, the

Above: Percy Alliss in his role as a golf writer at Scioto Country Club. Like Aubrey Boomer and Henry Cotton, the talented young player fell foul of the rule stating that professionals must be resident in Britain to qualify to play in the Ryder Cup against America – Alliss was based at Wansee Golf Club in Berlin at the time. He was then invited to write a report on a match he should have been playing in.

country they represented. Alliss was ineligible because of his post at Wannsee Golf Club in Berlin, and Boomer because of his association with St Cloud in Paris. The British side was denied three of its finest young players before the event had even begun.

Single-minded almost to the point of stubbornness, Henry Cotton had actually received his invitation to play in the Ryder Cup at Scioto. His argument with the British PGA concerned that part of the 'resident' clause that demanded that all the players must return to Britain with the team after the event had finished. A further condition stipulated that all exhibition money must be shared among the players during the trip. Win or lose, Cotton had intended to stay on in America to play in more tournaments and under no circumstances was he going to share his exhibition fees with anyone.

As the argument between himself and the PGA grew more acrimonious, Cotton gave in his defence the example of how the Americans had dealt with a similar situation two years earlier in England. Staying together as a team until the Ryder Cup was over, they were then considered, in his own words, 'individuals, free to do as they please'. The PGA, who took an equally intransigent view, considered Cotton's actions as not only disloyal but also unpatriotic. With little option left to him, Cotton sought to justify his actions in an article for *Golf Illustrated*, saying:

> It was pointed out to me that if I enjoyed the benefit of a free passage, it was not fair for me to use that benefit for my personal gain by staying after the team had returned and playing as a freelance. It was this that caused me to intimate to the Professional Golfers' Association that I was quite prepared to pay my passage out and back. Here again the Association found my suggestion unacceptable.

In a final gesture of defiance, Henry Cotton approached Alliss and Boomer about taking part in a private American tour. Alliss agreed and he, like Cotton, also made plans to appear at Scioto Country Club during the Ryder Cup, working as a correspondent for a daily newspaper. With only weeks to go before the British team were due to set sail on the *Majestic*, the PGA made it known that if Cotton was prepared to write a letter of apology, they would overlook his rebellious actions. The young Englishman adamantly refused to even consider it. Then on 6 June – only four days before the team was set to leave – the PGA approached Cotton during the Open Championship at Carnoustie.

Henry Cotton was re-invited to join the team on three conditions. He must submit himself to the authority of the Ryder Cup management committee, apply to stay on in America only after the match had ended, and agree to share all exhibition fees with other team members. For Cotton this was like a red rag to a bull. He refused to submit to the PGA's authority and, despite deputations from various parties, including George Philpot of *Golf Illustrated*, he stood firm and effectively ruled himself out of the Ryder Cup.

For British golf fans following the story in the golfing press, the whole controversy was highly confusing and somewhat distasteful. Frustrated at losing three of Britain's finest young players, they understood little about the conditions set forth in the Trust Deed that had prevented the inclusion of Boomer, Alliss and, effectively, Cotton. As the argument raged on, the original Ryder Cup Trust Deed signed by Samuel Ryder himself appeared not to make any stipulations concerning matters of qualification. When asked, Ryder commented that it was the Americans who had decided prior to the 1927 match that their team 'should consist entirely of native-born players and those residing in America at the time'.

In an attempt to explain the situation, Percy Perrins, Secretary of the PGA, wrote an open letter to *Golf Illustrated*, in which he disputed Sam Ryder's version of events. He stated that the Americans had brought this rule into effect shortly before the 1929 match at Moortown. This being the case, both Alliss and Boomer were entitled to participate in that particular match but not the current one in America. Examples were thrown back and forth in the media. It was argued that if the

resident rule were scrapped for both teams, then Scottish-born exiles living in the United States, such as Tommy Armour and Jim Barnes, would be eligible to play for Great Britain and Ireland. The fact that they were both now naturalized American citizens only served to confuse matters more.

Sadly embroiled in the controversy, Sam Ryder declared at the farewell banquet for the British team that 'the Cup is the sole property of the PGA and they can alter the terms in any way they think fit at the time'. By stating that qualification for the Ryder Cup was a domestic affair not open to scrutiny from outside, the statement brought howls of condemnation from long-time supporter of the event, *Golf Illustrated*. Somewhat haughtily, it replied, 'Very well, treat it [the Ryder Cup] as a domestic matter. But do not come to us when you are short of money.'

It was against this sorry background that the British team arrived, in the hot summer heat, in Ohio. An unlikely looking team on paper, they comprised new

Above: (Left to right) George Duncan and the ageing Arthur Havers line up against the strong American pairing of Densmore Shute and Walter Hagen in the second match in the foursomes. With hot humid weather a factor throughout the week, the British pairing struggled to compete, losing by 10 and 8. Sadly for Duncan, his Ryder Cup was a short-lived affair as he was dropped from the singles the following day.

boys Bert Hodson, W.H. Davies and Syd Easterbrook, along with veterans Archie Compston, Fred Robson, Abe Mitchell, Ernest Whitcombe and Arthur Havers. Havers, Open Champion from 1924, was called up as a replacement for the woefully out-of-form first-choice team member Herbert Jolly. Havers' late inclusion meant that only two members of the Great Britain and Ireland Ryder Cup team, Easterbrook and Hodson, were under thirty when the match began – a vital consideration in the hot weather expected over the two days at Scioto Country Club.

While Walter Hagen continued as US captain, the winning British captain of two years earlier, George Duncan, had inexplicably been replaced by Charlie Whitcombe. Undoubtedly, the 1920 Open Champion was past his best, but with all the infighting that had

Above: A smartly attired Walter Hagen in singles action against rival British Captain Charles Whitcombe. Unbeaten throughout the week, his presence on and off the course would dominate the Ryder Cup for some years to come.

preceded the match, strong leadership was needed and ultimately Whitcombe was not able to deliver.

Hagen, for his part, had a good blend of youth and experience. US team selection had been delayed until the last moment to include in-form players such as Craig Wood, Whiffy Cox, Denny Shute and Billy Burke – all of whom had qualified in a four-round tournament only the week before. From previous Ryder Cup matches came Gene Sarazen, Johnny Farrell, Horton Smith, Al Espinosa and Leo Diegel. The inclusion of Diegel, professional at the Agua Caliente Golf Club in Mexico, looked for a time to have broken the controversial resident rule that had caused so many problems for the British team. The problem was swiftly resolved when it was found that Diegel lived just across the border in the United States.

Almost predictably, the preceding unrest and hothouse conditions meant that the British team fell quickly behind on the opening day foursomes. The Americans forged ahead to a lead of 3–1 with first pair out, Sarazen and Farrell, defeating Compston and Davies (8 and 7). Hagen and Shute beat Duncan and Havers (10 and 9), and Burke and Cox beat Easterbrook and Charlie Whitcombe (3 and 2); only Mitchell and Robson won a point for the British team by defeating Diegel and Cox (3 and 1).

Ill-equipped for the torrid heat, the British team were offered little sign of a revival in the singles matches. Setting the pattern for the day, Burke demolished Compston by 7 and 6 in the top singles, while Sarazen beat Fred Robson by a similar score in the match that followed. With further defeats for British professionals Abe Mitchell, Bert Hodson and Ernest and Charles Whitcombe, the singles were lost and so was the Ryder Cup. Creditably, Arthur Havers put in a wonderful display, beating Craig Wood 4 and 3, as did young W.H. Davies in his win over Johnny Farrell by a similar score. However, the final 9–3 margin of defeat was a bitter blow to British morale.

On the team's arrival back in Southampton, the post-mortem began. Speculation raged about the effect that leaving out Cotton, Alliss and Boomer had had on the result. Yet, as time passed, discussion turned, more than to any other subject, to how significantly the hot weather had impacted on the British players' form. As *Country Life* later reported, these were not easy conditions in which to play golf:

So far as one can judge, our men, with one or two exceptions, played more or less as well as could be hoped against a very strong side under extraordinarily difficult conditions. The handicap of playing in another man's country is not perhaps sufficiently appreciated by those who have not tried it. Cold is the one and only thing which is likely to beat the Americans, and when our team won so fine a victory at Moortown, they were greatly helped by the raw and bitter weather. Similarly, heat is our worst enemy.

The Ryder Cup lost, the British PGA moved that the event should never again be played in the heat of an American summer. In four years time at Ridgewood, New Jersey, the Ryder Cup would be played in September. The Americans reluctantly agreed. At last the PGA had got their own way.

Above: The two captains, Charles Whitcombe [putting out] and Walter Hagen, battle it out in the singles. The visiting British team struggled in the mid-summer heat and fell to a heavy defeat at the hands of a strong American team. Not surprisingly, the British PGA moved that the biennial match should not be played in June again when the match returned to the USA four years later. Rescheduled for September, it continued to be played in June in England in 1933 and 1937 because it was thought that the summer conditions would not be 'unduly oppressive'.

1933

SOUTHPORT AND AINSDALE GOLF CLUB, SOUTHPORT, LANCASHIRE, ENGLAND

26–27 JUNE

The Ryder Cup at Southport and Ainsdale on the windswept West Coast of England was a landmark match in many ways. After the humiliating defeat two years earlier and the long-running 'Cotton' debacle that had preceded it, the British PGA were determined to maintain some degree of control. So while the United States stayed loyal to Walter Hagen as captain, the British elected the first non-playing captain, five-time Open Champion John Henry Taylor. Taylor was a past selector and noted disciplinarian and it was clear from the start that there was to be no repeat of past mistakes. 'J.H.' would help win the Cup back for Britain, but it would be done his way and no other.

A major figure in the formation of the Professional Golfers' Association in 1901, J.H. Taylor was widely regarded as a natural leader. Having begun his career as a caddie at Royal North Devon, he graduated into one of the most dominant professionals of his time. Along with Harry Vardon and James Braid – the other members of the 'Great Triumvirate' – he helped raise the social standing of the ordinary club professional in Britain.

Up until Southport, J.H. Taylor had taken a fairly passive role in Ryder Cup proceedings, but after the defeat in America he was determined to take control. The first matter to resolve was the same problem that had almost derailed the match at Scioto two years previously, namely the availability of professionals resident outside the British Isles, which inevitably included Henry Cotton. Fortunately for Taylor, Cotton was employed by the Royal Waterloo Golf Club in Belgium, which ruled out any possibility of him playing. This also applied to Aubrey Boomer who, unlike Percy Alliss, had continued working in France. Deputations were made about amending Sam Ryder's Trust Deed but Taylor and the PGA were adamant – there was never any question of changing the rules for Cotton and Boomer.

With Charlie Whitcombe and Abe Mitchell the only surviving members from the victory at Moortown in 1926, Taylor set about moulding his team. His first move was to employ a physical fitness expert from the British Army, Lieutenant Alick Stark, to lick his side into shape. With the average age of the team pushing thirty-four, early morning runs along Southport beach were made compulsory, along with strenuous rub-downs to loosen up the golfers' muscles. Quite what the more senior members of the British team, such as forty-six-year-old Abe Mitchell, thought of this new regime is unsure. However, it must have been an inspiring sight to find sixty-two-year-old J.H. Taylor regularly running alongside them.

For the Americans, there was no place in the team for the newly crowned United States Open winner Johnny Goodman. Five other team members were making their first appearance in Britain: Densmore Shute, Olin Dutra, Craig Wood, Billy Burke and Paul Runyan. Ably backed up by Gene Sarazen, Horton Smith, Ed Dudley and Leo Diegel, they amounted to what Bernard Darwin described in *The Times* as 'a very strong side, if anything stronger than that which our men so gloriously defeated on that freezing day at Moortown'.

In contrast with the opening day foursomes in previous Ryder Cup encounters, the British team took control from the start. Ending the day 2–1 up with victories for Mitchell and Havers and Davies and Easterbrook, confidence was high in the British camp. Yet in a curious incident between the rival captains, the first day matches – indeed the Ryder Cup itself – almost never took place. When the time came to exchange

Right: Abe Mitchell tees off at the short par-3 opening hole in his singles match against Olin Dutra. His 9 and 8 win over the 1932 PGA Champion contributed hugely to the British teams narrow one-point victory over the USA.

Above: Gene Sarazen escapes from the sand in his singles match against Englishman Alf Padgham. With poor shots greeted by cheers from the partisan British crowd, even the easy-going Italian American was forced to compare the atmosphere to more like that of a fairground than a golf course.

team lists setting out the order of play, American Walter Hagen proved strangely reluctant. Whether it was gamesmanship is unsure, but he twice failed to meet with Taylor at the appointed time. Taylor, refusing to play such games, let it be known that unless Hagen appeared on his third request he would call off the match. The lists were duly exchanged and the match went ahead as planned, but the relationship between the two men remained strained throughout the two days.

The opening day foursomes left Great Britain and Ireland needing just four of the eight singles matches to win. In anticipation of a famous home victory, an estimated 15,000 people, including Edward, Prince of Wales, turned out to watch. With the large crowds came an army of stewards to help with the flow of play. Not always able to control the stampeding galleries, they could be identified by the long bamboo 'lances'

they carried with red and white pennants at the tip. The Prince of Wales, a highly popular member of the British family, had intended to follow the Hagen versus Lacey match but was forced to take refuge in the clubhouse as the crowds became more boisterous. When one steward remonstrated a spectator for putting off the players, he replied, 'Players be damned, I've come to see the Prince'.

While adding greatly to the drama of the occasion, the crowds of holidaymakers from town brought their own problems. With only a basic knowledge of golf, they commonly greeted poorly played American shots and missed putts with loud cheers and claps. Gene Sarazen, who was first out in the singles against Englishman Alf Padgham, later referred to the atmosphere at Southport and Ainsdale as being nearer a fairground than a golf course.

After the morning eighteen holes, the British side held its slim lead from the previous day. The singles stood all square, with each team ahead in three matches and two even. In what was to prove a dramatic afternoon, this delicate balance was enhanced by American Horton Smith holding a 5-up lead on Charlie Whitcombe in the final match, with British professional Abe Mitchell also 5-up on Olin Dutra in the second. The stage was set. If the British team were to win, they had to manage it before the last match came into play.

In the opening singles, a determined Gene Sarazen eventually cruised to a 6 and 4 win over the luckless Alf Padgham. Despite the American having won the United States and British Open titles only a year before, he was thrown into the match against the in-form Padgham almost as a sacrificial lamb. It was no secret that relations had become strained between the tough little Italian and his greatest rival, the United States captain Walter Hagen. They were never the best of friends, but Hagen had paired them together in the opening match of the foursomes in an attempt to silence rumours of a feud between them. Then, after halving the match with British pair Percy Alliss and Charlie Whitcombe, Hagen had taken little time in blaming his partner Sarazen for the disappointing result.

In the second singles, Abe Mitchell confounded his critics by building on his large lunchtime lead and going on to crush American Olin Dutra 9 and 8. In this remarkable match, Dutra began by racing to a 3-up lead after nine holes in the morning, only for veteran Mitchell to win six holes in a row to gain the upper hand.

Following in the match behind, Walter Hagen eventually closed out Arthur Lacey by 2 and 1, while Craig Wood added to British misery by defeating William Davies 4 and 3 to take the Americans ahead for the first time. This left the British team needing to win three matches out of the four remaining on the course – Alliss against Runyan, Havers against Diegel, Easterbrook against Shute and, finally, Whitcombe against Smith.

Percy Alliss was the first to come up trumps. Winning the sixteenth hole, the Englishman looked on in amazement as the American star thinned a greenside bunker shot out-of-bounds on the next hole to give him an unexpected 2 and 1 win. Then came the news that despite a brave comeback by Charlie Whitcombe against Horton Smith in the final match, the American had beaten him 2 and 1. The Ryder Cup was now tied 5–5 with one game left on the course – Syd Easterbrook and Densmore Shute.

After a hard-fought battle, the pair came to the final hole at Southport and Ainsdale all square. Easterbrook had overcome an early spell of poor putting to finish the morning round only 1-down. Yet waiting on the eighteenth tee as the vast crowds were being ushered off the fairway, the club professional from Knowle in Bristol must have been secretly pleased to survive this long against the more talented Densmore Shute. Driving on the demanding par-4 finishing hole, both players found sand off the tee. Easterbrook played out safe, but Shute bunkered his second by attempting to go for the green. After their third shots, both players had ended up on the green, about five paces from the hole.

The match in the position it was, the Americans only needed a half to retain the Ryder Cup. Walter Hagen, accompanying the Prince of Wales by the side of the green, was rumoured to be considering asking Densmore Shute to play safely up to the hole with his putt to achieve this result. Having decided that it would have been an affront to the heir to the throne, Hagen remained silent and Shute raced his first putt six-foot past. An understandably nervous Syd Easterbrook left his approach putt only slightly less. Shute then missed the return and Easterbrook holed his to win not only his match, but also the Ryder Cup.

Standing on the clubhouse steps, the Prince of Wales presented the trophy to the victorious British captain J.H. Taylor and said, 'Naturally I am unbiased in these matters, but I can only say that we over here are delighted to have beaten you over there'. Hagen, for his part, said he was only 'slightly disappointed', but later admitted that he had reserved a special place onboard the *Aquitania* for the Ryder Cup trophy and the journey back to the States.

As the crowds milled away from the course, the British team could reflect favourably on how they had beaten the Americans. Unlike the bitter cold of Moortown four years earlier, the weather had not been a factor, despite Bernard Darwin's declaration in the press that every 'raging patriot will pray for a raging east wind, because it gets at the heart and liver, killing those who are not used to it'. It had been a brave and hard-won British victory inspired by a captain whose 'never say die' attitude had carried him to five Open Championships, and now his team to victory in the Ryder Cup.

Sir Guy Campbell described J.H. Taylor in an article for *Golf Illustrated* as a 'ringmaster'. It was an apt description for someone who inspired and cajoled those around him into performing greater and more extraordinary feats. Though no one knew it at the time, the British triumph at Southport and Ainsdale was to prove a watershed in the history of the Ryder Cup. In future years, the sheer depth in numbers would give the Americans an almost unassailable advantage, and while there would still be glorious moments to come, the balance of power had shifted forever.

Above: Following what was a hard-fought battle, the victorious British captain J.H. Taylor is presented the Ryder Cup trophy by HRH The Prince of Wales.

4

An Unwelcome Break

1935

RIDGEWOOD COUNTRY CLUB, RIDGEWOOD, NEW JERSEY, USA

28–29 SEPTEMBER

Long before the departure of the British team to the United States, a feeling of optimism pervaded the British press. The victory over the Americans at Southport and Ainsdale two years earlier had been followed by a British one-two-three at the recent Open Championship at Muirfield. The newspapers made much of how Henry Picard, a newcomer to the American Ryder Cup side, had been beaten into sixth place behind eventual winner Alf Perry and runners-up Alf Padgham and Charlie Whitcombe. Sadly, the fact that Picard was the only member of the team playing that year would offer a better insight into the final result.

The 1935 Ryder Cup at Ridgewood, New Jersey, was unusual in another respect. It would be the first and only time that three brothers would compete in the event. The Whitcombes – Ernest, Charles and Reg – were from a remarkable golfing family from Burnham, Somerset. Ernest, the eldest, had been runner-up to Walter Hagen in the 1924 Open Championship at Hoylake. Charles was an experienced Ryder Cup campaigner, having played in all four previous matches. His best chance to win the Open had come only weeks before at Muirfield, where he had taken a final round 76 to slip back into third place. Reg was the youngest and perhaps least talented of the three brothers. Yet despite never making the top eight of the Open Championship before finishing runner-up to Henry Cotton at Carnoustie in 1937, it would be his name on the trophy a year later at Royal St George's.

Prior to leaving for New York, a farewell banquet was staged for the British team at the plush Grosvenor Hotel in London. Each member of the ten-man side, including the Whitcombe brothers, Alf Perry, Percy Alliss, Bill Cox, Ted Jarman, Dick Burton, Alf

Padgham and J.H. Busson, was introduced to the assembled throng. Once again, both Henry Cotton and Aubrey Boomer were ineligible for selection because of working abroad but this hardly seemed to matter to anyone that night – least of all the newly appointed secretary of the PGA and British team manager, Commander Charles Roe RN. As he commented to the waiting journalists, 'Though my association with professional golfers in an official capacity is somewhat short, I feel that no team could go to America with a greater opportunity of success than Whitcombe and his boys'.

With the match pushed back to September to escape the torrid heat of the American summer, the weather was far more temperate than it had been at Scioto Country Club four years earlier. Never considered quite good enough to have staged the United States Open Championship, the course itself was in fine condition,

Above: The British team takes a break from practice prior to the opening match at Ridgewood. Boosted by the presence of the highly rated Whitcombe brothers in the side, the first away victory seemed possible. But even with the help of Ernest, Charles and Reg, the team could not stave off a heavy defeat at the hands of the Americans.

except for a large growth of clover that had pervaded the fairways. (After the subsequent result, this was mentioned but was never taken seriously as an excuse.)

For the Americans, Walter Hagen was once again elected captain. Hagen was coming to the end of his career and the match at Ridgewood would be his last as a player, but his position as captain was set to continue for another two years. His team contained only five professionals from the humiliating defeat at Southport and Ainsdale: Gene Sarazen, Paul Runyan, Olin Dutra,

Horton Smith and Craig Wood. Those brought in to bolster up the United States side were an unusual mix, which, apart from new boys Johnny Revolta, Sam Parks and Henry Picard, included one professional with a highly dubious American Indian heritage, Ky Lafoon. (Once asked if his high cheekbones were a sign of Red Indian blood, Lafoon gladly agreed, aware of the publicity it would generate.)

With American team members increasingly hardened by the rapidly growing tournament circuit in the United States, it was not surprising they raced to an immediate 3–1 lead in the opening foursome matches. The comparisons were difficult to dismiss. While British professionals competed regularly in the Open and prestigious *News of the World* Championships, the majority of the golfing year was spent at their respective Golf Clubs. Even British Open Champion Alf Perry was required to return to his post at Leatherhead in Surrey as soon as the Ryder Cup was finished.

With the only win coming from Charles and Ernest Whitcombe against Olin Dutra and Ky Lafoon, the British team once again faced an uphill battle in the singles. Sadly for Commander Roe, the size of the British defeats in the foursomes did not inspire confidence. Perry and Busson had lost to Sarazen and Hagen 7 and 6 in the first match, followed by Padgham and Alliss losing to Picard and Revolta in the second, and finally Cox and Jarman losing out 9 and 8 to Runyan and Smith. With nothing short of a mountain to climb,

the British set out in the singles the following day more in hope than confidence.

Seen as a sacrificial lamb, new boy Jack Busson was matched in the opening singles with recently crowned Masters Champion Gene Sarazen. Surprisingly, Busson found himself 1-up on the American at lunch before finally losing out 3 and 2. Effectively, this result set the tone for the day as the United States swept up the next three singles – Runyan beating Burton 3 and 2, Revolta beating Reg Whitcombe 2 and 1, Dutra beating Padgham 4 and 2 – and the Ryder Cup. Some consolation for the British team did arrive in the shape of an unexpected 1-hole win for Percy Alliss over Craig Wood, and halves for Cox and Perry with Smith and Parks respectively. This final match between the Open Champions of Britain and the United States – Alf Perry and Sam Parks – drew a surprisingly small crowd, despite its significance. Park, the surprise winner at Oakmont that year, was not highly rated by the American public and only managed to halve with Perry by holing a massive putt on the last green.

As news of the 9–3 defeat (followed by an equally humiliating 9–5 defeat in Toronto by the Canadians)

Below: Horton Smith putting on the eighteenth green during his singles match against W.J. Cox. Winner of the inaugural Masters tournament at Augusta National the year before, Smith was expected to win easily but could only manage a half with the plucky British pro.

filtered back to the British golfing public, the recriminations were not long in coming. Long-time supporter of the Ryder Cup, *Golf Illustrated* wrote in its editorial, 'The best team we have ever sent [to the United States] played about as badly as it knew how. Scores running into the high eighties tell their own tale, which must be one of summary defeat.' Equally critical, *Tatler* wrote, 'Better not to go at all than to be beaten like this every year', while the *Glasgow Herald* entered the debate by commenting, 'If we cannot face to the humbling of our pride in a sport which is spreading to every corner of the earth, we would be false to those who helped make the British sportsman acknowledged as the most gallant on earth.' Various explanations for the poor British performance were offered by various golf writers, some of whom, like Brownlow Wilson, were actually present at Ridgewood:

> We lost because we played golf so very much below our usual standard. If we had played as well as we can, the result might have been different. The team, except Alliss who had a stiff neck, were fit and had been playing well in practice. They had plenty of time for preparations, so we cannot blame it on that. The Ridgewood course is difficult but not too difficult for our men. It demands a type of golf not usually played in Britain. There is clover on the fairways and we discovered that we needed clubs with much more loft to play shots to the green with success. The spectators did not have any effect on us. They were as fair a crowd as anybody could wish to have following. They gave us every encouragement, but we needed more than that. We needed more clubs and a lot of luck to have won.

The legendary C.B. MacFarlane agreed with the effect that clover could have on a golfer's shot, describing it as 'a terror, as the ball may skid off the irons'. This feeble attempt to explain the British defeat was seized upon by the anonymous M.W. in the *Observer* who wrote that, 'a lamer excuse could not possibly be offered and from whatever source it sprang, the pity is that it was ever offered'. The writer then went on to blame the British defeat on simple 'stage-fright'.

However, the storm raged on unabated in Britain for some weeks after the team had arrived home. Brownlow Wilson's comments about Percy Alliss (who won his singles match with a stiff neck) were taken up

Above: Johnny Revolta chips his way to victory over his singles opponent Reg Whitcombe. Winner of the 1935 PGA Championship, he would end the year leading US money winner.

by Henry Longhurst when he scathingly said, 'The unkind critic cannot help remarking that if Alliss had a stiff neck, the best thing to do with the next lot would be to make them all sit in a draught before the match!'

Even the Americans took part in the debate. Conveniently forgetting the similar discussion that had followed their defeat at Southport and Ainsdale only two years earlier, an American reporter for the *Herald Tribune* wrote, 'With the exception of the Whitcombes, the British players seemed to have left their form on the practice ground.'

As for the players themselves, there were no excuses about either the weather or the condition of the course. New Jersey Governor Harold Hoffman had praised the sportsmanship of both teams and presented each professional with a commemorative medal at the farewell dinner at the Ridgewood Club. The United States PGA had similarly honoured them with an inscribed wristwatch. There would be future defeats for both nations, but the honourable way the British professionals handled themselves in 1935 set an example that has been followed ever since.

1937

SOUTHPORT AND AINSDALE GOLF CLUB, SOUTHPORT, LANCASHIRE, ENGLAND

29–30 JUNE 1937

Southport and Ainsdale Golf Club, the scene of a famous British triumph four years earlier, was once again the venue for the Ryder Cup in 1937. Despite the inquest that had followed the last match at Ridgewood, New Jersey, hopes were high for a home victory. The Great Britain and Ireland team had been undefeated in the previous two matches held on their side of the Atlantic, and this was also the first appearance of Henry Cotton since 1929. Acknowledged as the greatest British golfer of his generation, Cotton had recently returned to England from Belgium to take up a post at Ashridge Golf Club near London. Now eligible under the same rules that had kept him out for the last three Ryder Cups, he seemed ready for the challenge of taking on the Americans once more.

In a British team that also included Percy Alliss, Dick Burton, Alf Perry, Arthur Lacey, Alf Padgham, Dai Rees, Sam King and Bill Cox, the captaincy was

given to the only remaining Whitcombe brother, Charles. Still a competent enough player himself, Charlie Whitcombe had the unenviable record of having led two British teams to defeat in 1931 and 1935. Whitcombe was looking for a 'third time lucky' victory, but some of his unusual team selections made during the heat of battle would draw fierce criticism.

The ten-man British team was considered by the golfing press to have a good blend of youth and experience. New boys Rees and King were promising young professionals and the team also boasted the winners of the last four Open Championships – Cotton in 1934 and 1937, Perry in 1935 and Padgham in 1936. (Dick Burton would go on to win in 1939 at St Andrews.) The Lancashire course was seen as a lucky talisman in much the same way The Belfry would be in later years and the poor weather forecast for the two days also gave cause for hope – gale force winds and continuous rain were the kinds of conditions that were thought to favour British teams. Sadly, this was not to be the case.

As for the Americans, they would rely on quality golf to see them through. Once again Walter Hagen, now aged forty-five, would captain the United States side, but only in a non-playing role. With one of the strongest teams ever to play in the Ryder Cup, Hagen was fiercely determined to retain the trophy. And if that meant changing the selection system to get the side he wanted, then so be it.

Five of the ten-man squad, including the 1936 United States Open winner, Johnny Revolta, and PGA Champion from the same year, Densmore Shute, had already been selected some months before. They were

Left: The British team pose for the cameras prior to the match at Southport. A strong mix of youth and experience, it boasted recent winners of the British Open, including Henry Cotton, Alf Perry and Alf Padgham.

to be accompanied by Horton Smith, Henry Picard and the indomitable Gene Sarazen. With a shortlist of thirteen professionals, the remaining five places would be allotted after a strenuous series of six qualifying rounds starting in May at the PGA Championship at Pittsburgh Country Club. (The two qualifying medal rounds at the PGA Championship were added to all four rounds at the following United States Open at Oakland Hills, with the best six scores counting.) By the end of June those players battling it out for a Ryder Cup place included Vic Ghezzi, Jimmy Hines, Ralph Guldahl, Harold McSpaden, Byron Nelson, Sam Snead, Olin Dutra, Dick Metz, Ed Dudley, Craig Wood, Ky Lafoon, Lloyd Mangrum, Tony Manero and Paul Runyan.

Eventually, the professionals who emerged to represent their country were Ralph Guldahl (winner of the 1937 Open) and Sam Snead (runner-up in the same event). With the last two places filled by Ed Dudley, Tony Manero and newcomer Byron Nelson, it was a hugely strong side, and despite finalizing his line-up only four days before they were due to set sail for Britain, Hagen was understandably confident about his chances of retaining the trophy. He was not alone: *Golf Monthly* later described the American Ryder Cup team that left New York on 16 June on board the *Manhattan* as 'the greatest golfing force which has ever come to this country. A splendid spectacle of athletic youth.'

As for the British, Charlie Whitcombe's choice of first-day foursome pairings gave some clue as to how the match would progress. By putting out his strongest two players – Cotton and Padgham – against Ed Dudley and the inexperienced Byron Nelson, he had hoped to get his British team off to a winning start. Yet even before the match began the signs were not good. Since winning his British Open title the year before, Alf Padgham's form had fallen off alarmingly. Many believed he had played himself out by spending the previous winter competing in South Africa; some golfing pundits had even questioned his inclusion in the British Ryder Cup team.

The match itself began well enough for the English pair. The first nine holes of the morning round were halved, with the British side going ahead for the first time at the fourteenth. Then, after giving away the next two holes, the Americans took full advantage and finished 1-up at lunch. Despite the blustery conditions, the opening match was well supported. However,

Above: British captain Charles Whitcombe congratulates young maestro Henry Cotton after he defeated Tony Manero in the singles. Despite this, Whitcombe became a three-time loser after his team, were soundly beaten 8 to 4.

compared with the previous Ryder Cup at Southport in 1933, the crowd numbers were considerably down. The poor weather that greeted the players obviously contributed to the low turnout, but a raise in the spectators' entrance fee up to 5 shillings also had its effect.

While Cotton had shown good form in practice, he contributed as much as Padgham to the terrible 5–6 start (against par of 3–4) in the afternoon. Five-down with only fourteen holes to play, the pair would ultimately find the hill too steep to climb against Dudley and Nelson. The match finally came to a finish with another British double bogey on the sixteenth; Cotton and Padgham lost by 4 and 2. In hindsight, Whitcombe's strategy had failed. As expected, Padgham had played miserably and the recriminations were not long in coming, with noted golf correspondents like Bernard Darwin accusing the British captain of 'putting all his eggs in one basket'.

Yet the opening foursomes matches were not a complete disaster. Lacey and Cox had lost 2 and 1 to Guldahl and Manero, but Charlie Whitcombe and the highly combative little Welshman Dai Rees had played well for a halve against Sarazen and Shute. Then in the final match, Percy Alliss and Dick Burton had survived losing a 3-up lead at lunch against the tough American pairing of Johnny Revolta and Henry Picard. Eventually coming out 2 and 1 winners, the British pair had picked up a vital point, leaving the overall match result now standing at 2½–1½ to the United States.

The day of the singles was greeted with only slightly better weather. The rain had passed, but the fairways at Southport and Ainsdale remained rock hard after weeks of hot weather prior to the match. When the order of play was announced, it came as a surprise to find that Charlie Whitcombe had left himself out of the singles in favour of Sam King. King, making his first appearance at the Ryder Cup, had been omitted from the foursomes because of his poor showing in the practice rounds. But if the inclusion of the out-of-form professional from Kent was a surprise, Whitcombe's decision to play Alf Padgham in the lead singles came as a real bombshell. Matched against the big-hitting Ralph Guldahl, the diminutive Englishman struggled from the start. After some early exchanges, the American pulled away to be 6-up at lunch before going on to win by the biggest margin of the day, 8 and 6. It surprised no one when one newspaper described his performance as 'unquestionably bad'.

With British hopes waning, Sam King looked for a time as though he was about to produce the shock of the day by beating the current United States PGA Champion, Densmore Shute. Starting his morning round with three 3s in the opening four holes, he raced to a 2-up lead against the talented American. Then Shute came back to level the match at lunch before going on to build a 4-up lead of his own in the afternoon. To his credit, King fought back from this near hopeless position, holing a birdie putt on the final green for a much-needed half. In keeping with the fighting spirit of the side, the tigerish Dai Rees battled hard against the talented Byron Nelson. Rees had been 3-down to the Texan during the morning round but had clawed back four holes in a row to finish 1-up at lunch. With the rain now lashing down, Rees at one point lost control of a shot as the club slipped from his hand.

Despite this distraction, the young professional played near par golf to defeat Nelson by 3 and 1, and was carried shoulder high back to the clubhouse by his fellow Welshman.

In the following match, a determined Henry Cotton was building on his 2-up lunchtime lead over Tony Manero. Always seemingly in control, the English maestro finished off the 1936 United States Open winner by 5 and 3 to even the match overall. The Ryder Cup now revolved around the remaining four singles, but one look at the scoreboard showed Great Britain and Ireland down in all of them. Percy Alliss had been leading Gene Sarazen 3-up just after lunch but had fallen back to be all square with just four holes left. On the par-3, fifteenth hole Sarazen had the good fortune to bounce back onto the green off an unwitting spectator. Alliss, already on the green, then watched in amazement as the little Italian casually rolled in the putt for a 2 and ultimately a win. With his American teammates holding good leads going into the final few holes, Sarazen then held on to the eighteenth for a 1-up victory, effectively clinching the Ryder Cup for the United States.

With singles victories in the final three matches for Sam Snead over Dick Burton, Ed Dudley over Alf Perry, and Henry Picard over Arthur Lacey, the Americans completed an 8–4 victory. It was the first occasion in Ryder Cup history that a team from the United States had won on British soil and it was greeted with huge celebrations. President Franklin D. Roosevelt was cabled the good news and Walter Hagen was sent the following communication from the White House:

> To the greatest general in the world: Congratulations on leading the greatest golfers in the world to a wonderful victory which brings great honour to your Country, the PGA and your fellow professionals who are proud of you. Your achievement will go down in golfing history as the greatest of all time; we salute you, admire your courage and honour you as champions and heroes.

It was a buoyant Walter Hagen who congratulated his own team at the trophy presentation. Just as he was about to make his formal acceptance speech, his handwritten notes blew away on a gust of wind. Hagen, an accomplished public speaker, suddenly looked uncertain. Under the emotion of the occasion, he mistakenly began by saying, 'I am very proud and happy to be the

captain of the first American team to win on *home* soil.' Realizing his error, he raised four fingers to signify his four British Open titles and said, 'You'll forgive me I'm sure, for feeling so at home here in Britain.' As he was one of the most popular players ever to grace British shores, the crowd would have forgiven him anything.

With the onset of World War II, the 1937 match at Southport and Ainsdale would be the last Ryder Cup to be held for ten years. Though he did not know it at the time, Walter Hagen would never participate in another match, even as captain. However, two years later in September 1939 he was chosen to lead an American Ryder Cup team at Ponte Vedra in Florida. With the match scheduled for November, Commander R.C.T. Roe of the British PGA cabled the United States PGA to announce that the match had been cancelled due to the outbreak of war in Europe on 3 September 1939.

By this time the Americans had already picked their ten-man team to face the British. It consisted of Walter Hagen (captain), Ralph Guldahl, Dick Metz, Harold McSpaden, Byron Nelson, Vic Ghezzi, Henry Picard, Horton Smith, Jimmy Hines and Sam Snead. The Great Britain and Ireland selectors had also announced their team. It included Henry Cotton (captain), Dick Burton, Sam King, Jimmy Adams, Dai Rees, Alf Padgham, Charles Whitcombe and Reg Whitcombe.

Above: The US team that never played. The match was cancelled because of the outbreak of war in Europe, but a number of exhibition matches were played between amateurs and professionals, in which the Ryder Cup trophy was presented to the winning team.

The final four places were never filled and, unlike in the United States, honorary medals were never awarded to the players.

Two years later in 1941, the American PGA decided to honour their finest golfers by selecting a Ryder Cup team that they knew would never be able to play. The team included Walter Hagen as non-playing captain, Vic Ghezzi, Harold McSpaden, Lloyd Mangrum, Byron Nelson, Jimmy Demaret, Ben Hogan, Horton Smith, Craig Wood and, finally, Ryder Cup veteran Gene Sarazen (who had inexplicably been left out of the side two years earlier).

Unlike in 1939, this United States team, captained by the great Bobby Jones, did actually play against a team of British-born professionals, including Tommy Armour, and raised over $25,000 for the Red Cross. The result hardly mattered; what did matter was that the Ryder Cup had continued to survive in one form or another. So by the time the War ended in 1946, plans were immediately put into action to resume the matches on a home and away basis.

5

The Hogan Era

1947

PORTLAND GOLF CLUB, PORTLAND, OREGON, USA

1–2 NOVEMBER

After a decade of inactivity, the Ryder Cup once more took centre stage. Following six years of war, golf in the United Kingdom was recovering only slowly from closed golf courses and club members on active service. With many club professionals also in the armed forces, there were effectively no competitive tournaments between 1940 and 1945. In 1946, after the barbed wire that surrounded the greens at St Andrews had been removed, professional competition got underway with the staging of the first Open Championship since Dick Burton's win there in 1939.

In the United States, professional golf had gone on much as before. In deference to American soldiers fighting overseas, sports such as baseball and American football had in general kept a low profile. Golf took a similar path, and while the United States Open was cancelled between 1942 and 1945, and the Masters tour-

nament between 1943 and 1945, there were enough professional tournaments to have warranted an order of merit throughout the war years (apart from 1943, when no money winner records were kept).

In stark comparison to Ben Hogan, who was the leading United States money winner between 1940 and 1942, young British professionals like Charlie Ward were serving in the Royal Air Force. While a professional tour of sorts continued in America, Ward and his contemporaries almost had to re-learn the game in readiness for the challenge ahead. For two years after the war had ended, professional golf in Britain struggled to survive in a time where rationing of food, clothing and petrol was still commonplace. Therefore it came as a surprise to many that a November date had been agreed by the respective associations for the next Ryder Cup match.

The British PGA found itself poorly equipped to accept the invitation from the Americans to play in Portland, Oregon. An appeal was considered, but in a time of national austerity the idea was sensibly dropped. Perhaps more surprisingly, the United States PGA were struggling to raise enough funds to put on the event. Potential sponsors had shown little interest in the match and for some months the Ryder Cup was in real danger of dying. Finally, after weeks of skilful and secret negotiation by the executive director of the United States PGA, Fred Corcoran, the Ryder Cup was saved by the unlikely figure of Robert A. Hudson.

Hudson was a wealthy American industrialist whose company annually sponsored the Portland Open. A member of the United States PGA Advisory Committee, he was approached by Corcoran and convinced of the rich potential such an international event had to offer. On the understanding that the event be played in Portland, Hudson himself agreed to underwrite the expenses incurred by the British team on their journey to New York on board the *Queen Mary*. Welcoming the British professionals and their captain, Henry Cotton, to America, Hudson proved a generous if slightly flamoyant host. At a reception banquet in New York he invited film stars like Dorothy Lamour to entertain the visitors and made gifts of clothing and even a radio to each of the British team. He then accompanied them on the arduous three-and-a-half-day rail journey to the north-western state of Oregon where the first Ryder Cup match for a decade would finally get underway.

The British team included only three survivors from its defeat at Southport in 1937 – Dai Rees, Sam King and Henry Cotton. With the exception of Cotton, a selection committee was appointed by the British PGA to draw up the shortlist of fourteen players from which nine would be selected. Looking for a more youthful blend of professionals to take on the Americans, the remaining places were filled by Charlie Ward, Eric Green, Reg Horne, Max Faulkner, Jimmy Adams, Arthur Lees and, finally, Fred Daly, the newly crowned Open Champion.

Below: Suited, booted and ready for action, the 1947 British Ryder Cup team prepares to leave England and head for America. Despite the confident impression they gave off, they were woefully under prepared after six years of war and ran headlong into a powerful USA team that had no such problems.

For the American side, a complex new selection process had been introduced. Invented by George Schneiter, Chairman of the United States PGA Tournament committee, it involved points being awarded to any professional finishing in the top ten of a tour event. Running from January 1946 to September 1947, the winners of the United States Open and PGA Championship were awarded 100 points, with 95 for the Masters, 80 for the prestigious Western Open and 70 for all other PGA co-sponsored events. Team places were then decided by the executive committee of the PGA based upon points awarded during this period. The system was greeted with a certain amount of scepticism – not least by the British PGA – but it was deemed to be fair and later formed the basis of the current selection process.

Ben Hogan was appointed playing captain for the United States and his team was a typically strong one.

Below: Ben Hogan (left) looks on as British professional Jimmy Adams putts up from the front edge of the green during their foursome match at Portland. Hogan was captaining the USA for the first time and the war years had dented neither his skill nor competitive spirit as he led his talented team to an emphatic 11 to 1 victory.

According to the *Daily Telegraph* it was as 'good a side as any that has ever played against Great Britain and probably better'. It included some real stars with players such as Jimmy Demaret, Herman Barron, Lew Worsham, Lloyd Mangrum, E.J. Harrison, Ed Oliver, Herman Keiser, Sam Snead and possibly the best player in the world at that time, Byron Nelson.

Born in Texas, Nelson had been the leading United States money winner in 1944 and 1945, and had accumulated an amazing record of tournament titles. Excused from military service because of haemophilia, he won thirteen out of twenty-three tournaments in 1945 and eighteen out of thirty-one a year later. Including a world record of eleven consecutive professional tournament wins, he went into semi-retirement because of ill health and failed to play a single event during the later stage of the Ryder Cup qualification period. Consequently, Nelson was offered a special invitation to play; he duly accepted.

Perhaps the biggest problem with bringing the Ryder Cup to Oregon in November was the weather. Portland had experienced its wettest October for sixty-five years, with more than an inch of rain falling the night before the match was due to begin. The course was playable but overall conditions were terrible, with

flooded bunkers, drenched fairways and soaked greens. 'Toots' Cotton, wife of team captain Henry, remarked, 'no club in England would consider even holding a monthly medal in such weather'. Dai Rees later compared the climate with that of India during a monsoon. Even during practice, large galleries turned up to watch the action. With spectators allowed to roam unchecked, the rough soon churned up into a muddy morass, which the players were happy to receive relief from during the match itself.

Despite the British-style conditions, it was the American professionals who adapted best. Much was made in the golfing press about their amazing ability to spin the ball backwards on the greens, while British players' shots just seemed to have 'burrowed straight into the turf'. American journalist Robert Caldwell also described how advances in golf equipment in the United States had contributed to the players' ability to control the ball. This was too much for Henry Cotton. On the last afternoon of practice he demanded that the American team's golf clubs be inspected for illegally deep grooves. With the two captains looking on, an American PGA official inspected all the clubs in secret and nothing untoward was found. Ben Hogan and his teammates had submitted to Cotton's request without complaint, but two years later at Ganton the incident was to have its repercussions.

Another odd request from Henry Cotton came the following morning, shortly before the opening four-somes were due to get underway. Gathering the British team together for what was thought to be a tactical discussion, Cotton held a bible aloft and asked for a period of 'meditation'. How the other players greeted this is unsure, but it appeared to make little difference to the whitewash that followed.

At lunch on the first day the British team was narrowly up in two matches but heavily down in the other two. In the opening match, Henry Cotton had paired himself with newcomer to the Ryder Cup Arthur Lees. Competing against Ed Oliver and Lew Worsham, Lees, a tenacious little golfer from Sheffield, performed well on his debut but was let down by his partner's erratic putting. Lunching 6-down to the Americans, they failed to mount a recovery in the after-noon, losing by the huge margin of 10 and 8. Playing behind them were the British pairing of Charlie Ward and Fred Daly against Sam Snead and Lloyd Mangrum.

Above: (Left to right) Jimmy Adams and Max Faulkner line up in the rain before their match against Ben Hogan and Jimmy Demaret. The tree-lined course was playing long due to the poor weather that week and the British pair proved no match for Hogan and the big-hitting Demaret, eventually losing 2-down.

Mangrum, decorated for his part in the D-Day landings, combined well with the relaxed easy style of Snead and they ran out eventual winners by 6 and 5.

The third game matched Jimmy Adams and Max Faulkner against Jimmy Demaret and American captain Ben Hogan. The extrovert Faulkner relished the challenge of taking on Hogan and began by striking a majestic two-iron second shot to the first green. Playing the opening nine holes of the match in 33 gave the British pair a 4-up lead. After cutting the gap to only 2-down at lunch, Hogan, in typical style, forced the pace in the afternoon with partner Demaret and managed to win on the final green 2-up. In the last match of the opening foursomes, Dai Rees and Sam King were up against Byron Nelson and, possibly the weakest link in the American team, Herb Barron. After losing the early advantage, the British pair finished only 1-up at lunch. Then in the afternoon round, Nelson began to assert his authority on the game with vital putts on the eleventh, twelfth and thirteenth greens. A fine tee-shot on the par-3 seventeenth hole by Nelson culminated in a useful 2 and 1 victory over the dejected

Rees and King. The result on the first day was a clean sweep of all four foursome matches to the United States.

With the singles considered something of a formality by the American press, Ben Hogan demonstrated his faith in his team by dropping out in favour of E.J. 'Dutch' Harrison. Continuing the tradition set by previous American captains, including Walter Hagen, of playing all ten members of the team, he also replaced Sam Snead with Herman Keiser. As the opening singles match got underway with Harrison against Irishman Fred Daly, it was to prove one of the most disastrous days in Ryder Cup history for the British team.

In contrast to the United States policy of giving everyone a game, Henry Cotton ignored the claims of Eric Green and Reg Horne in favour of more experienced players who had lost badly the day before. It would prove a huge mistake. Beginning with Harrison beating Daly (5 and 4) and ending with Jimmy Demaret's defeat of Dai Rees (3 and 2), the British team would lose seven out the eight singles – eleven matches

Above: Dai Rees congratulates Jimmy Demaret after suffering a heavy defeat in the singles. Interestingly, the Welsh firebrand met the flamboyant American four years later at Pinehurst with much the same result!

in a row, counting the foursomes. With only one match in the whole series reaching the final hole – Hogan's and Demaret's 2-up win over Adams and Faulkner – the ignominy of defeat was complete.

There had been occasional moments of hope for the British team. Arthur Lees had battled well against Byron Nelson to only lose by 2 and 1. Dai Rees had given Jimmy Demaret the shock of his life by going into the final nine-holes 1-up before the American found an extra gear to win 2 and 1. Even the experienced Henry Cotton was no match for the youthful Sam Snead. Looking increasingly frustrated at his inability to hole a putt, Cotton battled back after going into lunch 3-down. Closing the gap to 1-down, the smooth swinging Snead pulled away once more to win by 5 and 4. With further defeats for Charlie Ward at the hands of Ed 'Porky' Oliver (4 and 3) and Jimmy Adams loss against Lew Worsham (3 and 2), the match started to take on embarrassing proportions.

Cotton and the British team were finally saved at the last gasp from a complete 12–0 defeat by a late win for Englishman Sam King. Level after the morning round, King played steady rather than spectacular golf, but his 4 and 3 victory over Herman Keiser proved a welcome distraction from the criticism a complete whitewash would have drawn. Considering the lack of competitive golf the British squad had played in recent years, few had expected them to win. Yet the size of the defeat had come as an unpleasant surprise to the British golfing public; even the continuation of the Ryder Cup was coming into question.

Some time later, Robert Caldwell addressed the basic differences between the British and American players during the Ryder Cup at Portland. Offering the opinion that the British style of play had advanced considerably from ten years earlier, he wrote:

> They [the British team] drove just as straight as our players, if not quite as far. Their second shots were adequate but lacked the consistent accuracy of the Americans and consequently, over thirty-six holes, the British were all under far greater pressure on and around the greens. The modern American professional excels in the trap-shot, the chip of any description and with his putter, which more than any club earns him his living.

It was a lesson from which the British golfers would do well to learn.

1949

GANTON GOLF CLUB, SCARBOROUGH, YORKSHIRE, ENGLAND

16–17 SEPTEMBER

Arriving in Southampton for the first Ryder Cup match played on British soil for twelve years, the United States team ran straight into a storm of controversy. Robert Hudson, the American industrialist whose personal fortune had saved the event from dying out two years earlier, had taken the unusual step of transporting $1300 worth of fresh meat over to England. Hudson reasoned that, with food rationing still in force in Britain, the cost of feeding the American squad would be spared their British hosts if they brought in their own food. When approached by the press over the growing scandal, he intimated his hope that the British players would help them eat a haul that included six hundred steaks, twelve sides of rib-eye beef for roasting, a dozen hams and twelve boxes of smoked bacon!

The meat might well have gone unnoticed except that it was stopped by customs officials, who immediately demanded an import licence. Not everyone welcomed the gift of food, however, believing that it smacked of charity. In a row that seemed to rumble on, the controversial fare was later served at an American-sponsored banquet for the two teams in London. On finding out about the meat that was to be served, the wives of British team members all refused to take part – unlike their husbands, who appeared to tuck in heartily.

One American who was not feeling particularly generous towards his British hosts was Ben Hogan. Like Henry Cotton in 1947, he questioned the legality of some of the golf clubs being used by certain members of the British side – most notably Dai Rees and Dick Burton. Hogan claimed that the grooves did not conform to the rules and demanded they be filed back to lessen their potential for backspin. The British PGA, placed in a highly embarrassing situation, hurriedly drove to a Scarborough hotel to consult with Bernard Darwin, Chairman of the Royal and Ancient's Rules of Golf Committee. Summoned from his pre-dinner bath, Darwin was asked to inspect the clubs and, in typically

Above: Captain Ben Hogan in his team uniform. Considered the most competitive professional of his or any other era, he caused controversy from the moment he arrived by questioning the legality of the clubs used by members of the British team, much to the disgust of the press and public alike.

succinct manner, proclaimed that 'it was nothing a little filing would not put right'. Hogan's complaint thus upheld, the suspect clubs were then spirited back to Ganton, where club professional Jock Ballantine spent the night filing the grooves to the required depth. Dai Rees considered the whole affair a waste of time, claiming that rough filing would sharpen the edges of the grooves, effectively imparting more spin rather than less. With the iron clubs belonging to Arthur Lees and Sam King also coming under close scrutiny, the whole affair left a sour taste in the mouths of the British players. They also objected to the publicity surrounding the matter, which contrasted markedly with the discreet way in which a similar matter had been handled at Portland two years earlier.

Surprisingly, press opinion generally supported Hogan's request for an inspection. *Golf Illustrated* rumbled on about how clumsily the whole affair had been handled and how 'no captain should be put in the invidious position of having to make the request'.

Refusing to blame Hogan for the controversy, they ended with a call to introduce compulsory checks at all major professional events. On the same subject, British golf journalist Leonard Crawley wrote:

Too much emphasis has been laid on Hogan's insisting on an inspection of clubs before the match. The fact that Bernard Darwin saw fit to agree with Hogan's objections to certain British clubs is proof beyond doubt that Hogan was right. I would have done exactly the same myself in Hogan's position.

As the storm raged on unabated, both the British PGA and their newly appointed non-playing team captain, Charlie Whitcombe, failed to show any strong leadership. Following the withdrawal of Henry Cotton from the British squad only weeks before the match was due to begin, the chances of a home victory were lessening day by day. (Cotton had also refused to play under Whitcombe as captain because he felt he should have been given a second chance by the PGA after the 11–1 thrashing two years earlier.) As for the players, they were told to continue practising and ignore the squabble as best they could.

Below: Max Faulkner clowning around at the welcoming banquet. A smiling Ben Hogan gets the joke but British professional Arthur Lees, seated second from the right, obviously does not.

Despite all the distractions, the British team members showed some fine form in practice. Chosen from a 'merit-list' devised by the PGA, the original shortlist of sixteenten players was then narrowed down to ten players. The selected team consisted of Max Faulkner, Charlie Ward, Sam King, Arthur Lees, Dick Burton, Jimmy Adams, Ken Bousfield, Dai Rees, Laurie Ayton and Fred Daly. Both Sam King and Charlie Ward had rounds of 62 in final practice.

In many ways, the United States side was an unknown quantity. Surprisingly, only three members of the team had played in Britain before – Jimmy Demaret, Sam Snead and Lloyd Mangrum. Out of the remaining team of Ed Harrison, Johnny Palmer, Bob Hamilton, Clayton Heafner, Chick Harbert and Skip Alexander, only 'Dutch' Harrison had any Ryder Cup experience. Probably the most notable omission from the side was the new United States Open winner, Cary Middlecoff. The American PGA considered that he had not been a member of their association long enough and decided against his automatic inclusion in the side for 1949. This ruling brought howls of protest from Gene Sarazen, among others, who later described the PGA as 'archaic as the hickory-shafted baffy, the sand-tee and red golfing jacket'.

Another competitor missing from the action was non-playing captain, Ben Hogan. He had suffered multiple injuries in a severe car accident six months earlier – he was in hospital for fifty-eight days after crashing head on into an overtaking bus in Phoenix – and was considered fortunate to even be at Ganton. In total, Hogan would be out of golf for a year – he would make a legendary comeback a year later by winning the United States Open at Merion – but during the Ryder Cup match he was just able to walk with the aid of crutches. Restricted to the holes within easy reach of the clubhouse, the determined American still managed to drive on his players in the later stages of each match.

Huge crowds of spectators greeted the opening day foursomes. In the first match, Max Faulkner and Jimmy Adams stepped up to face the American pairing of Harrison and Palmer, and for once British play matched the crowd's expectations. Amid scenes of great excite-ment, the first Ryder Cup foursomes match to be played in Britain for a decade ended in a home win. Inspired by Faulkner's superb iron-play, the two Englishmen finished the first eighteen holes 3-up before eventually

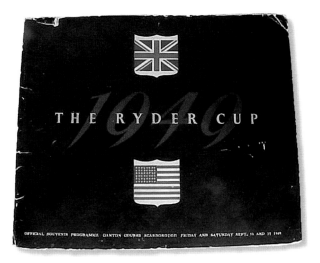

Above: The official programme for the 1949 match at Ganton Golf Club. Often discarded after the match, early Ryder Cup programmes have become highly collectable in recent years with any copy in mint condition fetching a high premium at auction.

going on to win 2 and 1. Maintaining the wonderful form they had shown in practice, Faulkner and Adams went round Ganton in 69 (the Americans in 71).

This high standard was matched by the game behind involving Ken Bousfield and Fred Daly against Skip Alexander and Bob Hamilton. Round in 69 in the morning, the British pair gained a two-hole advantage on the Americans at lunch. With the experienced Irishman Daly encouraging the newcomer Bousfield to even greater heights, they ran out eventual 4 and 2 winners. With two points in the British bag, there were great hopes for the in-form pairing of Charlie Ward and Sam King in their match against Jimmy Demaret and Clayton Heafner. Sadly, they were unable to handle the American pair, who played their last eight holes in 3–4–4–3–3–4 to win by 4 and 3. Shortly after, memories of another home victory, similar to the one at Southport in 1933, were rekindled after Dick Burton and Arthur Lees beat Sam Snead and Lloyd Mangrum on the final hole.

With a 3–1 advantage from the first day foursomes, things looked to be going Britain's way. Needing only 3½ points from the remaining eight singles matches, hopes were understandably high. Captain Charlie Whitcombe decided to put Max Faulkner out in the first match, where he faced the relatively inexperienced American 'Dutch' Harrison. Having already beaten him in their opening foursome match, the Englishman should have had the advantage, but Harrison began the morning round with four birdies in the first six holes. This remarkable start of 3–3–4–3–3–3 destroyed Max Faulkner and to some extent the British players behind him. Considered the best player on the British side, Faulkner would go on to win the Open Championship in 1951, but for now his 8 and 7 defeat at the hands of Harrison was to prove a severe blow to his team's morale.

Even with Jimmy Adams' 2 and 1 defeat of Johnny Palmer in the second game, American wins for Sam Snead over Charlie Ward (6 and 4) and Clayton Heafner over Dick Burton (3 and 2) left the Ryder Cup result balancing on a knife-edge. In the fourth singles match, Dai Rees's wonderful round of 65 contributed to his 6

Below: Lloyd Mangrum plays his approach to the opening hole during his singles match against Irishman Fred Daly. A five-time Ryder Cup player, Mangrum would captain the American team four years later at Wentworth.

and 4 win over Bob Hamilton. With the little Welshman in unstoppable form, his American opponent had called for divine help on the twenty-eighth hole when faced with a long putt. 'You up there,' Hamilton cried out, 'come on down and help. But don't send your son this time. This is a man-sized job!' The putt went in.

With the crowds scampering back and forth between the games, the final three singles matches became vital. In what transpired to be one of the great American comebacks in Ryder Cup history, Sam King was the first to fall to Chick Harbert (4 and 3) and was quickly followed by Jimmy Demaret's demolition of Arthur Lees by 7 and 6. With the British team needing to win the final match to gain a half, hopes were raised when Fred Daly led Lloyd Mangrum by 1-up shortly after lunch. All square with nine to play, the talented American surged to a 4-up lead with a run of 3–2–4–3–4 from the eleventh hole onwards. Losing 4 and 3, Irishman Fred Daly and his team could only look on as the Ryder Cup disappeared once more to the United States.

1951

PINEHURST COUNTRY CLUB, PINEHURST, NORTH CAROLINA, USA

2–4 NOVEMBER

After losing the last two matches, the British travelled to Pinehurst more in hope than expectation. With the gap in ability between the two teams now perceived to be a yawning chasm, Leonard Crawley described how 'the British would be out-hit to such an extent that they would be unable to cope with their opponents on such a fearfully long course'. Dismissing any thoughts of victory, Henry Longhurst wrote in *Golf Illustrated* that the 'best the British team could expect was one win in the foursomes and possibly two in the singles'.

Crawley was correct about one thing – the frightening length of Pinehurst No. 2. Soaked by heavy overnight rain, the majestic course, designed by Donald Ross, played every inch of its 7200 yards. So much so that it was decided to move the competition tees forward for the week. A pine and sand golf course, it resembled Sunningdale in parts and probably suited the British team more than their American opponents. The unusually cold weather also favoured the visitors, with American professionals like Clayton Heafner forced to wear an overcoat between shots; even Ben Hogan chose to wear pyjamas under his golfing shirt and trousers.

Apart from the weather, the American team was also unhappy about arrangements for the prestigious North and South tournament due to be played at Pinehurst immediately after the Ryder Cup had finished. With the star-name American players already at the venue, the sponsors had gone back on their promise to increase the prize-fund to $10,000. To keep them there, the Ryder Cup had been extended over a period of three days, with a rest day between the foursomes and singles matches so that both teams could attend a game of American football. (The United States team later boycotted the game at the University of North Carolina in protest.)

With Sam Snead taking over as American captain from new Masters Champion Ben Hogan, the side

Above: Pinehurst has long been considered one of the premier golf resorts in the United States and was chosen as the venue for the first Ryder Cup of the 1950s. This was also the first time the match had been played over three days rather than two.

remained much as before. With Hogan now playing, the team offered a good blend of youth and past Ryder Cup experience. Along with new boys Jack Burke and Henry Ransom, the team comprised Jimmy Demaret, Lloyd Mangrum, Clayton Heafner, Skip Alexander, 'Dutch' Harrison and Ed Oliver.

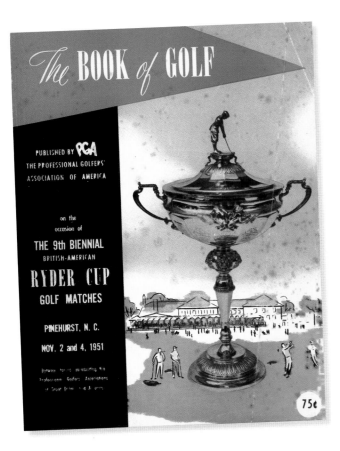

Above: The official programme for the 1951 Ryder Cup at Pinehurst. Offering a hole-by-hole view of the course and player profiles, it provided the visiting public with an insider's guide to the biennial match.

Like the Americans, who had first introduced a 'points for performance' selection process in 1947, the British PGA had devised a merit system of its own. A panel was appointed to choose eight players to represent Britain with the final two places delayed until after the *News of the World* Match Play tournament. From a shortlist of sixteen, the team included Arthur Lees, Jimmy Adams, Jack Hargreaves, Ken Bousfield, Charlie Ward, Dai Rees, Max Faulkner and Fred Daly. Experienced Ryder Cup veteran Arthur Lacey was appointed non-playing captain, and two new players, Harry Weetman and John Panton, were taken on. Once again, Henry Cotton was a possible candidate for the British team. His last Open Championship win had come only three years earlier in 1948, but his tournament appearances had been limited in recent years by increasingly poor health. The British PGA felt this was reason enough to omit him from the team.

The first day foursome matches were greeted by a heavy mist that hung about the pine trees and reduced visibility to a few hundred yards. The British opened their campaign with the pairing of Dai Rees and their newly crowned British Open Champion, Max Faulkner. Playing against Clayton Heafner and Jack Burke, they struggled on the dew-covered greens and found themselves 3-down after nine holes of the morning round. Despite reducing the deficit with a 3–4–3–4 finish, they could not sustain the pressure and eventually went down 5 and 4.

The second match between Charlie Ward and Arthur Lees against the American pairing of Henry Ransom and Ed Oliver enjoyed some of the best golf seen in the 1951 Ryder Cup. The British players finished the first round 3–3–2–5–3–3 to finish 3-up with an approximate round of 69, a lead they sustained until the end, finally winning by 2 and 1. Playing behind was the strongest American partnership: Sam Snead and Lloyd Mangrum. Not expected to lose, they duly defeated the sadly outclassed Jimmy Adams and John Panton by 5 and 4. The same margin of victory applied to Ben Hogan and Jimmy Demaret in their win over Fred Daly and Ken Bousfield (a result made a little more respectable after the British pair had fought back from being 9-down).

After the 3–1 first-day drubbing, the British team probably welcomed the rest day before the singles got underway on November 4. The press, while sympathetic to the British team's plight, seemed more interested in lionising the American players. Hogan's legendary reputation as a cold, calculating golf machine was first introduced to the British golfing public by Henry Longhurst in an article for *Golf Illustrated*:

> Among the gallery in the fourth match, bearing no outward and visible sign connecting him with the proceedings, is a small dark man with grey raincoat, grey cap, grey trousers, and inscrutable expression, looking somewhat like a Pinkerton detective on watch for Pickpockets. This is the world's greatest golfer, Ben Hogan, participating in a Ryder Cup match.

Going into the singles, any hopes of a British comeback relied on Jimmy Adams beating Jack Burke in the opening game. He lost by 5 and 4. In the second match, Dai Rees faired slightly better against Jimmy

Demaret. All square with nine to play, the Welsh professional performed well, but every time he thought he had won the hole, the flamboyant American hit back with a series of fantastic sand saves to halve or win the hole. Getting up and down from sand ten times out of eleven, Demaret reeled off four birdies in five holes to run out winner by 2-up. Demaret later gave his sand wedge to the Welshman as a keepsake!

Falling 5–1 behind to the USA, the British team knew the Ryder Cup was effectively over as Weetman lost to Mangrum (6 and 5), Ward lost to Hogan (3 and 2), Panton lost to Alexander (8 and 7) and finally Faulkner lost to Snead (4 and 3). Apart from the well-

deserved half for Fred Daly against Clayton Heafner, the only British success was Arthur Lees's singles win over Ed 'Porky' Oliver. Though Lees was the only British player to ever win all his matches in the USA, it did little to soften a humiliating 9–2 defeat at the hands of the Americans, the first of many more to come. The Ryder Cup was in danger of losing its competitive edge.

Below: British professionals Max Faulkner and Harry Weetman. Winner of the British Open at Royal Portrush earlier that year, Max (left) was an extrovert individual, who was known to have entertained the crowds at British tournaments by walking down the fairway on his hands when things got a little quiet!

6

False Dawn

1953

WENTWORTH CLUB, VIRGINIA WATER, SURREY, ENGLAND

2–3 OCTOBER 1953

After a gap of twenty-seven years, the Ryder Cup returned to its spiritual home at Wentworth, bringing back memories of that first unofficial match. The West Course had changed little in the intervening time but the Ryder Cup certainly had. Professionals from both sides now struggled hard throughout the season just to qualify. Strong public interest on both sides of the Atlantic brought glory to the victors and ignominy to the losers. While both teams treated the event with great respect, the almost casual air of previous years had been replaced with an intense rivalry. The Ryder Cup was no longer an event to enjoy, it was something that was either won or lost.

In 1953 there was a feeling of optimism throughout Britain that extended to the Ryder Cup. Queen Elizabeth had been crowned at Westminster Abbey, Edmund Hillary had conquered Everest and England

had beaten Australia to win the Ashes at cricket. A middle-aged Stanley Matthews had rolled back the years to gain his only FA Cup winners' medal at Wembley and popular Czech tennis player Jaraslov Drobny had won at Wimbledon. As for our chances of beating the Americans at golf, the best possible news – Ben Hogan was not playing.

In a surprise decision, Hogan had refused an invitation to play at Wentworth. Having come back from the near-fatal car accident that had ruled him out of the 1947 Ryder Cup at Portland, Hogan nevertheless didn't consider his legs to be strong enough to play thirty-six holes in a day – the standard requirement for matches at Wentworth. For British golf fans, the omission of Hogan from the United States team was a double-edged sword. Having won the Masters at Augusta in the spring, Hogan had gone on to win both the

American and British Open Championships in the summer and was generally considered to be the world's greatest golfer. While his presence would have been welcome at Wentworth, it would have lessened considerably the chances of a home win.

Having accumulated three of golf's four major titles in 1953, Hogan declined to play in the United States PGA Championship for the same reasons he gave for not playing in the Ryder Cup. Apart from the logistical problems involved in getting back in time after the British Open at Carnoustie, the event scheduled thirty-six holes of match play per day.

Certainly the new PGA winner Walter Berkemo was not among those who would have been pleased to see Hogan competing at Birmingham Country Club in Michigan. Along with Dale Douglas, Ted Kroll, Fred Haas and Cary Middlecoff, Walter Berkemo was among five newcomers to the United States team. With experienced Ryder Cup veteran 'Dutch' Harrison also declining an invitation, the American PGA had little choice in fielding a comparatively weak side at Wentworth. Lloyd Mangrum was appointed playing captain and the remaining places were filled by Jack Burke, Sam Snead, Jim Turnesa and Ed Oliver.

Above: Captained by war hero Lloyd Mangrum, the American team that took on the British at Wentworth had a decidedly jaded look about it, with many of the players, including Oliver, Turnesa, Burkemo and Kroll, aged 35 or older.

In contrast, the Great Britain and Ireland team had a fairly good look about it. Henry Cotton had been persuaded to take the role of non-playing captain and team selector. Taking this position perhaps more seriously than he did as a player, Cotton was present at Wentworth during the Ryder Cup trials instigated by the British PGA, which took place a few weeks before the real competition was due to begin. A newly formed Tournament Committee was to choose ten players from a shortlist of seventeen. With professionals of the calibre of John Jacobs, Ken Bousfield, Sam King and Arthur Lees all missing out, the final team included newcomers Peter Alliss, Eric Brown, Harry Bradshaw and Bernard Hunt. The more experienced members consisted of Fred Daly, Dai Rees, Max Faulkner, Jimmy Adams, Harry Weetman and John Panton.

The forward-thinking Henry Cotton insisted on only the best for his team, who were staying at the Dormie House in Sunningdale. With the American

Above: Led by three-time British Open winner Henry Cotton, the British team were convinced they could reverse the trend of Ryder Cup defeats and came very close to achieving that aim on the final day.

squad resident at the luxurious Kensington Palace Hotel in London, the British captain made sure his players received both fine food and five-star treatment. A great believer in a good lifestyle breeding good golf, Cotton even managed to take his men to a West End theatre to see *Guys and Dolls*. Keeping his team under one roof was an important part of his plan. Despite some of the professionals being local to the area (Harry Weetman was at Croham Hurst and Jimmy Adams at nearby Wentworth), Cotton wanted them to bond as a team. Not unlike J.H. Taylor back at Southport in 1933, the three-times Open Champion wanted to foster a strong team spirit by making sure his team practised together, ate together and discussed how to beat the Americans together.

Convinced they could pull off a surprise, Cotton started his campaign by leaving out his two most expe-rienced players, Faulkner and Rees, from the opening foursomes. Instead he chose to play Harry Weetman and the youngest professional ever to play Ryder Cup golf, Peter Alliss. Quite what the young player – the son of four-times Ryder Cup stalwart Percy Alliss – was thinking as he stood on the opening tee about to face Dale Douglas and Ed Oliver is unsure.

The match itself was a close affair, with the British pair holding a 1-up lead at lunch. Three holes into the afternoon round, one of the most curious refereeing decisions in Ryder Cup history occurred when the Americans' tee-shot was lying unplayable at the base of a tree. The match adjudicator, Admiral Sir Charles Forbes, ruled that as it was in a rabbit scrape a free drop was allowed. After they had holed a huge putt and escaped with an undeserved win, this inaccurate ruling gave Oliver and Douglas just the luck they needed and they went on to take full advantage. Standing on the famous seventeenth tee, the Americans stood dormie 2-up before promptly driving out of bounds on the left. With the door now wide open, the British pair then contrived to halve the hole in six and lose the match by 2

and 1. For a frustrated Henry Cotton, standing by the edge of the green, it was to prove sadly typical of what was to follow.

With the remaining British pairs struggling throughout the day just to keep level with their American opponents, the first day score of 3–1 down was probably the best they could hope for. In a wonderful exhibition of golf, Jack Burke and Ted Kroll scored 66 in their morning round against Jimmy Adams and Bernard Hunt before winning by 7 and 5. This was almost matched by Sam Snead and Lloyd Mangrum with a 67 on the way to defeating Eric Brown and John Panton by 8 and 7. With three matches lost, British honour was saved by the Irish double act, Fred Daly and Harry Bradshaw.

The first Ryder Cup pairing drawn from both Northern and Southern Ireland, Daly and Bradshaw battled hard against the strong American partnership of Walter Berkemo and Cary Middlecoff. After being 3-up with just nine holes left to play, the Americans had cut it back to only 1-up with three. However, it proved to be just enough of an advantage for the two Irishmen,

Above: A smiling Max Faulkner shows off his skills to American team members Sam Snead and Porky Oliver prior to the singles. Despite having won the British Open at Royal Portrush only weeks before, he and the highly rated Welshman Dai Rees were inexplicably dropped from the opening day foursomes by Captain Henry Cotton. In retrospect, it was a decision that possibly cost the home team victory.

eventually running out 2-up winners. Despite the tongue-lashing that Cotton later gave his team, it was a welcome victory that had stopped the possibility of a highly embarrassing United States' whitewash in the opening foursomes. The crowds at Wentworth also felt the tide had turned. After Portrush-born Daly had holed his winning putt on the final green, the delighted gallery enthusiastically clustered around the two players. The feeling was that anything was possible, and in the singles the following day, they almost were.

After being dropped from the foursomes, Welshman Dai Rees was given the task of playing against Jack Burke in the opening singles. Still convinced that Britain could win, Henry Cotton had emphasized the

Above: An historic Ryder Cup keepsake: the official menu for the welcoming banquet held prior to the Ryder Cup at Wentworth. The banquet was a grand affair, at which players from both teams went around the tables asking for their fellow professionals' signature as a memento.

importance of a flying start against the Americans during his captain's team talk the night before. Unfortunately, other less tactful comments about a need to 'kick the team's asses', had also been picked up by the press, resulting in every news-stand carrying the quote in banner headlines. ('Toots' Cotton had been so incensed that she had spent the morning tearing them down wherever she could find them.)

Putting his toughest competitors out early, Cotton followed Dai Rees in the singles with the in-form Fred Daly against Ted Kroll, followed by Eric Brown against Lloyd Mangrum. Next came Harry Weetman against Sam Snead and Max Faulkner against Cary Middlecoff. The two young professionals Peter Alliss and Bernard Hunt followed. They were out against Jim Turnesa and Dave Douglas, while the dependable Harry Bradshaw

was in the final game against Fred Haas. Cotton knew that his strategy of putting his experienced players out first could backfire as the match drew to a close, but it appeared a risk worth taking. Equally, leaving out John Panton and Jimmy Adams after their poor showing in the foursomes was a difficult decision, as was putting Faulkner out against the talented Middlecoff. The 1951 Open Champion had performed badly in practice but Cotton believed he would come through under the pressure of competition.

After a two-hour delay because of fog, Dai Rees set out in the opening singles. Still unable to see more than 200 yards, the Welshman mistook the line to the first and second greens to find himself 2-down after five to Jack Burke. To his credit, by the time the mist had lifted, Rees had fought his way back to all square by lunch. Sadly, erratic putting by Rees, combined with some steady golf by Jack Burke, derailed the great British comeback. With little to choose between the two players in terms of skill, the American stood 1-up playing the par-5 seventeenth. Playing his downhill approach to the green from 80 yards, Burke surprised the gallery by reaching for his putter and striking his ball along the ground in what was later described as a 'Texan wedge' shot. The ball finished only a foot away for a tap-in birdie and a 2 and 1 victory over Rees.

Losing the opening singles was a severe blow to British hopes. The overall match score was 4–1 to the Americans, but there was better news for Cotton in the second game. The magnificent Irishman Fred Daly had been 6-up on Ted Kroll after the first eighteen holes, going on to beat him by a margin of 9 and 7. This result echoed around the tree-lined West course at Wentworth and appeared to inspire his fellow teammates in the afternoon round. In the next match, Eric Brown had a battle on his hands against the Ryder Cup veteran Lloyd Mangrum. Before the match had begun, Brown had actually promised a point to his captain, Henry Cotton. True to his word, the gritty Scotsman had held onto his 2-up lead at lunch to win by the same margin in the afternoon.

With the remaining five singles in the balance, rapid calculations showed that the match could indeed be won. Despite Max Faulkner losing out 3 and 2 against Cary Middlecoff, Harry Weetman had made one of the greatest comebacks in Ryder Cup history against Sam Snead: from being 4-down with five to play, Weetman had won all five and the match. The sudden realization that Britain could actually win came with Harry Bradshaw cruising to a 3 and 2 victory over Fred Haas in the final match. It all depended on the final two matches and the possibility that Peter Alliss, 1-down with one to play, could halve, and that Bernard Hunt, 1-up with one to play, could win.

In the full ghastly light of publicity, the young Peter Alliss had already suffered poor fortune over the previous two holes. After being 1-up with three holes to play, he had watched his American opponent, Jim Turnesa, slice violently off the tee on the par-4 sixteenth only to strike a spectator and fall safe. Building on his good luck, Turnesa then escaped with a par from a greenside bunker to win the hole and square the match. Alliss suffered the indignity of driving out of bounds on the following hole to go dormie 1-down. His growing anguish can only be imagined as he stood a hole later by the side of the last green faced with a delicate pitch. With Turnesa struggling to make par after three badly hit shots, Alliss had struck a two-iron second just to the left of the green and looked in a good position to halve the match despite being close to the small grandstand that flanked the green. Setting up the ball, Alliss later described how his mind 'was full of nothing but feet, rows and rows of feet – brogues, moccasins, sneakers, boots, shoes, spikes, rubbers, the shoes of the people perched on the front seats of the grandstand'.

Feeling apprehensive, he then remarked how 'all those boots and shoes kept popping idiotically in and out of my mind'. The result was a predictable skuff that only managed to move his ball just a few yards ahead. Still short of the green in three, he gathered himself long enough to play a trim little run-up, just over a yard short of the hole. Still with a chance of winning the hole and the match, Turnesa then missed his putt for a five and made bogey. Then, from short range, Alliss missed his putt! It was a half in six and, as Henry Longhurst later conjectured, 'if he had quietly lost his match out in the country, the rest of his golfing life might have been different'. Certainly, it must have been a devastating blow to the confidence of the young British professional. While he would never fulfil his dream of winning the Open, Alliss would go on to become one of the best-known commentators on the sport.

Even with the defeat of Alliss, the Ryder Cup was still there to be tied. Bernard Hunt had been all square

with Dale Douglas at lunch before edging his way to a precious 1-up lead playing the par-5, eighteenth. With Bradshaw having lost, British hopes now depended on the lanky Englishman stealing a last-minute victory that would halve the entire match, but once again nerves would play a big part in the outcome. With both men on the green in regulation, Hunt had two putts to win his match and took three! Faced with a three-foot putt for glory, he lost the hole to par, and once again the Ryder Cup was gone.

Winning by a single point – 6 to 5 – Lloyd Mangrum said afterwards that he would, 'never, never captain an American team again because of the nine thousand deaths I suffered in the last hour'.

For many players the pressure encountered at Wentworth that day would stay with them for the rest of their careers.

Above: Henry Cotton (right) can only look on in envy as fellow captain, Lloyd Mangrum, shows off the golden trophy his USA team has just won after a nail-biting finish. Ending a fragmented history with the event that dated back to 1929, this was the last time that Cotton would play an active role either as a player or captain in the Ryder Cup.

7

Swings and Roundabouts

1955

THUNDERBIRD RANCH AND COUNTRY CLUB, PALM SPRINGS, CALIFORNIA, USA

5–6 NOVEMBER

Even before play got underway in the eleventh Ryder Cup at Palm Springs, the match was seen as a sporting non-event. Not only had the British side failed to win since the war, but they had also managed to accumulate only three points in the last two visits to the United States! And while the Ryder Cup continued to be well supported in Britain, the actual match had survived only because of the financial generosity of Robert Hudson. With America seemingly able to produce any number of teams capable of beating the British, it was obvious that something needed to be done if the Ryder Cup was to survive.

First to act was Sam Snead, who suggested that fourball matches replace the traditional foursomes. With more golf to see, Snead believed that American audiences would favour the move but, not surprisingly, the British golfing press and PGA balked at the mere

suggestion. Despite the fact that the score stood at 7–2 in favour of the United States since the event began, they preferred instead to hang onto the widely held myth that British teams were more accustomed to playing them than their American counterparts. The match would go on as before.

Yet even the British PGA was not immune to the criticism. Hoping to produce a more competitive team, it had evolved a new system of team selection for the forthcoming match in America. Following a meeting with top tournament professionals, it was decided that the first seven places would be filled from an order of merit based around the Open Championship in July. It was a totally new concept: only five tournaments would go towards Ryder Cup selection in the hope that only in-form professionals would be making the trip to America. To bolster the team, the remaining three places would then be decided upon by the PGA tournament subcommittee on an invitation-only basis.

With the United States side chosen over a two-year period, it was considered by many that this new British system would result in a weakened team made up of 'Johnny-come-latelys'. This view was further strengthened by the omission of two of Britain's brightest young professionals, Peter Allis and Bernard Hunt. Despite the chastening experience of Wentworth two years earlier, both players had come back well. Alliss had won both the 1954 Daks tournament and the 1955 Dunlop Masters event prior to the qualification period and expected to be picked in the PGA's final choice of three.

Unfortunately for the twenty-four-year-old professional from Parkstone Golf Club in Dorset, it was not to be. Like most talented golfers, Alliss was considered inconsistent, and he suffered more than most on the PGA's new rule that points were to be deducted if a player failed to make the final day of a tournament. For Alliss, the final straw came at the Open Championship at St Andrews, where he failed to even qualify for the event proper.

Along with Dai Rees as captain, newcomers to the Ryder Cup team consisted of Johnny Fallon, Christy O'Connor, Syd Scott and John Jacobs. Making up the rest of the team were three survivors from Wentworth: Harry Weetman, Eric Brown and Harry Bradshaw, who were joined by Arthur Lees and the newly crowned PGA Match Play Champion, Ken Bousfield. There had also been some talk about Henry Cotton making a Ryder Cup comeback. Still competitive at forty-eight, Cotton was ultimately thought to be 'too old', which, considering the average age of the British team, seemed faintly ridiculous. With Alliss and Hunt not in the side, only John Jacobs was under the age of thirty, while the oldest player in the side was Arthur Lees at forty-seven.

The US team also had a decidedly middle-aged feel about it. Although the team included five newcomers to the Ryder Cup – Jerry Barber, Marty Furgol, Doug Ford, Chandler Harper and Tommy Bolt – the average age of the players was thirty-seven. Taking over as non-playing American team captain from Lloyd Mangrum was Chick Harbert. He also inherited four previous team members from Wentworth: Cary Middlecoff, Ted Kroll, Jack Burke and Sam Snead.

The opening series of foursome matches was greeted by bright blue skies and marching music from the kilted

Above: The 1955 British Ryder Cup Team. With no victories on American soil in the entire history of the event, the British introduced four rookies in Fallon, O'Connor, Scott and Jacobs in the hope of changing their woeful record.

band of the American Sixth Army. From the fleet of electric buggies that followed each game to the Californians in their multi-coloured attire and huge straw hats, everything at the Thunderbird Ranch and Country Club was larger than life. At a time when golf in the desert was a comparative novelty, the newly built course nestling between vast mountain ranges near the Palm Springs resort was in wonderful condition. Unlimited water had been discovered a few hundred feet down and, to quote the locals, all you had to do was 'spread the seed, apply the water and jump back'.

Sam Snead had observed that at only 6314 yards the course was a little short and would perhaps favour the British. However, this touch of gamesmanship was also qualified with the comment about how difficult they would find playing from the Bermuda grass fringes around the greens. In contrast to many golf courses – even in the United States at that time – the designer, Jimmy Hines, had put water hazards around the greens where before there would have been sand. His theory was that you could 'splash' out of sand but certainly not out of water. For British players facing this type of golf for the first time, it would prove a novel experience.

The first day foursomes saw three new faces in the visiting team's line-up. The opening pair, Johnny Fallon

Above: Lacking many of the big name players from the past, such as Hogan and Nelson, the 1955 US Ryder Cup team had an average age of 37 and was considered among the weakest American sides ever to play in the Ryder Cup.

and John Jacobs, were both accomplished tournament players, as was Syd Scott, who partnered Eric Brown in the second match. Facing Chandler Harper and acknowledged short-game wizard Jerry Barber, the two Englishmen acquitted themselves well in the lead-off game. Even with Barber holing out three times from off the green, Fallon and Jacobs found themselves only 2-down at lunch. With the help of some fine putting by Fallon, they managed to forge a 1-up lead with only nine holes to play before the American partnership did a little fighting back of their own. After the British pair three-putted the eleventh hole, missing the opportunity of going 2-up, the pressure was always going to be on them down the closing stretch. Jerry Barber chipped in again at the thirteenth to reduce the gap, but Fallon and Jacobs' iron play stayed rock solid all the way to the final hole. Yet even here there was a sting in the tail.

Standing dormie 1-up on the eighteenth green, Fallon and Jacobs were only four feet from the hole in three. With an opportunity to chip-in for a match-saving birdie, Chandler Harper nervously fluffed his shot. Then, just as Fallon was expecting to have two-putts from no distance for the game, Barber calmly stepped up and holed his chip from off the green. To his credit, the British professional ignored the loud cheers from the American gallery and holed his short putt for a half and a 1-up win.

The opening match was not the only cliffhanger in the foursomes. In the third game out, Harry Weetman and Arthur Lees had played superbly in the morning round for 68 to be only 1-up on Tommy Bolt and Jack Burke. In what must have proved a frustrating experience, they went out in 34 in the afternoon to find their lead had not improved. Tommy Bolt, playing in his first Ryder Cup, was a determined competitor known for his short fuse when things were not going his way. 'Lightning' Bolt, as he was known, revelled in the battle and it was his second shot within feet of the last hole that finally turned things around for the American pair. Now holding a 1-up lead playing the eighteenth, Jack Burke was forced to hole the putt as just moments earlier Weetman had made birdie for the British team.

Considered a turning point in the whole Ryder Cup match, the 1-hole victory for Tommy Bolt and Jack Burke made the first day score 3–1 to the United States. With Brown and Scott losing to Ford and Kroll 5 and 4, and Bradshaw and Rees losing to Snead and Middlecoff 3 and 2, the scoreboard had a familiar and disappointing look about it. The series of eight singles due the next day offered little hope, but as the escape from the hurricane had proved, miracles were possible.

With vocal support from good-size crowds, the United States team had taken a strong hold on the singles by lunch. Tommy Bolt had raced to a 3-up lead on Dublin-based Christy O'Connor, Chick Harbert was 6-up on Syd Scott, Sam Snead was 5-up on Dai Rees, Middlecoff was 2-up on John Jacobs and Doug Ford was 1-up on Harry Weetman. The remaining games were evenly balanced, with both Lees against Furgol and Bradshaw against Burke all square. The only notable British success after the morning eighteen was the redoubtable Eric Brown, who was 3-up on Jerry Barber.

The British comeback, when it came, was surprising in its compass. The British captain, Dai Rees, started the fight back by winning four of the opening six holes of the afternoon round. Having faced a barrage of birdies in the morning, Rees had the opportunity of going level with Snead after the American had sliced his drive at the long seventh. With the straw-hatted Snead hard up against a palm tree and Rees reaching the edge of the green for two, it looked like a tied game. Instead, the 1946 British Open Champion pulled off a miracle recovery, which resulted in an eagle-three and a sudden two-hole swing. It was a bitter blow, but the tigerish Welshman still managed to fight all the way before eventually going down 3 and 2.

As Dai Rees was winning holes against Snead, Syd Scott was steadily pulling holes back from Chick Harbert, but the finest performance of the day was coming from John Jacobs in his match against Cary Middlecoff. Despite scoring a 69, Jacobs found himself 2-down at lunch to the qualified dental surgeon Dr Cary Middlecoff. With the help of a razor-sharp short game, Jacobs had pulled back to level after the first nine holes in the afternoon, before consecutive birdies at the twelfth and thirteenth took him 2-up. A huge birdie putt across the seventeenth green by Middlecoff halved the deficit, before Jacobs finally holed out from six feet

on the last green for a well-deserved 1-hole victory. Jacobs' final round 65 remained the unofficial course record for some years after.

The golf played in the 3 and 2 defeat of Marty Furgol by Arthur Lees was hardly in the Jacobs/Middlecoff class, but it proved an exciting bonus as holes started to run out for other British team members. With Scott finally losing 3 and 2 to Harbert, and O'Connor losing 4 and 2 to Bolt in the opening match, the writing was on the wall. Even with Eric Brown's 3 and 2 victory over Jerry Barber, further British defeats by Burke over Bradshaw (3 and 2) and Ford over Weetman by the same score saw the Ryder Cup still in American hands.

Despite the disappointment of losing, Lord Brabazon of Tara, President of the British PGA, gave a rousing address at the closing ceremony. With Churchillian overtones, he remarked, 'We have learnt a lot, although we have lost, and we are going back to practise in the streets and on the beaches.' Brave words, but they would come back to haunt the Americans two years later at Lindrick.

Above: 'The man who saved the Ryder Cup', Bob Hudson, stands between US captain Chick Harbert (holding trophy, left) and British captain Dai Rees. The matches were becoming a one-sided affair with yet another American win.

1957

LINDRICK GOLF CLUB, SHEFFIELD, YORKSHIRE, ENGLAND

4–5 OCTOBER

Lindrick Golf Club in Yorkshire was an unpopular choice of venue for the 1957 Ryder Cup. A heathland course with tree-lined fairways, it was thought to favour the United States team far more than a links course such as Southport and Ainsdale might have done. Questions were also raised about using a course that was bisected not once, but twice by a main road. However, the main point of contention was its lack of length. Measuring only 6541 yards, it had too many holes requiring just a drive and wedge. With the American players acknowledged

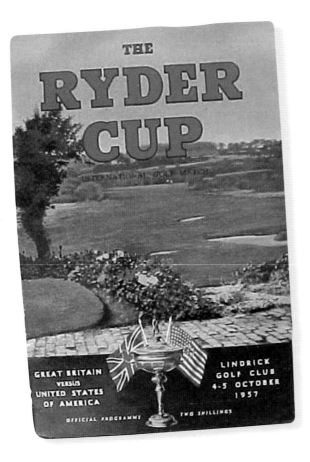

experts with the short irons, two extra tees were built to lengthen the course, but the calls from the British press for a change of venue went on unabated.

In hindsight, the British PGA who accepted Lindrick as a Ryder Cup venue had little choice in the matter. With the last British victory over the United States back in 1933, interest in the event was sadly waning. While the Ryder Cup proved to be a well-supported event locally, financial backing had proved more elusive and this was still the case only a few months before the match was due to be played in Britain. The Ryder Cup was in mortal danger and desperately needed a saviour in the same mould as Robert Hudson. Thankfully, one was at hand: a last-minute sponsor was found in Yorkshire industrialist Sir Stuart Goodwin.

Like Sam Ryder, Stuart Goodwin had found golf late in life. After a luncheon engagement had been cancelled at short notice, he had watched an exhibition match at Lindrick involving Dai Rees and Fred Daly. Intrigued by the skill shown by these professionals, the fifty-eight-year-old magnate met with the Secretary of the British PGA, Commander Roe, to discuss the possibility of bringing a major tournament to Lindrick. Agreeing to underwrite a three-year, £15,000 deal to sponsor a professional tournament, Sir Stuart Goodwin was approached about funding the forthcoming Ryder Cup. Coming up trumps once again, Goodwin gifted the British PGA the sum of £10,000, with the pledge that they would also receive all gate money. The Ryder Cup was saved, the only condition being that the match should be held at Goodwin's home club of Lindrick.

Left: The official Ryder Cup programme for 1957. Despite complaints that Lindrick in the north of England was not a suitable venue to host such a prestigious event, it proved the perfect choice for the Great Britain and Ireland team.

On balance, the British team was fairly strong compared with the one that had played at Palm Springs two years earlier. The entire team was now selected via a new system that involved scoring points for top-twenty finishes in all professional stroke-play tournaments, including the Open Championship. Further points were then awarded for high finishes in the Dunlop Masters and PGA Match Play events. Dai Rees was elected playing captain of a side that now included Ken Bousfield, Eric Brown, Christy O'Connor, Harry Bradshaw, Max Faulkner and Harry Weetman. With newcomer to the Ryder Cup Peter Mills, plus younger players such as Peter Alliss and Bernard Hunt coming back into the side after a four-year absence, the overall feeling was one of surprising confidence.

The American team, in contrast, showed little of the depth and quality of past years and lacked many of the more familiar star names – both Sam Snead and Ben Hogan, winners of the 1956 Canada (later World) Cup, had declined to play. Cary Middlecoff and Julius Boros had also been omitted from the side because they had

Above: The British team that faced the USA in 1957 included such seasoned players as Faulkner, Rees, Alliss and Bousfield. Selected via a new order of merit system, the team had a mix of youth and experience that would eventually prove far too strong for its American rivals.

chosen to play in a lucrative exhibition match instead of competing in the United States PGA Championship. Even with three-time Ryder Cup veteran Jack Burke elected as playing captain, the team had a weakened look about it. Along with Doug Ford, Tommy Bolt and Ted Kroll, the American team included six newcomers: Dow Finsterwald, Fred Hawkins, Dick Mayer, Art Wall, Lionel Hebert and Ed Furgol.

With defeat considered an unlikely proposition even in Britain, the American PGA put little pressure on its golfing superstars like Hogan and Snead to play. After seven victories in a row, they were understandably complacent about winning; but as in Britain after the era of Vardon, Braid and J.H. Taylor, the professional game in the United States was in a curiously transitional period. With the gradual decline in prowess of Hogan and Snead over the previous five years, apathy had begun to set in. However, for now at least, the American team gave the clear impression that to win the Ryder Cup, all they had to do was turn up. At Lindrick they were in for a major shock.

Perhaps recalling what happened during the later stages of the match at Wentworth in 1953, when both Peter Alliss and Bernard Hunt had faltered in their crucial single matches, Dai Rees sent Peter Alliss and Bernard Hunt out first in the foursomes. Now established as leading tournament professionals in Britain, they were matched against the comparatively weak American pairing of Doug Ford and Dow Finsterwald. Whether nerves played a part is unsure, but failing to even match par in the morning, the two Englishman lost a close match 2 and 1.

Paired with the soft-spoken Ken Bousfield in the second match, Dai Rees found himself 2-down early on before squaring his match by lunch against Art Wall and Fred Hawkins. After losing both the third and fourth hole in the afternoon, the British pair played wonderfully to claw five holes back from the Americans to run out 3 and 2 winners. Having levelled the overall match, Rees made his way out to the course to offer his support to the remaining two British pairs.

In the third match, Max Faulkner and Harry Weetman were both struggling to find any form against Ted Kroll and Jack Burke and eventually lost by 3 and 2. There was equally bad news in the final foursomes between Eric Brown and Christy O'Connor against the United States' strongest team of Tommy Bolt and Dick Mayer. Despite the British pair playing par-golf throughout, the two Americans built on a morning round of 67 to demolish Brown and O'Connor by 7 and 5.

Losing the opening four matches was considered a real disaster by Dai Rees. Looking to fight back in the singles the next day, Rees called his men together to discuss team selection. He also wanted to know who had performed badly and called for the day's scorecards to provide the information. They probably told him what he already knew – Max Faulkner and Harry Weetman had struggled to break 80 in the morning and showed even less form during the afternoon. After Rees asked for an open discussion, Faulkner immediately told the gathered assembly that his playing had been 'rubbish' and asked to be excused from the singles. Harry Weetman is said to have followed shortly after. With the matter thought to have been settled amicably, the controversy that followed must have come as quite a shock to the British captain.

Shortly after Rees had exchanged the order of play list with American captain Jack Burke, Harry Weetman allegedly told a waiting journalist how he would never play under Rees as Ryder Cup captain again. Asked about the matter, Rees was understandably dumbfounded. The two men had been long standing friends and travelling companions, and as the

Left: With Harry Weetman looking on, Max Faulkner lines up a putt near the end of their alternate shot match against Ted Kroll and Jackie Burke. They lost out to the American pair and both men were later dropped from the singles.

controversy gathered pace, Rees refused to make any further comment until the match was over. Weetman was later called before a PGA disciplinary hearing and banned from PGA-sanctioned tournaments for a year.

On the morning of the singles, conditions at Lindrick were in direct contrast to those of the previous day. The greens, dried out by a brisk easterly wind, were cut much shorter on the orders of the British PGA to speed them up. (Incredibly, the course green-keeper believed the Ryder Cup was starting a day later than it did, resulting in much slower greens than was normal.)

As for the golf, the acrimonious encounter in the opening singles match between Eric Brown and Tommy Bolt appeared to set the tone for the day. 'Lightning' Bolt, like many of his teammates, had been upset by the vocal way in which the Yorkshire crowds had cheered missed American putts during the four-somes. Continuing to complain throughout the match, Bolt found himself 3-down after just seven holes to a determined Eric Brown. The Scotsman had built on his 4-up lead by lunch and he eventually won by a margin of 4 and 3. Bolt, who had broken a club shaft over his knee in frustration shortly after the game had ended, complained to fellow team member Ed Furgol, 'They cheered when I missed a putt and sat on their hands when I hit a good shot.' Furgol, to his credit, told the fuming American to 'Pipe down – you were well and truly licked.'

After the defeat of Tommy Bolt, perhaps the biggest shock of the day came in the second match between Peter Mills, Ryder Cup newcomer, and Jack Burke. Along with Harry Bradshaw, Mills had been brought into replace Max Faulkner and Harry Weetman in the singles. In this battle of the 'substitutes' – Jack Burke only decided to play after Ted Kroll had fallen ill the night before – Peter Mills surprised everyone by taking an early 4-up lead on his vastly more experienced opponent. Helped by some poor putting by Burke, Mills moved 5-up by lunch and never looked back. Winning by 5 and 3, his victory over the 1956 United States PGA Champion had levelled the overall match score at 3–3.

With Ken Bousfield 5-up early in the afternoon round against Lionel Hebert, Bernard Hunt 5-up against Doug Ford with nine left to play, and Irishman Christy O'Connor winning six out of the first eight holes against Dow Finsterwald, an upset was definitely in the making. As the crowds scrambled across

Lindrick to get a view, occasional roars would fill the air from different parts of the course as yet another British win was registered on the wooden scoreboards. For all the headlines in the morning newspapers about the row between Rees and Weetman, all that interested most British supporters was winning the Ryder Cup.

A defeat for Peter Alliss by Fred Hawkins in the third match out was a severe blow. Alliss had reeled off four wins in six holes to claw his way back from being 3-down early in the afternoon round. Unfortunately, he

Below: Scottish professional Eric Brown contemplates his approach to the first. The singles match against the equally fiery Tommy Bolt ended in defeat for the American by the margin of 4 and 3. As they shook hands, Bolt commented how little he had enjoyed the game. Typically, Brown replied in blunt style, 'No, neither would I if I had been given the hiding I just gave you!'

could not maintain his tight lead after Hawkins had birdied the long fourteenth and sixteenth holes. After halving the seventeenth, the American registered his team's first win by 2 and 1. Almost unbelievably, it was also to be their last. In a remarkable series of results, Christy O'Connor (using a putter newly purchased from the pro shop at Lindrick during lunchtime) had beaten Dow Finsterwald by 7 and 6. Like the first match between Tommy Bolt and Eric Brown, this encounter had some unsporting moments. As early as the third hole in the morning, Finsterwald had raked his ball away after missing his putt. The hole having not been conceded, the match referee immediately awarded it to O'Connor. Later in the game, the American angrily marched off after his losing tap-in was conceded, leaving the Irish professional standing alone on the green. Thinking the hole had been given, O'Connor

rolled his first putt up to the hole and picked it up. On the next tee, Finsterwald asked what had happened and promptly claimed the hole. With the remaining match played in this edgy atmosphere, both men refused to shake hands after the game had ended.

The win for Christy O'Connor was closely preceded by Dai Rees's 7 and 6 demolition of Ed Furgol. Realizing that victory was now possible, the British captain quickly shook hands with Furgol, then raced off around Lindrick in pursuit of the vital two points from the final three matches that would give him the Ryder Cup. The first point was not long in coming. Playing behind Rees, Bernard Hunt redeemed himself for the defeat at Wentworth two years earlier by crushing Doug Ford 6 and 5. One look at the scoreboard told Rees what he wanted to know. Harry Bradshaw was tied with Dick Mayer with only four holes to play, but out on the fifteenth green Ken Bousfield was about to beat Lionel Hebert by 4 and 3. Bousfield had been 7-up at one stage during the afternoon round but had given away three consecutive holes in what looked suspiciously like a

Below: Triumphant British professional Bernard Hunt leaves the course accompanied by his wife after dealing a hammer blow to American hopes with a surprise 6 and 5 victory over Doug Ford.

Above: With dejected members of the American team looking on, Dai Rees gives his victory speech outside the Lindrick Clubhouse. The first British win since the matches resumed after the war, it would prove a short-lived triumph as the USA resumed their dominance over the coming decade or more.

collapse. Faulkner and Rees had come charging through the crowds to inform him of the state of play. The British team needed his point and moments later the young Englishman obliged with a 4 and 3 victory. The vital seventh point had been won and even with Harry Bradshaw halving his match with Dick Mayer, the Ryder Cup was back in Britain.

It had been a hard-fought and well-won victory for the British team. With a celebratory mood sweeping through Lindrick clubhouse for some hours afterwards, the American team headed back to their hotel. Tommy Bolt and other team members continued complaining about everything from the hotel they were staying in to the food they were eating. Bolt also described the partisan Yorkshire crowds as 'the worst in the world' – a comment that was later disowned by Harry Moffitt, then President of the United States PGA. Despite the diplomatic comments from the American camp, the

final discourtesy to their British PGA hosts came when three professionals from the USA team refused to attend the prize giving and reception that followed.

When Tommy Bolt's remark filtered back through the American press, Moffitt also put on record how, 'several of the team had come to me and said how the crowd had been very fair. They had applauded their good shots as well as those of their opponents'. He was also generous enough to say how the result would prove a wonderful boost to the competition and how the Ryder Cup would go on for 'years and years'. How prophetic those words would prove.

8

A Non Contest

1959

ELDORADO COUNTRY CLUB, PALM DESERT, CALIFORNIA, USA

6–7 NOVEMBER

Fresh from victory at Lindrick two years earlier, the British Ryder Cup team boarded the *Queen Elizabeth* at Southampton in confident mood. Captained by Dai Rees, the team that had defeated the Americans had stayed intact apart from Max Faulkner and Harry Bradshaw. Both players were considered too old to withstand the pressures of the Ryder Cup and their places were taken by two newcomers, Norman Drew and Dave Thomas. It was a strong British side that set sail for the United States, but with the 1958 Munich air disaster that killed twenty-one still fresh in the public's minds, this was one British Ryder Cup team that almost never made it.

The decision to sail across the Atlantic rather than fly was intended to foster team spirit, but a heavy buffeting in the Atlantic saw many of them violently seasick before the ship docked in New York. The sea journey was followed by a gruelling trip across country,

and the British players and representatives of the PGA arrived in Los Angeles on 29 October 1959, seven days before the match was due to begin. Climbing onboard the twin-engine Convair for the forty-minute flight to Palm Springs, the team was expecting little more than a short hop across the San Jacinto mountain range to the air-conditioned splendour of the Desi Arnaz Hotel at Palm Desert. However, flying into the tail end of a hurricane that had devastated parts of Mexico, the small plane was tossed around, with baggage flying around the cabin. In fact, the movement of the Convair was so violent that an air stewardess was knocked senseless. During what must have felt a terrifying ninety minutes or so, the plane pitched and tossed until, suddenly, it literally fell out of the sky, plummeting from its normal height of 13,000 feet down to 9000 feet in a matter of seconds. Golf journalist Ronald Haeger, who was on the flight, later described the experience in the 1977 Ryder Cup brochure:

> The reality proved to be the nightmare none of the twenty-nine passengers would forget. 'Keep your seat belts fastened. There may be some rough weather ahead', our captain warned us. Rough? A little? A few minutes away as we approached the jagged peaks of the San Jacinto Mountains the plane began to toss like a cork as we met the storm that lit up the vivid purple skies. The bumps were mild at first but sufficient to turn bronzed golfers ashen. Heads ducked down between knees. Collars were loosened. In the eye of the storm the jolts increased in frequency and violence. We were trapped in a big lift racing up and down, berserk. The climax was still to come. It arrived with a new dimension of violence. There was a sickening downward plunge. We were a stone dropped in a well. Anything not strapped down took off and floated to the roof of the plane. Weightless. A grinding, crunching agonised sound of metal on metal heightened the horror. We didn't know it then but this was the brink of calamity. From that robots' wrestling match of sound we inched back from the edge of disaster. The metallic judderings of the aircraft were beautiful noises to the grappling pilot. He had regained command of the ship. He had won his battle with the furies of the elements.

Below: The British Ryder Cup team who almost never made it. Following a laborious journey over to America's West Coast, they were involved in a terrifying air incident that saw the plane they were in plummet thousands of feet in a matter of seconds.

After getting through the violent storm, fate had one last ironic twist for the British team. Only minutes from landing at the destination, the pilot was forced to return to Los Angeles as the severe weather had closed the Palm Springs Airport. After landing back at their original departure point, several of the players understandably fell to their knees to kiss the tarmac and thank heaven for their deliverance. Amazingly, not long after the Convair had landed, they were offered another flight back to Palm Springs. It came as no surprise to anyone that Dai Rees declined the offer, preferring instead to travel by Greyhound bus.

For those who had been onboard the ill-fated flight to Palm Springs, John Letters, of the famous John Letters Golf Company, formed a society aptly entitled 'The Long Drop Club'. Apart from the British players

themselves, it included other notable members, including Commander Roe, Secretary of the PGA, and Frank Pennink, golf course architect. Also among its number were a liberal sprinkling of Americans, including Lou Freedman, Vice-President of the United States PGA, and Doug Ford, an American Ryder Cup player who was hitching a ride from Los Angeles!

Complete with their own club tie, the members would meet over dinner whenever possible in the years to come to enjoy each other's company and perhaps relive their experience. One British team member who escaped the horrific journey was John Panton. He had been called out as a last-minute replacement for Peter Mills, who had complained of a bad back after arriving at Eldorado Country Club. (Bernard Hunt was also doubtful after wrenching his shoulder during the flight from Los Angeles.) As things turned out, neither Mills nor Panton took part in the actual match.

The American team also had selection problems. Determined to exact revenge for the defeat at Lindrick, they appointed Jerry Barber as non-playing captain with a completely revamped team from two years earlier. With reigning United States Open Champion Billy Casper, plus Ken Venturi, Gene Littler and the emerging Arnold Palmer all ineligible because they had not completed the statutory probation period for membership of the PGA, they turned instead to proven tournament winners. With only Cary Middlecoff, Dow Finsterwald, Art Wall and Doug Ford surviving from the 1957 Ryder Cup, the team now included Sam Snead plus newcomers Julius Boros, Jay Hebert, Bob Rosburg and Mike Souchak.

Prior to the match at Eldorado, professionals from the United States and British teams ran up against two curious problems. Unlike today, when the Ryder Cup course is closed for at least a week before the event, Eldorado left the course open to members and the occasional paying guest right up to the day of the match! Often held up during play, Dai Rees complained bitterly but to no avail. The other problem concerned the tees from which the Ryder Cup was to be played. Both sets of professionals had practised from the back tees, only to find that on the first day of the match, officials at Eldorado had moved them in line with the ladies' markers. The reason for their decision was that television executives had wanted to guarantee low scoring for their audience, a novel

Above: Having made his debut at Lindrick two years earlier, American professional Dow Finsterwald won both his matches at Eldorado Country Club and went on to record a fine Ryder Cup record of 8–4–1.

concept that had the opposite effect because players were no longer sure of their yardages.

The match itself was an undistinguished affair, played on a less than testing golf course that included seven artificial lakes and imported citrus and palm trees, and failed to measure up to previous Ryder Cup encounters. The weather was pleasantly warm and the first-day foursomes were closer than expected. As in previous Ryder Cups, the British team made its customary slow start, losing both of the opening matches before Christy O'Connor and Peter Alliss restored some pride by defeating Art Wall and Doug Ford by 3 and 2. The score line was also eased by a draw in the final match between the strong American pairing of Sam Snead and Cary Middlecoff against Dave Thomas and Harry Weetman, leaving the match score at 2½–1½ to the Americans.

The foursome result appeared to confirm what everyone had thought – that Britain may have a fighting chance at home but in the alien conditions of America they had none. Even compared with previous Ryder Cup venues like Pinehurst and Portland, Eldorado Country Club was unlike anything the British players had encountered. The widespread feeling among the press was that the British professionals were exhausted by the time the match had begun. Leonard Crawley wrote in the *Daily Telegraph*:

> I regard it as essential that the British part should fly out one week beforehand and get rid of the present two weeks unnecessary preliminaries wandering about the United States and tiring themselves out like the Children of Israel in the desert before getting to the promised land. Travelling, and getting the kindest hospitality, is all great fun but is nevertheless frightfully exhausting.

Driven on by captain Dai Rees, the team's determination to mount a fight back on the scale of Lindrick two years earlier was just not there. By lunch on the day of the singles, Britain was down in six of the eight matches. Only Eric Brown, 3-up on Cary Middlecoff in the final game, along with Peter Alliss, who had a slender 1-up lead over Jay Hebert, looked to be mounting any sort of challenge against the Americans.

The afternoon saw occasional flashes of revival as the British team struggled hard to avoid a humiliating defeat. Dai Rees made a typically brave fight back in his match against Dow Finsterwald – coming from 6-down to all square before finally losing on the eighteenth 1-down. Ulsterman Norman Drew, making his first Ryder Cup appearance, hit a remarkable three-wood at the final hole to halve the opening singles match against Doug Ford. At the opposite end of the playing order, Alliss eventually halved with Hebert, while Eric Brown kept up his remarkable record in the singles by beating Middlecoff by 4 and 3. Unfortunately, by the time these two final results came in, the Ryder Cup had already been lost.

A string of five singles defeats in a row meant that the United States had won by 8½–3½. Learning from the match at Lindrick, American team captain Jerry Barber put his strongest players out early to ensure victory long before the final two games became important. Starting with Mike Souchak's 3 and 2 win over Ken Bousfield in the second match and following with Snead over Thomas by 6 and 5, Wall over O'Connor by 7 and 6 and finally Finsterwald beating Rees in the fifth game out, it was a solid performance by the United States team.

Afterwards, there was much talk on both sides of the Atlantic about the future of the Ryder Cup. Even though Britain and America had shared the honours over the last four years, it was felt that something must be done to improve the competitiveness of the event. Suggestions were made about bringing in players from the Commonwealth to compete – golfers such as the emerging Gary Player and three-times Open Champion Bobby Locke, both from South Africa, Peter Thompson and Kel Nagle from Australia and Bob Charles from New Zealand.

In the end, the British PGA deferred to Sam Ryder's original idea that the match should be contested solely between teams of professional golfers from Great Britain and Ireland and the United States. However, the pressure from America to make the Ryder Cup more 'audience friendly' was growing ever stronger. The thirty-six hole matches in both foursomes and singles were considered too long to hold the attention of American galleries and changes were made. The British PGA resisted as best they could, but if the Ryder Cup was to survive, the playing format had to be adapted in time for the next match at Royal Lytham St Annes. It seems that times, along with the Ryder Cup, were changing.

1961

ROYAL LYTHAM AND ST ANNES, ST ANNES, LANCASHIRE, ENGLAND

13–14 OCTOBER

The 1961 match at Royal Lytham and St Annes was a landmark event in the history of the Ryder Cup. After consultation between the respective professional associations, it was decided to introduce some new changes in the playing format. Scrapping the old thirty-six hole matches in favour of an eighteen-hole challenge, there would now be two sets of foursomes on the first day – four in the morning and four in the afternoon. Then eight singles matches would take place in the morning followed by eight in the afternoon. This revolutionary move to streamline the Ryder Cup for the modern era was proposed in March 1960 by Lord Brabazon of Tara, President of the British PGA. Under pressure from the

Americans to provide a more 'marketable' format, various suggestions had come forward but this was deemed the most practical. More importantly, it avoided the possibility of turning the Ryder Cup into a possible match between United States and Britain *plus* the Commonwealth to make it more competitive, which was something the British PGA wanted to avoid at all cost. Finally agreeing to the proposal in September, the United States PGA made a further recommendation for the match to be extended to three days so a series of fourball matches could be included.

Having gone so far, the British PGA would go no further. The new format had been agreed for Lytham and they would only consider further changes after the 1961 tournament was over. Surprisingly, the changes were universally welcomed by the golfing press – and later by the paying public who went to watch the match at Lytham. Writing for *Golf Illustrated* in 1959, Henry Longhurst originally accused the British PGA of being 'forced to it for economic reasons', primarily because the Americans had wanted a 'three-day show'. Four years later he had apparently changed his tune when he wrote:

> For years I have been pressing the case for having two 18-hole matches each day instead of one of 36, whether it be in the Ryder Cup, the University match, or any other Cup. It had so often happened that a couple of the four foursomes were virtually over by lunchtime and thus fifty percent of the interest disappeared from the spectators' point of view.

Prior to the match at Royal Lytham and St Annes – incidentally the first Open Championship venue to stage the Ryder Cup – press speculation on both sides of the Atlantic centred on which team these eighteen-hole 'sprint' matches would favour most. In theory, the new format should have favoured the weaker British team,

Above: Commander R.C.T. Roe, head of the British Professional Golfers' Association, and his counterpart from America join forces to promote the 1961 Ryder Cup match at Royal Lytham and St Anne's on England's windswept east coast.

whose players were quite capable of beating any of the top Americans on the day over the shorter distance. Of course, the fact that there were now 24 points available instead of 12 meant the team with greater strength in depth would win, which inevitably pointed towards the United States. It proved to be a fascinating conundrum, which generated more pre-match interest in the Ryder Cup than ever before.

Another story that captivated the golfing press, which broke only weeks before the match was about to start, was the omission of Sam Snead from the US team. Snead – one of the world's most famous golfers – had taken part in an unauthorized Pro-Am tournament in Cincinnati, Ohio. Despite the player's attempt to obtain permission before teeing off, this was considered a clear breach of PGA policy, which banned its members' participation in an event that conflicted with a legally sanctioned tournament. Snead later explained:

> I figured it wasn't anything more than a glorified exhibition. Five minutes before I am about to tee-off, someone tells me I'd better get permission from the Portland Sponsors, so I sent off a wire right away. When I finish 18 holes, I come into the clubhouse and there's the answer. Permission not granted.

Realizing his error, Sam Snead immediately withdrew from the thirty-six hole event in the hope that this would count in his favour. Shortly afterwards, another telegram arrived from the United States PGA disciplinary committee, which informed him that he would be fined $500 and banned from tournament golf for six months. It was a brutal punishment that was later amended to forty-five days, but for now it also meant the possibility of losing his Ryder Cup place in October. Three days after the Pro-Am had finished, a telegram arrived confirming that Doug Ford, who was eleventh in the Ryder Cup points list, had been chosen to replace Snead in the forthcoming match in England.

As newspapers in Britain and America blasted out the headlines 'Snead out of Ryder Cup', the player himself was understandably angry. After lodging an official appeal and threatening to get lawyers to fight the ban, Snead commented, 'This is the worst slap in

Below: The Yanks are here! The American Ryder Cup team, including debutante Arnold Palmer, boards the train in London en route to Liverpool. It was a relatively young side, and fitness would be important as the format of the match had been doubled from 12 matches to 24 by reducing each game to just 18 holes rather than the marathon 36 of previous years.

Above: The 1961 British Ryder Cup Team. Standing, left to right: John Panton, Ralph Moffitt, Bernard Hunt, Harry Weetman and Christy O'Connor. Sitting, left to right: Ken Bousfield, Neil Coles, Dai Rees, Tom Haliburton and Peter Alliss.

the face I have ever had. I went out of my way to enter enough tournaments to qualify for the Ryder Cup and I won't take it sitting down.'

Unfortunately for Snead, his appeal would be heard at the PGA's annual meeting *after* the Ryder Cup had ended. It proved a sad finish to a wonderfully competitive Ryder Cup career. In seven competitions stretching back to Southport and Ainsdale in 1937, Sam Snead had played thirteen matches, winning ten, halving one and losing only two. It was a remarkable record that few players on either side have ever come close to matching. Although he would be made non-playing captain at Royal Birkdale in 1969, his omission from the side at Lytham was more than enough reason for many golf fans to stay away in 1961.

Even without Sam Snead in the side, the general opinion was that this was one of the strongest American teams to have ever played in Britain. With the home side giving Dai Rees the captaincy for the fourth time in succession, the United States PGA continued their policy of sharing it around. It was decided, because of the extended format, that an honorary non-playing captain should be chosen, along with elected captain Jerry Barber. The idea was that with Barber out playing and unable to see who the in-form players on his team were, the task of keeping him informed would fall to past Ryder Cup veteran Ed 'Porky' Oliver.

The United States team offered a strong mix of youth and past Ryder Cup experience and included Mike Souchak, Doug Ford, Dow Finsterwald, Art Wall and Jay Hebert, along with newcomers Gene Littler, Bill Collins, Billy Casper and, perhaps the greatest of them all, Arnold Palmer. Now eligible to play in the Ryder Cup after serving the statutory PGA probation period, Palmer was already a big-name golfer in the United States. Two-time winner of the Masters in 1958 and 1960, United States Open Champion in 1960 and reigning British Open Champion, Palmer was already a highly popular visitor to British shores.

In contrast, the British side had a familiar look about it. The PGA had stipulated that all professionals had to have competed in seven of the nine British tournaments to be eligible. With few professionals able to enter this number of competitions, the list of players from which to choose was limited. The final team, picked shortly after the Open Championship, consisted of Peter Alliss, Bernard Hunt, Ken Bousfield, Harry Weetman, John Panton, Christy O'Connor, plus newcomers Neil Coles, Ralph Moffitt and Tom Haliburton.

With the new eighteen-hole format in place for the opening foursomes, it was essential to get off to a flying start. Alliss and O'Connor out in the first match against Americans Doug Ford and Gene Littler gave Britain the start they wanted by winning 4 and 3 despite a poor outward 9. After a successful start, the British collapse that followed was unexpected and demoralizing. In order of play, Panton and Hunt lost 4 and 3 to Art Wall and Jay Hebert, Rees and Bousfield lost 2 and 1 to Billy Casper and Arnold Palmer, and finally Haliburton and Coles lost by 1 hole to Bill Collins and Mike Souchak.

Incredibly, no sooner had the British side lost 3–1 in the morning than Dai Rees ordered the same pairings out in the afternoon with exactly the same result! Now 6–2 down after the first day, the press went looking for blood. Unlike the Americans, British playing captain Dai Rees decided against having someone to help with advice on team selection during the match. It was a decision he would later come to regret when the British golfing press used it as an excuse to criticize his captaincy.

Pairing himself with Ken Bousfield in the opening series of foursome matches, Dai Rees had hardly finished his morning game against Billy Casper and Arnold Palmer when he was called upon to select his team for the afternoon. In contrast, the United States team captain Jerry Barber had left himself out in the morning so that he could see exactly how his players were shaping up. No matter that Rees and Bousfield had won their afternoon match against Bill Collins and Mike Souchak by 4 and 2, Henry Longhurst summed up the feelings of many when he wrote:

Below: Big-hitting American Mike Souchak proved a real match winner. Pictured here driving on the tenth hole, he followed up a win and a loss on the opening day with singles victories over Ralph Moffitt in the morning and the experienced Bernard Hunt in the afternoon.

If we are to have 18-hole matches, which I most devoutly hope, then either the order of both morning and afternoon matches must be announced overnight, or we must have a non-playing captain, or the captain must not play himself in the morning. Or the captain, if he plays in the morning, must have a sort of assistant-cum-advisor with whom to consult at lunchtime. In the foursomes Rees had hardly got in when the first match was due to go out in the afternoon, and this threw an impossible burden of selection upon him. He could have seen nothing of the other players; he had only minutes to decide; and he had to get his own lunch and rest. He thus made what most critics deemed an error of selection which he later defended on the grounds that the players concerned could hardly play so badly twice running.

Unconcerned by the barrage of press criticism, Rees defiantly picked himself for the morning singles the following day. His other overnight decision was to replace the out-of-form Scottish professional John Panton with Ralph Moffitt, and Tom Haliburton with Harry Weetman. Ultimately, it was to make little difference, as the morning singles matches went the same disastrous way as the foursomes the previous day. The two replacements, Weetman and Moffitt, were put out in the opening two games against Doug Ford and Mike Souchak respectively. In a close match, Weetman played well enough to earn himself a putt to win on the eighteenth green. That missed, he failed to hole an even shorter return to lose by 1 hole. It was a devastating double blow that was quickly followed by Ralph Moffitt losing out to Souchak by 5 and 4. There was slightly better news in the third game between Peter Alliss and Arnold Palmer, who in the best spirit of the Ryder Cup had conceded each other a yard-long putt on the final green for a creditable half.

Another halved match between Littler and Coles failed to arrest the slide to defeat in the singles. In typically battling fashion, United States Open Champion Gene Littler had made a birdie 3 at the final hole to rob Neil Coles of his first win in the Ryder Cup. Captain Dai Rees then collected his second consecutive victory with a 2 and 1 win over Jay Hebert, with Bernard Hunt beating Jerry Barber by 5 and 4 in the penultimate match. Balanced against these results were further defeats for Ken Bousfield by Billy Casper (3 and 2) and Christy O'Connor by Dow Finsterwald (2 and 1).

After the morning singles were lost by the Brits 5–3, the criticism of Dai Rees's tactics was becoming more vocal. Following defeat in both sets of foursomes the previous day, the British team now found themselves 11–5 down in the overall match. With nothing short of a miracle needed in the final eight singles, the British captain defiantly placed himself in the middle order. Replacing Moffitt with the club professional at Wentworth, Tom Haliburton, Rees needed only the briefest glimpse at the scoreboard to see that his team needed to win all eight singles to hold the Ryder Cup.

Peter Alliss playing in the second game provided the first point with his 3 and 2 victory over Bill Collins. Weetman had played superbly in the opening match against Art Wall to make the turn in 33 strokes, only to find the American had scored 31 to be 2-up. With Bernard Hunt 1-up on Mike Souchak after nine holes in the third game, the impossible dream was still alive, but only barely. Weetman eventually pulled himself back to level with Wall before losing on the eighteenth, but the record books show that it was Souchak who finally sealed the match for the United States. From the turn, he made three 3s and five 4s in eight holes to beat Hunt by a score of 2 and 1. The Ryder Cup was in American hands once more.

To their credit, the British team performed well enough to win the last eight singles by 4½–3½. Whether the American team became complacent after retaining the trophy is unsure, but there were some fine individual performances, which gave some hope for the future. In the remaining matches Palmer was given a real fright by the indefatigable Tom Haliburton, who took him all the way to the seventeenth before finally losing by 2 and 1. In the last four matches there were British wins for Rees over Ford by 4 and 3, Bousfield over Barber by 1 hole and Coles over Finsterwald by 1 hole. The final game between Christy O'Connor and Gene Littler ended in a half.

With the final match score 14½–9½ to the United States, the post-mortem began in earnest. Tom Scott, editor of *Golf Illustrated*, wrote, 'It's the old story. Our men regard the match as something so special that they are unable to play their regular golf at the start and when they come to their senses, their opponents are one or two holes to the good.'

The *Daily Mail* was the first newspaper to produce statistics showing how close the match had actually been. In a strangely futuristic article, they studied the 399 holes played and worked out technical details like the amount of fairways hit (GB & Ire. 234 – USA 214), greens hit in regulation (GB & Ire. 153 – USA 157), and even the amount of single putts made (GB & Ire. 117 – USA 110). However, the most revealing fact of all concerned the final holes. For instance, out of the 24 matches, only seven failed to go to the sixteenth, and out of the ten games that went the full distance, the United States won three matches, halved six and lost only once!

Quite what these final statistics reveal is uncertain. Perhaps the amount of tournament play in the United States had prepared their professionals better for the nerve-jangling climax to the ten games that did reach the final hole. What is certain, however, is that if the British players had held their nerve better and the final hole result had been reversed, they would have walked away with a famous Ryder Cup victory instead of another ignominious defeat.

Below: Captain Jerry Barber is lifted aloft by team members, including Arnold Palmer, after guiding the USA to victory at Royal Lytham, signalling a sustained period of American dominance in the Ryder Cup. The emergence of other young stars, such as Billy Casper and Gene Littler (far right), meant that the golden trophy would stay in America for years to come.

1963

EAST LAKE COUNTRY CLUB, ATLANTA, GEORGIA, USA

11–13 OCTOBER

Among the many thousands of Americans who had watched the Ryder Cup on home soil, few understood the intricacies of foursome play. 'Scotch foursomes', as they preferred to call it, was hardly ever played in a country where singles or fourball match play was the chosen game. Indeed, it was not that common outside of its native Scotland. Looking to attract a future television audience, the United States PGA had proposed as early as 1960 that the format of the Ryder Cup be altered to reflect this situation. A formal request to replace foursomes with fourball matches was put before the British PGA, but it was understandably loath to give up foursomes and declined. Now, two years later at East Lake, the request had become a demand that the British authorities could no longer resist. After protracted discussion and an alteration to Sam Ryder's original Trust Deed, the match would now include two series of fourballs, two foursomes and one singles, all over eighteen holes. With 32 points at stake instead of the 24 on offer at Lytham, the Ryder Cup, for the first time in its history, would be played over three days.

Coming up to the match at East Lake – known for being the boyhood home of the immortal Bobby Jones – the British PGA had made some changes of its own. After the criticism that had followed the match at Lytham concerning Dai Rees, it was decided that a non-playing captain would be appointed to lead the British side. No longer would a captain be put under pressure to select the right players for the afternoon matches only moments after finishing his own game. Rees, who had doggedly defended his position as playing captain since 1955, was quietly replaced by Johnny Fallon.

A former Ryder Cup team member who had played under Rees at Thunderbird, Fallon was a soft-spoken man who had followed his father as club professional at Saddleworth Golf Club in Yorkshire. After his solitary foursomes win, partnered by John Jacobs, over Chandler

Harper and Jerry Barber in the opening match of the 1955 Ryder Cup, Fallon remains one of the few professionals on either team to boast a 100% record. Left out of the singles that year by Rees, Fallon must have felt some satisfaction in replacing the Welshman as British captain.

Another change from previous Ryder Cup matches in the United States concerned travelling arrangements. Acting on advice, the British PGA had reduced the pre-match exhibition matches, social engagements and assorted distractions to a minimum. The journey to America would be by air instead of sea and would include, for the first time, an official PGA delegation. Agreed in December the previous year, the decision was considered important to show the team's American hosts just how far the British had come since those austere days of post-war Ryder Cup matches.

Flying first class, the party now included the president of the PGA, various vice-presidents, the Secretary of the Association, Commander R.C.T. Roe, the managing director of the newly-formed PGA Co-operative, George Gibson, the captain and chairman of the PGA and assorted executive committee members. Wives were also invited, but in a curious twist to this lavishly funded trip, it was later found that a huge saving of £2000 could have been made if the party had flown tourist class. It was decided that on future trips, wives, though welcome, would have to pay for themselves.

Arriving at East Lake, the British team set hard at practice. Along with familiar faces from previous Ryder Cup matches, the side now included three newcomers: George Will, Brian Huggett and Geoffrey Hunt – the younger brother of fellow team member, Bernard Hunt. The remaining team consisted of Peter Alliss, Christy O'Connor, Harry Weetman, David Thomas, Tom Haliburton and Neil Coles. (Coles had been the only British professional to sail over to the United States because of a morbid fear of flying).

In contrast, the American team, captained by the great Arnold Palmer, had a formidable look about it. Selection was now based on a two-year points system, which tended to eradicate any one-off wonders who might once have made the side. Along with experienced past-Ryder Cup players like Bob Rosburg, Gene Littler, Dow Finsterwald, Billy Casper and Julius Boros, the team included first-timers Billy Maxwell, Johnny Pott, Dave Ragan and Tony Lema. With many of his side at the peak of their powers, playing captain Arnold Palmer boasted in the American press that his team 'would beat the rest of the world combined'. Writer Henry Longhurst was later quoted as saying that 'any team which gets twenty-five percent in America is doing quite well'. As the match result at East Lake was to show, he was probably right.

Above: The British Ryder Cup team disembark at Atlanta Airport ready to take on a powerful USA team at East Lake Golf Club. Travelling in first-class comfort, they were followed down the steps by their wives, who were later informed they would have to pay their own way on future trips!

The opening series of foursomes went well for the visiting side. With a surprising 3 and 2 win by Brian Huggett and George Will over Arnold Palmer and Johnny Pott, the British campaign got off to the perfect start. Despite Alliss and O'Connor losing 1-down to Casper and Ragan in the second game, two halved matches for Coles and Bernard Hunt against Boros and Lema and Thomas and Weetman against Littler and Finsterwald, the first-morning score was tied at two all. As this was the first occasion on which this had happened in the United States, the British team now approached the afternoon matches with renewed confidence. Sadly, however, it was to prove a false dawn.

Choosing his pairings for the afternoon, Fallon inexplicably broke up the partnerships that had done so well in the morning. Neil Coles later recalled the amazement felt by all the players concerned when he said:

> We were as chuffed as anything as we ate lunch and then up comes Johnny Fallon and says 'you boys played so well this morning, I'm going to split you up this afternoon – Neil to play with Geoff Hunt and Bernard [Hunt] with Tom Haliburton.' We couldn't believe our ears. We just sat and gaped.

As the afternoon foursomes came to a close, the worst fears of Coles and his fellow team members came to pass – they had been whitewashed 4–0 by the Americans. With British morale in tatters, the second-day fourballs offered little hope for a comeback. Long before the match began it was thought likely that such a format would prove an ideal stage for American skills – and so it was to prove. With so much strength in depth, the United States won the eight matches by 5–1 with two matches halved. In the morning games, Johnny Fallon had refused to repeat the successful partnerships of the day before, choosing instead to mix and match to no great effect. It was only under pressure from PGA officials that he kept together Coles and O'Connor (1-up winners over Goalby and Ragan) and Alliss and Bernard Hunt (half with Littler and Boros) for the afternoon matches.

Below: US playing Captain Arnold Palmer encouraging his team prior to taking on the British at East Lake Golf Club. Talking to the press in the run up to the match, he confidently predicted that his players could beat 'the rest of the world combined'.

Whatever the combinations, the British approached the final day series of singles matches needing to win thirteen of the remaining sixteen matches scheduled for the morning and afternoon. It was always an unlikely prospect, made all but impossible by the 5 and 3 defeat of Geoff Hunt by Tony Lema in the opening match. Yet as victory slipped out of their grasp, the British team began to perform to their potential with wins for Huggett over Pott, Alliss over Palmer, Weetman over Boros and Bernard Hunt over Dow Finsterwald.

As they basked in the glory of a 4½–3½ win over the Americans, perhaps the biggest surprise of the day came in Peter Alliss's 1-up victory over Palmer. In a replay of their halved match at Lytham two years earlier, the young Englishman had battled hard to reach the final hole with a 1-up lead. After holing a difficult three-yard putt to halve the seventeenth in birdie, Alliss hung on well at the last for a notable victory over the three-time Masters Champion. Then, in the penultimate match of the morning, Harry Weetman secured a valuable point for his team with a magnificent win over reigning United States Open Champion Julius Boros.

This acted as a wake-up call for the United States team, who came out with all guns blazing in the afternoon singles. Arnold Palmer, keen to avenge the two unexpected defeats he had suffered at British hands, beat George Will by 3 and 2 in the opening match. He set a good example for the rest of his team: with the USA winning seven of the remaining eight matches with one halved, this was to prove one of the most disastrous sets of results for any British team in the Ryder Cup. The final match score saw a humbling defeat for the British by 23–9.

In the post-match interviews the blame was widespread. Avoiding the thorny issue of team selection, Johnny Fallon believed the American players had a superior short game, while Palmer accused the British players of not practising enough. Whatever the cause, questions concerning the fairness of such a competition began to resurface. In an item for *Golf Illustrated*, three-times Open Champion Henry Cotton summed it up best when he wrote:

> I repeat what I have often said, that we cannot win this match in America. Despite the advantage we have in playing our own small-sized golf ball on these short visits to play in international encoun-

Above: Arnold Palmer (left) lines up next to the match referee shortly before his singles encounter against Peter Alliss on the final day. Alliss later moved on to a hugely successful career in the golf media and it is easy to forget what a talented player the young Englishman was in his youth. Indeed, he sprung a major surprise by beating Arnie in the morning before halving with Tony Lema in the afternoon.

> ters, we again were outclassed. We know, and have known all along, since the game of golf got underway in the twenties, that good players were in great numbers there, and with the sun throughout the year, practice facilities and huge rewards, we were up against an insoluble problem. The present top home players, by no means poor performers, are leagues outside the tough American ones.

It would not be the first time that Britain had been 'outclassed'. Nor would it be the last.

9

America Brings Out the Big Guns

1965

ROYAL BIRKDALE GOLF CLUB, SOUTHPORT, LANCASHIRE, ENGLAND

7–9 OCTOBER

Among the huge crowds that scrambled across the sandy hills of Birkdale, few people could have realized how close the event had come to not being staged at all.

For years, the cost of sending British teams to the United States and entertaining American teams back in the UK had been a biennial headache. Samuel Ryder had generously donated the golden trophy and given the event his name but was never asked to make an endowment, which could have saved the Ryder Cup from the financial problems it faced over the years.

With the British PGA bearing the cost of staging the event before the war, American industrialist Robert Hudson had stepped in from 1947 onwards to underwrite the match. A decade later, Stuart Goodwin had stepped in to save the day. Now, as the match approached its sixteenth staging, the Ryder Cup desperately needed another far-sighted sponsor

to take it through the start of the modern era. Fortunately, yet again, the right man came forward at exactly the right time.

Brian Park was a successful businessman, vice-chairman of the British PGA and former captain of Royal Birkdale. With the Ryder Cup lacking a sponsor for the forthcoming match in Britain, he had stepped in to underwrite the contest as early as autumn 1963 with a guarantee of £11,000. An innovative man, Park was determined that the event should set new standards in golf organization and presentation, not only in Britain, but also for the world. He travelled to tournaments in the United States to see what the Americans had to offer and returned with numerous ideas, which he looked not only to implement, but also to better. Forming a Ryder Cup committee to discuss his new ideas, he sought to revolutionize the staging of golf tournaments, with the Ryder Cup at Royal Birkdale the first to feel the benefit.

As interest in professional golf tournaments increased and the crowds grew, it became evident that the sponsors had given little consideration to the viewing public. Prior to the Ryder Cup at Birkdale, golf spectatorship in Britain had changed little since the era of Vardon, Braid and J.H. Taylor. Crowd control was almost non-existent, toilets were little more than a sheet of flapping canvas strung between two poles in some obscure woody corner and refreshment was usually the sole domain of a local baker, who was asked to provide a few sandwiches. Even the Open Championship had little in the way of exhibition space for golf manufacturers looking to show off their latest wares. Stewards were provided by the home club to marshal the galleries, but in the main, facilities for players and spectators alike were basic at best.

Looking to change the amateurish way golf tournaments were run in Britain, Brian Park hired the enterprising company that had organized the 1962 Senior Service tournament at Dalmahoy, near Edinburgh. In a spacious area next to the clubhouse, designer R. Binnie-Clark had erected an attractive village of white canvas with every possible facility, including luncheon marquee, rest and social pavilions, toilet facilities with hot and cold running water and even a television area. It was considered extraordinarily extravagant at the time, but Park saw it as his blueprint for the Ryder Cup at Birkdale and set about improving upon the formula.

As an executive member of the British PGA, Park had travelled to the United States to watch the 1963 Ryder Cup at East Lake in Atlanta. Impressed with the organizational skills of the Americans, he had returned with many ideas that he looked to realize. Coming from a still shortage-ridden Britain, one of the aspects of American tournament golf that appealed to him most was the lavish size of the souvenir programme. He immediately commissioned George Simms of Exclusive Press Features Ltd to provide a 160-page programme that included a colour pullout plan of the course, interesting features on golf, player profiles and photographic studies. It was far and away the most ambitious golf publication ever attempted, but he managed to attract enough advertising revenue to make a substantial profit – even before the programme went on sale for five shillings. Golf, it seems, was big business.

Above: The official Ryder Cup programme for 1965. Designed by George Simms, who was the press officer at the British Open for many years, it ran to 160 pages and included features on individual players along with a detailed breakdown of the changes that had been made to the Royal Birkdale course.

The crowds that finally arrived at Royal Birkdale for the 1965 Ryder Cup – two years in the planning – must have been amazed. If the magnificence of the programme were not enough, they would have been astounded by the facilities on offer. On the large stretch of ground between the clubhouse and the main road running into Southport, a vast tented village of white canvas had sprung up as if by magic. As at Dalmahoy some years before, there were luncheon areas provided for both the paying public and the exhibitors' guests. With a dozen marquees all surrounded by a resplendent flower border, facilities included an information tent, a first aid area, a lost property tent, a mobile Post Office and, perhaps most impressive of all, a huge Trade Exhibition, where the public could roam at will, picking up the latest in golf equipment.

The golfing media were also given the five-star treatment, with innovative ideas such as an observation tower for photographers and press giving extensive views

Above: American Ryder Cup player Tony Lema practising his chipping at Royal Birkdale. Known as 'Champagne' Tony for his love of the good in things in life, Lema was tragically killed in an air accident less than a year after this tournament.

across the course. This unusual feature complemented the biggest press area ever seen at a golf tournament in Britain. Sited close to the final green to allow easy access to the players after their round, the wooden structure housed the largest number of golf writers ever assembled on this side of the Atlantic. With twenty-four matches scheduled over three days, information was considered at a premium and no expense was spared in relaying hole-by-hole scores from the course to the awaiting reporters. To aid the flow, Mini-Mokes were pressed into service as up-to-the-minute scoreboards, driven by female golfers with orders to follow each match at a discreet distance so as not to disturb the players.

Amid the carnival-style atmosphere of Royal Birkdale, the sixteenth Ryder Cup finally got underway. The British PGA elected one-time bad boy Harry Weetman as their non-playing captain in a split vote with Eric Brown. With the order of merit points system weighted more towards tournament winners and higher place finishes, the side remained much as before. There were four newcomers in Lionel Platts, Peter Butler, Jimmy Martin and Jimmy Hitchcock, and the remaining six places were filled by Neil Coles, Bernard Hunt, Peter Alliss, Christy O'Connor, George Will and David Thomas.

With the defeat at East Lake nothing but a distant memory, British confidence was high. The Open held at Royal Birkdale in July had seen only one American – defending Champion Tony Lema – finish in the top six, while Irishman Christy O'Connor had finished runner-up. Then there was the remarkable 11–11 draw achieved by British amateurs in the Walker Cup at Baltimore only weeks earlier. Showing that it was possible to get a result on American soil, Harry Weetman had sent a cable to British team captain Joe Carr saying, 'Great golf. Well done. Don't destroy the recipe. Keep it for me.'

Meanwhile, the United States had problems of their own. Still denied the talents of Jack Nicklaus because of the strict eligibility rule imposed by the American PGA, they had to find a last-minute replacement for Johnny Pott, who had damaged his ribs before coming to Britain and failed to respond to treatment. Mike Souchak was put on stand-by, but in the end American captain Byron Nelson decided to pick from the players he had. Asked about the pressure his weakened team was under, the lanky Texan responded by saying that his players had accumulated more than $4 million in prize money and had to be 'used to holing pressure putts on the big occasion'.

In retrospect, this act of bravado by Nelson could have backfired if the early results had gone against him. One of his star-name players, Ken Venturi, had developed circulatory problems earlier in the year and had been forced to wear gloves on both hands while playing. (Venturi in fact went on to lose all three of his games.) However, the American team did have enough strength in depth to field a side that included Gene Littler, Billy Casper, Arnold Palmer, Julius Boros, Dave Marr, Tommy Jacobs, Don January and Tony Lema.

Something else that favoured the Americans was the way Birkdale had been set up for the Ryder Cup. Heavy rain immediately prior to the match had softened up both the fairways and greens and removed the luck of the bounce so prevalent at British seaside links. The parkland quality of the course meant that reaching the par-five holes in two was now out of the question. This meant that the finishing stretch of fifteen, seventeen and eighteen now required a short pitch to the green to make birdie – a shot at which the American professionals were far more skilled than their British counterparts. Handing the American team a big advantage, George Will suggested it would be over these three holes that the final result would hinge. He was right.

In contrast to previous Ryder Cup encounters, the British team made a solid start in the opening day foursomes. With a 6 and 5 victory for Dave Thomas and George Will over Marr and Palmer, followed by a 5 and 4 win for Peter Alliss and Christy O'Connor over Venturi and January, the spoils were shared 2–2 in the

morning. It could have been even better if Julius Boros, paired with Tony Lema, had missed his difficult putt for a half on the final green to beat Lionel Platts and Peter Butler. Similarly, Neil Coles and Bernard Hunt had made a good start against Venturi and January before finally succumbing on the seventeenth by 2 and 1.

The afternoon foursomes began with a remarkable reversal of the shock result of the morning. Arnold Palmer had been so incensed by his lack of form in the 6 and 5 defeat that he spent most of lunch working on the practice ground. Partnered again by Dave Marr, and drawn against his earlier opponents Thomas and Will, the hard-hitting American seemed determined not to make the same mistakes. Instead, he and Marr began in

Below: Captained by the legendary Byron Nelson, the 1965 United States Ryder Cup team was one of the most powerful ever to have arrived on British shores. Despite this, British confidence was high after a poor showing by the Americans over the same course in the British Open in July.

Above: Memorabilia from the 1965 Ryder Cup. Showing how popular the match still was in Britain, this pennant was signed by all the great stars with the orders to hang it in the 'Bedroom or Hall – Just right for your wall'.

blistering style with six consecutive 3s from the second hole onwards for an outward nine of 30 – 6 under par. Reversing the morning result, it had been an awesome display from Palmer whose iron shots rained in on the flag along with his putts. Afterwards, the only comment George Will could muster was, 'blimey!'

Two matches behind, Billy Casper and Gene Littler faced a similar assault from the increasingly confident pairing of Peter Alliss and Christy O'Connor. In a high-quality match, the British double raced out in 31 strokes to find themselves only 1-up. With the Americans drawing level four holes later with yet another birdie, the issue was finally settled with birdies on the sixteenth and seventeenth for a 2 and 1 triumph for the British. With a confidence-boosting win for Coles and Hunt versus Venturi and January, against a United States victory for Boros and Lema over the two Jimmys – Hitchcock and Martin, the day drew to a well balanced conclusion at 4–4.

Fine weather and large crowds greeted the morning matches at Royal Birkdale. As expected, by the end of the day the American team would have

pulled away by 5–3; yet for once the result failed to tell the whole story. With seven of the eight fourball matches going to the final green, it became a simple matter of which team played better golf under pressure. Two matches stood out in the afternoon. Firstly, Dave Thomas and George Will were 4-up with only eight holes to play against January and Jacobs and then lost! This was followed by an even more demoralizing result in the match between Platts and Butler and Casper and Littler. Dormie 4-up with four holes left, the British pair contrived to lose all four to give the US team an undreamed of half.

There were some bright spots for the home team in the morning, such as a well-deserved 2 and 1 win for Neil Coles and Bernard Hunt over Boros and Lema. Then in the first match of the afternoon came yet another triumph for the successful duo of Peter Alliss and Christy O'Connor over Palmer and Marr. As the final day singles matches approached, the Ryder Cup was still there to be won by either side. The United States had a superior record in the singles but with so little to choose between the sides, the press called upon the Lancashire people to provide the same sort of support they had shown at nearby Southport and Ainsdale during the memorable British victory of 1933.

The third day dawned bright and sunny with only a little breeze. It was in many respects the perfect day for playing golf, and indeed watching it. Crowds at Birkdale had been estimated at more than 50,000 for the three days of competition and, as they flooded through the gates on Saturday, there was an overwhelming feeling of optimism around the place. Although the British press had dubbed the previous day as 'Black Friday', there was still hope that the British team could save the day with another Lindrick-style comeback. But the 14,000 spectators attending the final day singles matches were soon to be sadly disappointed.

From the closely fought battle of the previous two days, the Americans rapidly raced to a six-point lead by taking the four opening singles matches. Starting with an easy 3 and 2 win for Palmer in his opening game against Jimmy Hitchcock, further US victories followed in quick succession. First there was Julius Boros (4 and 2) over Lionel Platts, then Tony Lema, 1-up on Butler, followed by Dave Marr, 2-up on Neil Coles. To their credit, the British fought back with wins for Peter Alliss, 1-up on Casper, and Bernard Hunt, 2-up on

Above: The distinctive white-walled clubhouse at Royal Birkdale, home to the Ryder Cup in 1965 and 1969. The venue was popular with the players and fans alike and the matches played here remain two of the best attended in Ryder Cup history.

Gene Littler, but it was never going to be enough. The final nail in the coffin came with Tommy Jacobs' 3 and 2 defeat of Dave Thomas in the final game of the morning. Taking the USA even further ahead, the five-point lead was always going to be enough with only eight singles matches left to play, and so it proved.

At 14½–9½, needing just two more points for victory, the United States set about the task in ruthless fashion. To avoid the crowd getting behind any potential British comeback in the final eight games, American captain Byron Nelson put his four strongest players out first. In the opening game, Lema played brilliantly and was six under par in his 6 and 5 execution of Christy O'Connor. (Charming, popular and stylish, Lema had been labelled 'Champagne Tony' by the British press after he shared a bottle with them shortly after his Open victory at St Andrews the previous year. His victory over O'Connor was his last competitive appearance in Britain, as early in 1966 he was tragically killed in an air crash.)

Even with Palmer and Venturi following up in games three and four, the American team confirmed its superiority by taking the vital second point in only the second game. The 1963 United States Open Champion Julius Boros's 2 and 1 defeat of Jimmy Hitchcock won the Ryder Cup for his team and rendered the matches behind meaningless. The USA had won again.

Later that day, British Prime Minister Harold Wilson presented the Ryder Cup trophy to a smiling Byron Nelson and his team. Nelson admitted to the press that the margin of seven points bore no relation to the closeness of the match. Henry Longhurst confirmed this when he wrote, 'The 1965 match was so close that if the Americans had missed half a dozen putts that they holed, and the British had holed half a dozen that they missed, the result might well have been reversed.'

While the final 12½–19½ result flattered the visitors, the final surprised no one. In the post-mortem that followed, Henry Longhurst berated the British players for their lack of skill around the greens, commenting that the American players often had the ability to 'roll three shots into two'. This call for a change in technique was stubbornly resisted by the British players, who cited the inconsistent conditions under which they played as the reason for their poor showing. Even though they had a point, the fact remained: unless the British team players improved their performance, the Ryder Cup would become a biennial humiliation.

1967

CHAMPIONS GOLF CLUB, HOUSTON, TEXAS, USA

20–22 OCTOBER

If there was ever a mismatch in the seventeen-year history of the Ryder Cup then the encounter at Champions Golf Club in Houston was it. It was perhaps best summed up at the pre-match banquet, when British captain Dai Rees introduced his team by listing their individual careers. After Rees had finished 'making rather a meal of it', according to team member Peter Alliss, American captain Ben Hogan stood up to introduce the United States side. Standing up slowly, the legendary golfer gestured towards his men and said 'Ladies and Gentleman – the finest golfers in the world.' Alliss later admitted that after the storm of applause that greeted Hogan's words the British team felt 'ten-down before a ball had been hit'.

ARNOLD PALMER

Welshman Dai Rees had been brought back as captain by the British PGA, who were looking to recapture the glorious victory at Lindrick a decade before. While his players responded to his committee-style decision-making about team selection and the like, his appointment was not universally welcomed. One-time friend and travelling companion Harry Weetman had walked out in 1957 after Rees had dropped him from the singles following a poor performance in the foursomes. Having commented that he would never again play if Rees were captain, Weetman had been banned from all PGA tournaments for a year. Obviously still at odds with Rees, Weetman now refused to sign an undertaking as an official member of the PGA party travelling to the States that he would be under the British captain's control. Brian Park, Executive Director of the Association, sided with Rees, and Weetman was left at home.

In contrast to the disharmony that pervaded the British camp, the American team had absolutely no doubt who was running the show. As early as the first practice day, Ben Hogan had ordered his players to use the still-optional 1.62 British-size ball. Arnold Palmer light-heartedly questioned his choice, saying that he had brought none with him. The tough little Texan replied, 'Who said you are playing?' (Palmer had flown into Houston in his own private jet and was only a few thousand dollars away from becoming the first American to win $1million in prize-money.)

A disciplinarian by nature, 'Bantam' Ben decreed that his team must be in bed by 10.30 p.m. and ruled out all but official social events. Unlike Dai Rees, Hogan

Left: Arnold Palmer has long piloted his own aircraft to golf tournaments but he caused a rift between himself and captain Ben Hogan after offering British professional Tony Jacklin a lift to the 1967 Ryder Cup in Houston.

made his team selections alone, offered no explanations and brooked no criticism before or after – win or lose. Long hours of practice were compulsory and, after driving his team hard, he was not beyond a little psychological torment; walking down the line he would utter, 'I've never seen so many god-awful shots in my life.'

Because of the five-year probationary rule strictly adhered to by the United States PGA, the Americans were still denied the considerable talents of Jack Nicklaus – despite the fact that by then he was two times US Open Champion, three times Masters winner, one time PGA Champion and 1965 British Open winner at Muirfield. As his agent Mark McCormack said, 'Americans playing on their home ground are no more likely to lose to the British than Boston is likely to apologize for the tea party!'

Even without Nicklaus, however, it was a formidable American team. In addition to Palmer, there were several experienced competitors from past Ryder Cup matches: Billy Casper, Julius Boros, Gene Littler and Johnny Pott. They were joined by five talented newcomers to the Ryder Cup – Bobby Nichols, Al Geiberger, Gardner Dickinson, Doug Sanders and Gay Brewer. The gap in ability had widened into a chasm: as was noted in the British press, this was an American side that looked almost unbeatable on paper.

The British team, in contrast, had little to feel confident about. Unrestricted by the rule that stated that an American professional had to serve a probationary period before being eligible for the Ryder Cup, they had three bright young hopefuls in the side. Tony Jacklin was fresh from his glorious win at the Dunlop Masters event at Royal St George's, Sandwich, where he had scored the first televised hole-in-one on the sixteenth. Along with Jacklin, the other newcomers were the stylish Malcolm Gregson and Irishman Hugh Boyle. The remaining seven places were filled by experienced professionals: Peter Alliss, Brian Huggett, Christy O'Connor, Bernard Hunt, George Will, Neil Coles and David Thomas.

In the opening game of the foursomes, the British side got off to a surprisingly good start. Brian Huggett and George Will won the first two holes against Billy Casper and Julius Boros and led the Americans through the first twelve before relinquishing their lead at the thirteenth. A poor drive into a tree at the next meant the British pair fell behind for the first time and suddenly

Above: Julius Boros had made his Ryder Cup debut at Eldorado Country Club in Palm Springs back in 1959. A hugely talented golfer, he was noted for his straight hitting and wonderful short game, which made him ideally suited to alternate shot golf.

all the good work looked as through it might be undone. To their credit, the British pair battled away, winning the sixteenth with a birdie-3 before going on to halve the remaining holes.

In the following game, Christy O'Connor and Peter Alliss slipped to a 2 and 1 defeat against Arnold Palmer and Gardner Dickinson, despite being all square at the turn. Restoring British pride in the third game were Tony Jacklin and Dave Thomas against the new pairing of Doug Sanders and Gay Brewer. With both American professionals performing poorly because of nerves, the British pair raced to a 2-up lead after nine holes. Unable to mount a fight back, Sanders and Brewer went down by 4 and 3. With the overall match now tied, the final

Above: Doug Sanders is arguably the most gifted professional never to have won a major. An unpredictable talent at the best of times, he lost both his singles matches in Houston but is probably best known for missing a short putt on the final green at St Andrews that would have won him the 1970 British Open.

game between Bernard Hunt and Neil Coles and Johnny Pott and Bobby Nichols took on even more significance. Despite Hunt having played in seven previous matches, he felt so much pressure on the opening hole that he turned to his partner and said, 'You know – I don't think I can hit it.' The English pair eventually made too many errors and lost by 6 and 5.

In the afternoon, Dai Rees attracted huge criticism from the press with some of his foursome pairings. Coles and Hunt were kept on despite the earlier mauling they received at the hands of Nichols and Potts. Alliss and O'Connor were inexplicably replaced by the inexperienced pairing of Malcolm Gregson and

Hugh Boyle, who then lost by 5 and 4 to Palmer and Dickinson. Things were not going well for the British, especially after Huggett and Will lost a close match 1-down to Boros and Casper. Thankfully, the flow of American victories was temporarily halted by the confident partnership of Tony Jacklin and David Thomas, who scored their second win of the day, beating Gene Littler and Al Geiberger by 3 and 2. (Jacklin admitted being racked by nerves in both his matches but credited Thomas for helping him along.) With a comfortable 2 and 1 win for Nichols and Pott over Coles and Hunt in the final game, the match result now stood at 5½–2½ to the Americans.

The fourball matches on the second day appeared to offer little hope for the British, who were trailing by three points. Having never even won a single four-game session since they were introduced at East Lake four years earlier, the British team were not confident, and it showed in the final result. Racing through the morning fourball matches 4–0, the United States team looked about to inflict another embarrassing whitewash in the afternoon when, at the last gasp, Jacklin and Thomas secured a half with Littler and Geiberger. The excuses were not long in coming, but despite four of the games reaching the final hole, there was no hiding from the truth – the Americans were just so much better in technique and temperament.

With a humiliating defeat on the cards, the third-day singles offered only a slight improvement on the day before. Neil Coles turned in two good performances to beat Doug Sanders in the morning and afternoon, while Brian Huggett (in the morning against Julius Boros) and Peter Alliss (in the afternoon against Gay Brewer) played well enough to earn a point each for their side. For the Americans, there were wins in the morning round for Brewer, Casper and Palmer and in the afternoon for Palmer, Dickinson, Nichols, Pott and Geiberger. There were also three creditable halves, between Thomas and Littler plus Hunt and Nichols in the morning and between Bernard Hunt and Julius Boros in the afternoon. The result over the sixteen singles was 10½–5½, giving a final match score of 23½–8½ to the United States.

In many people's eyes, the humiliation was now complete. Since 1947, the Ryder Cup had been lost ten times out of eleven, and the future of the competition was once again being thrown into doubt. Prior to the event, American television had turned down the opportunity to cover the match because it was perceived to be so one-sided in favour of the United States. Once again, there was discussion about bringing in foreign players to bolster up the competition, but, not surprisingly, the British PGA turned this suggestion down flat. Dai Rees proposed reducing the sides to eight men a side, which he felt would even up matters a little. Later, as criticism grew about his captaincy, Rees even reverted to the age-old argument about technique with the short-irons and wedges and said that British pros should stop flicking at the ball and develop an American-style method.

As the team arrived back in England, the debate raged on. Rees defended himself by saying that the result flattered the Americans and cited how eighteen of the thirty-two matches had reached the final two holes. However lame an excuse this was, it was Rees who also made the revolutionary suggestion that the larger size American ball should be made compulsory at British tournaments. Included in a list of improvements to be introduced into the British game, it was closely linked with raising the standards of British greens. Rees felt that watering the greens and making them more receptive to iron shots would help British professionals 'to master the only department of the game in which the Americans consistently beat us'. He then said, 'If we do that we might decide to go absolutely for the bigger ball.'

With golf ball manufacturers like Dunlop turning out millions of 1.62 golf balls each year, Rees's comments caused a storm of protest. Hundreds of enraged amateur golfers wrote to *Golf Illustrated* asking whether they should discard their golf balls in favour of the larger American balls. Respected administrator P.B. 'Laddie' Lucas wrote to the editor of the *Daily Express*, saying:

> Dai Rees has given a lead, now let the PGA plead with the Royal and Ancient, the National Golf Unions and the manufacturers that there is at the moment only one practical policy for Britain's survival as a first-class golfing power. Play the big ball exclusively in an agreed list of selected tournaments, championships and international matches in this country.

After further discussion, it was agreed a year later by the PGA to introduce the American-size ball into

Above: Official programme for the 1967 Ryder Cup at The Champions Golf Club in Houston, Texas. The tournament was a complete mismatch in terms of the teams' quality and experience and it came as no surprise when American captain Ben Hogan introduced his team at the welcoming banquet as 'the finest golfers in the world'.

professional tournaments in Britain for a three-year trial period. For the vast body of amateur golfers, the Royal and Ancient Rules Committee would ultimately have the final word on whether the smaller 1.62 ball would be made illegal in the future. Despite strong opposition from golf-ball manufacturers to the possible widespread use of the American size ball in Britain, the Royal and Ancient said they would monitor the situation closely and decide only then whether to introduce it into major Amateur competitions. In the end, it would be more than a decade before the larger ball came into common use, by which time the Ryder Cup would no longer be fought out between old enemies the United States and Britain, but between the United States and Europe.

10

Pushed to the Limit

1969

ROYAL BIRKDALE GOLF CLUB, SOUTHPORT, LANCASHIRE, ENGLAND

18–20 SEPTEMBER

In one of the most celebrated finishes in any Ryder Cup, two opposing professionals would shake hands on the final green in a gesture that has since gone down in sporting history. For many who had gathered around Royal Birkdale's eighteenth green in the semi-darkness of a September evening, the sportsmanship shown by Jack Nicklaus and Tony Jacklin that day would live in their memories forever. What greater pressure can two players ever have faced than having the fate of the Ryder Cup on their shoulders? The last match out on the course and all square. Teammates watching nervously from the sidelines and the match result lying on the outcome. Surely this was the Ryder Cup at its ultimate best.

Unlike any other professional contest in golf, or any other sport, the Ryder Cup is unique. The reasons are simple enough: for both sets of players this is the one occasion where they put sporting pride ahead of

monetary value. Receiving nothing apart from expenses and a selection of team clothing, all the professionals gladly place their golfing reputations on the line in a tension-packed battle for team and country. Quite how much this biennial contest affects the players concerned was perhaps best summed up by United States PGA President Leo Fraser prior to the match at Royal Birkdale:

> I have known players who will stand over a four-foot putt that may be worth $50,000 to them, looking as though they have stepped right out of the icebox. Not a trace of nerves. Yet I have seen these same players in a Ryder Cup match get so tensed up that they have asked to be rested.

Long before the match at Birkdale had reached its dramatic conclusion, it had already proved a ground-breaking contest. In addition to the larger American-size ball being made compulsory, it was also the first Ryder Cup to include twelve-man teams. Opposing Dai Rees's suggestion that the teams should be cut to eight players to give the British side a better chance of winning, both professional associations agreed that the Ryder Cup would be better served by expanding, rather than reducing, the amount of golf on show.

Another by-product of having larger teams was the amount of exciting newcomers that were introduced. For Great Britain and Ireland, under the captaincy of Eric Brown, there were Maurice Bembridge, Alex Caygill, Peter Townsend, Brian Barnes and Bernard Gallacher (who at twenty was the youngest professional to represent either side). They joining a team that included experienced players Brian Huggett, Neil Coles, Peter Butler, Bernard Hunt, Christy O'Connor and Peter Alliss. But the real jewel in the British crown was Tony Jacklin. Having triumphed in the Open Championship at Royal Lytham only weeks before, Jacklin had given the British game a real shot in the arm with an unexpected win just when it needed it the most. Fresh-faced and talented, the Scunthorpe-born Englishman had followed Henry Cotton's advice some years before and had spent the last few months playing tournaments on the PGA Tour in the United States. With him in the side, anything seemed possible.

As for the Americans, under captain Sam Snead, their team included perhaps the greatest player in the world at this time – perhaps of all time – Jack Nicklaus. Now available for Ryder Cup duty after serving the statutory five-year membership, his achievements were staggering and already included one British Open Championship, two United States Open titles, three Masters and one PGA Championship. Nicklaus was joined by two other players destined to become house-hold names in the future – Lee Trevino and Ray Floyd. This would be a tough team to beat, especially consid-ering the fact that neither George Archer, who was the reigning Masters Champion, nor Orville Moody, the reigning US Open winner, had scored enough points to make the team!

There were even more surprises once the match began. Deciding to omit Jack Nicklaus from the opening foursome matches, Snead chose newcomers Ray Floyd and Miller Barber to lead off against the experienced British pairing of Neil Coles and Brian Huggett. It was exactly this type of tactical mistake that

Above: Jack Nicklaus in full flow. Having served five years as a member of the American Tour, this was the first time his talents could be showcased in the Ryder Cup.

marked his debut as captain. Inspired by a win in the first match, the British were unstoppable, with further victories for Bembridge and Gallacher (2 and 1) over Trevino and Still, Jacklin and Townsend (3 and 1) over Hill and Aaron and a halved point for O'Connor and Alliss against Casper and Beard. Finishing the morning 3½–½ up, the spectacular start raised hopes of a rare home victory and the crowd quickly got behind their players. Sadly, the euphoria did not last long as the United States made a stirring fight back after lunch to win three matches out of four to close the gap.

Any momentum the British team had built up now seemed to have evaporated, as the Ryder Cup appeared to be taking on a familiar pattern. But British captain Eric Brown was having none of it, and reminded his team that it was *they* who were still leading by a single point – 4½ to 3½.

Calling for a lightning quick start on day two, that is exactly what his players gave him. Winning the morning fourballs 2½–1½, the British now moved two points ahead and, as the pressure began to tell, the American team reacted badly with a number of surprisingly bad-tempered encounters. Then the news broke that the British team were under orders from Brown not to help their opponents search for balls lost in the rough. Snead and his team considered this unsporting and the atmosphere between the two camps was not as cordial as it should have been, either on and off the golf course. Trouble had started the previous day after American Ken Still had been asked by Maurice Bembridge to move out of his eye-line on the thirteenth tee. Taking the opportunity to make a drama out of the incident, the combative Still demanded that everyone, including caddies, spectators and officials, should be moved from the side of the tee. Then, at the same hole, Trevino had bunkered his partner under the lip and watched as Ken Still attempted to explode the ball out. Falling backwards, the ball appeared to strike Still on the shoulder, but the American made no acknowledgement to either Bembridge or Gallacher. Taking control of the situation, Trevino asked if the ball had hit him. Still failed to answer, and the talented Mexican gestured to his partner to pick it up, conceding the hole.

Dropped by Sam Snead for the afternoon foursomes, Ken Still was soon back in trouble in the fourballs. Partnered by David Hill against Brian Huggett and Bernard Gallacher in the second match of the afternoon, he was involved in a series of minor incidents that threatened to sour the entire Ryder Cup. With the game close throughout, the aggression that had bubbled beneath the surface between Huggett and Still in the previous day's foursomes exploded into rancour. On the seventh green, Dave Hill accidentally played out of turn when he tapped in a small putt for a half. Huggett brought this to the attention of referee David Melville and the hole was awarded to the British pair. Not able to improve on his partner's score, Ken Still had picked up his own putt only moments earlier. On hearing the hole had been lost, the volatile American protested to the referee and

accused Brian Huggett of using unsportsmanlike tactics to win the match. With voices raised, David Melville sent for a mediator to help quieten matters down a little. Standing on the green, the frustrated American professional then snatched up Gallacher's ball marker and stormed off shouting, 'You can have hole and the goddamn Cup.'

By the time Lord Derby, President of the PGA, had arrived, the incensed Birkdale crowds were actively jeering Hill and Still for their behaviour. Things were calmed down a little, but the rest of the match was played in an icy silence. After falling behind, the two Americans became somewhat inspired by the whole argument and went on to beat the British pair by 2 and 1. Not surprisingly, there were few handshakes at the end. (As a postscript to this story, Huggett and Hill were known to have continued their personal feud in the corridor of the Prince of Wales Hotel that night.)

With the Ryder Cup now finely balanced at 16–16, the match was set for a tension-packed third day. With eight singles scheduled for both morning and afternoon, the Americans were still considered favourites to retain the trophy. Peter Alliss, playing in his last Ryder Cup, was called upon to lead off for the British side against Lee Trevino in the morning, with Tony Jacklin going out last against the great Jack Nicklaus. By lunch on the third day, the overall match was still up for grabs after Britain beat the United States in the morning matches by 5–3. With individual wins for Neil Coles, Christy O'Connor, Maurice Bembridge and Peter Butler, a triumphant morning for the British side was sealed by a magnificent 4 and 3 win for Tony Jacklin over Nicklaus.

The afternoon matches began in seesaw fashion: there were British victories for Gallacher and Butler in matches two and four, while Hill and Barber picked up points in games one and three. Yet with Britain needing just a half in the final four games, the United States came storming back. Dan Sikes beat Neil Coles 4 and 3 after the Englishman struggled to the turn in 40, while Christy O'Connor was somewhat flattered by the 2 and 1 defeat by Gene Littler, having struck the ball so badly throughout. Now, with the match score all square, the Ryder Cup would be decided over the final two games.

In the penultimate match between Brian Huggett and Billy Casper, the tigerish Welshman squared a close match on the sixteenth before halving the par-5 seventeenth in birdie. With loud roars coming from the

Jacklin/Nicklaus match one hole behind, Huggett and Casper were on the long eighteenth in two and were both putting for eagle. After the American had missed from around twelve yards, Huggett raced his approach putt at least five-foot past. Moments before he settled down to putt for a half, a huge roar came from the seventeenth green. Mistakenly assuming that Jacklin had won, Brian Huggett was convinced he had his putt to win the Ryder Cup. Bravely holing out, an emotional Huggett shook hands with Casper before falling tearfully into the arms of British captain Eric Brown. Minutes later the tension returned – Jacklin had holed a huge eagle putt just for a half.

Brian Huggett, like the rest of his teammates, gathered around the final green accompanied by 10,000 spectators all desperate for a British win. As the fading evening light bathed the eighteenth fairway, Nicklaus and Jacklin hit their tee-shots at the last. With never more than one hole between the two players throughout the whole match, the tension was at last beginning to tell. Now passed into golfing folklore, the story goes that Nicklaus asked Jacklin how he felt? Jacklin replied, 'Bloody awful.' Nicklaus agreed and said, 'If it's any consolation, so do I.' With this, both professionals manfully struck their second shots onto the green, now fully aware of the match situation.

Jack Nicklaus went for his eagle putt from around fifteen yards and watched anxiously as it slipped a few feet past. Putting downhill from the back of the green from around the same distance, Jacklin was unable to go for his putt and left it three-foot short. With the clubhouse clock showing 6.00p.m., Nicklaus stepped up to putt first and crouched slowly over the putt. The tap of the ball on putter head could be heard in the cathedral-like quiet of the final green. Despite the poor display of short putting he had given throughout the day, the ball went unerringly into the back of the hole. Quite what Tony Jacklin was thinking at this point can only be imagined. Then, as Jacklin prepared to study the line, Nicklaus strolled across and, after picking up his marker, handed it to the astonished young Englishman. Summing up the spirit of the Ryder Cup in once sentence, Nicklaus said, 'I don't think you would have missed that putt, but in the circumstances I would never give you the opportunity.'

With Tony Jacklin's short putt conceded, the Ryder Cup ended in a gracious draw. While Jacklin sent

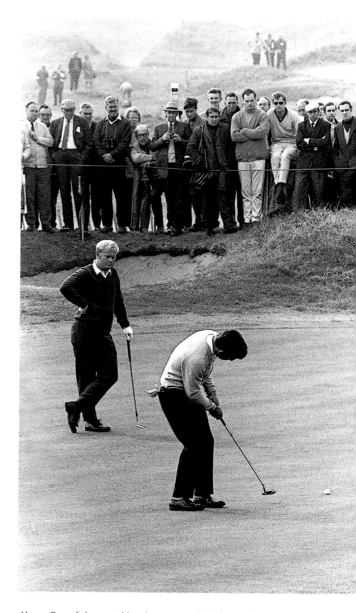

Above: One of the most historic moments in Ryder Cup history. Jack Nicklaus is an interested spectator as Tony Jacklin hits his approach putt to within a few feet on the final green. With the entire match resting on the outcome, the Golden Bear added to his growing legend by generously conceding his opponent's short putt after holing one twice the length.

Nicklaus a letter thanking him for the sporting nature of his actions, some of Nicklaus's American teammates were not so pleased with the gesture. Fortunately, among those professionals that did criticize his actions, few would ever play in the Ryder Cup again.

1971

OLD WARSON COUNTRY CLUB, ST LOUIS, MISSOURI, USA

16–18 SEPTEMBER

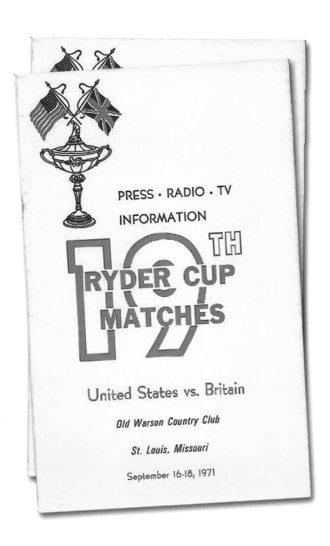

Above: A media guide from the Ryder Cup at Old Warson. After the dramatic draw two years earlier at Royal Birkdale, interest in the Ryder Cup was strong and accreditation was given out to dozens of news agencies and printed press.

After they landed in St Louis, the main talking point for the British players was the exceptionally hot weather – and they were given just five days to acclimatize. During the practice days at Old Warson, the temperature had exceeded the 100°F (38°C) mark with even hotter weather to come. Then, typically for the Midwestern states, a sudden change in conditions brought a torrential downpour on the first day, which resulted in the opening ceremony having to be abandoned for the only time in Ryder Cup history. Taking the opportunity to speak to their counterparts from the American PGA, the British PGA proposed a small variation in the playing format. Rather than play all eight foursome matches on the opening day, then all eight fourballs on the second day, the suggestion was made to split them up. The call for change, which had been led by non-playing British captain Eric Brown, was rejected on the grounds that it had not been put before the relevant committees before the match got underway. (Brown privately thought it might help break up the rhythm of the American team.)

The visiting team, who welcomed the change to more British conditions, had three newcomers in their side – John Garner, Harry Bannerman and Peter Oosterhuis. Offering a good blend of youth and experience, the remaining nine players consisted of Brian Barnes, Peter Townsend, Bernard Gallacher, Maurice Bembridge, Brian Huggett, Christy O'Connor, Peter Butler, Harry Bannerman and Tony Jacklin. Boasting seven players from the dramatic draw at Royal Birkdale two years earlier, hopes were high. Never in the history of the Ryder Cup had a British side come to the United States and won, but with double major winner Tony Jacklin in the side, such a win seemed possible.

In contrast to the pre-match rhetoric coming from the British camp, the United States side seemed quietly confident. Not surprising, considering that they had the top four professionals in the world playing for them –

Jack Nicklaus, Billy Casper, Arnold Palmer and Lee Trevino. Captained by Jay Hebert, this so-called 'invincible quartet' was joined by other top-class professionals – Gardner Dickinson, Miller Barber, Frank Beard, Mason Rudolph, Dave Stockton, Jesse Snead, Charles Coody and Gene Littler. Seven of the American team were still in their twenties. The only niggling worry Hebert had was over small injuries sustained by both Casper and Trevino. Casper had broken his toe in a bizarre incident in his hotel room, while Trevino had been a doubtful starter after suffering from an attack of appendicitis. Unfortunately for the large group of travelling British supporters, both players had been given the all clear by the time the match started.

After long delays because of the inclement weather, the morning foursome matches began with an unexpected 2 and 1 victory for Neil Coles and Christy O'Connor over Billy Casper and Miller Barber. Stalwart of eight previous Ryder Cup encounters, Irishman O'Connor had missed a number of tournaments in Britain through injury and had been a late choice for the match in St Louis. Relishing the challenge, he and Coles had given Britain the perfect start and by lunch on the opening day the 'away' team led 3–1.

The Americans were stunned. Having levelled the score in match two after Palmer and Dickinson beat Townsend and Oosterhuis, the British had bounced back to win the remaining two matches. In the third game, Bembridge and Butler had found themselves 4-up after ten against Charles Coody and Frank Beard. Despite playing over-par golf themselves, they had managed to close out the American pair on the final green to win 1-up. Then came the biggest surprise of all as Jacklin and Huggett defeated Nicklaus and Stockton by the unbelievable margin of 3 and 2. With the American pair failing to register a single birdie, Eric Brown spent most of lunchtime trying to calm his players down.

After leading 3–1 in the morning, the British side approached the second series of afternoon foursome matches in high spirits. Maintaining their advantage, Bannerman and Gallacher extended the overall lead to three points after beating Casper and Barber in the first match out. Sadly, it was the last good news the British camp enjoyed for some time. With Brown inexplicably deciding to drop the successful pairing of O'Connor and Coles, a narrow defeat for Townsend and Oosterhuis against Palmer and Dickinson was quickly

Above: Brian Huggett in action on the opening day against the powerful American pairing of Jack Nicklaus and Davis Stockton. Huggett and partner Tony Jacklin managed to pull off one of the biggest surprise victories in Ryder Cup history winning by 3 and 2.

followed by a 5 and 3 defeat for Bembridge and Butler against Nicklaus and Jesse Snead. Ending the day with a well-deserved half for Jacklin and Huggett against Trevino and Rudolph in the third game, the scores were now evenly balanced at 4½–3½ to the British. As Brown said later, 'Everything was still to play for.'

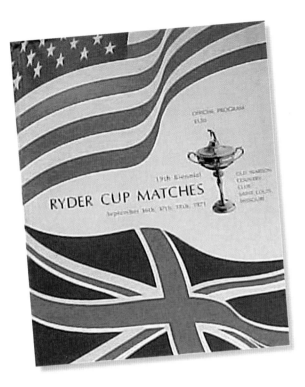

Above: The colourfully designed programme for the 1971 Ryder Cup at Old Warson Country Club in St Louis.

Having answered that 'it was a 5-iron', the astonished British pair were then penalized for breaking Rule 9a, which deals with requesting advice. To his credit, Palmer petitioned the match referee to ignore the matter, but under the rules of golf this was never possible and the hole was given to the Americans. Whether Gallacher or Oosterhuis actually benefited from knowing what club Palmer had used is unsure, but it was certainly enough to cost them the match. The incident upset both of them and, only 1-down at the time, they finally lost by 5 and 4.

In stark contrast with two days earlier, morale in the British camp could not have been lower going into the singles. A brave but ultimately futile performance in the morning still left them trailing the United States by five points going into the afternoon matches. Winning 4½–3½, the home team now needed only two more points to retain the trophy, and they lost little time in achieving that target with a crushing 7 and 6 win by Lee Trevino over Brian Huggett in match one followed by a 1-hole victory for Snead over the increasingly dispirited Tony Jacklin in match two. With the Ryder Cup lost to the USA once more, the remaining six singles became meaningless in terms of winning or losing. However, with nothing more than pride to play for, the British team showed what was possible by halving the afternoon singles 4–4 with creditable wins for Barnes, Gallacher, Oosterhuis and Bannerman.

The record books show a final score of 18½–13½ to the United States. When questioned by the press, Eric Brown boasted that it was the best performance by a British team on American soil. (It was later reported that Brown and his wife Joan had led a celebratory sing-song on the flight back to England.) Not surprisingly, the questions continued unabated. Why, for example, did Brown make a point of selecting John Garner, then play him only once during the entire Ryder Cup match? Why was the successful first morning pairing of Coles and O'Connor left out in the afternoon foursomes? Why was the in-form Jacklin dropped for the morning fourball matches? Why was the talented Maurice Bembridge omitted from the last two days after winning his opening foursomes match with Peter Butler? The Ryder Cup was lost and, despite being one of the finest head-to-head golfers in the world, Eric Brown was never asked to be captain of the British Ryder Cup team again.

Traditionally stronger in the fourball matches, the United States quickly gained the upper hand. A clean sweep in the morning – with successes for Trevino and Rudolph, Beard and Snead, Palmer and Dickinson, and Nicklaus and Littler – was followed by two wins and a half point in the afternoon. Trailing by four points going into the final day of singles, it was Eric Brown's erratic team selections that received most attention from the bemused press. Almost unbelievably, he had decided to leave out Jacklin and Huggett from the morning fourballs, and Britain had paid a huge price. A major talking point at Old Warson, the in-form pairing of Huggett and Jacklin had been undefeated on the opening day and people wanted to know why they were now being dropped. Typically stubborn, captain Brown refused to give any reason, but it would certainly count against him when the post-match reports were filed.

Another curious incident on the second day concerned the Palmer and Dickinson versus Gallacher and Oosterhuis game. Bernard Gallacher's college-boy caddie had asked Palmer what club he used after he had hit the green on the 208-yard, par-3 seventh.

1973

MUIRFIELD, GULLANE, SCOTLAND

20–22 SEPTEMBER

For the first time since its inception in 1927, the Ryder Cup was being played at the 'Home of Golf' – Scotland. Looking out on the majestic Forth of Firth, Muirfield had played host to one of the most remarkable Open Championships in living memory only a year before. American Lee Trevino had broken the heart of Tony Jacklin and many of his British supporters by making birdies at each of the last five holes in the third round, then doing much the same in the final round. With the help of outrageous luck and miraculous recovery shots, he had robbed the young Englishman of his second Open title and condemned him to a third place finish behind the great Jack Nicklaus.

As the British team settled into the Marine Hotel at North Berwick, it was a bitter memory that would haunt Jacklin and his team throughout the match. Having won the Open Championship two years running, and the 1971 United States Open at Merion, Lee Trevino was considered probably the most in-form golfer in the world. Yet, in an American team that also

Below: Home to the Honourable Company of Edinburgh Golfers, Muirfield consistently ranks among the very best golf courses in the world. Originally laid out by the immortal 'Old' Tom Morris, it was considered an unusual choice to host the Ryder Cup, especially as it had been a venue for the British Open for decades.

included Jack Nicklaus, Billy Casper and Arnold Palmer, the talkative Trevino was not even sure of a place in the starting line-up. With the recently crowned British Open Champion Tom Weiskopf also in the American side for the first time, it was certainly a daunting team. There were three other first-timers – Homero Blancas, Lou Graham and Chi Chi Rodriguez – and the remaining four places were filled by Tommy Aaron, Gay Brewer, J.C. Snead and Dave Hill.

For once, the golfing press on both sides of the Atlantic were in agreement – this was probably the strongest American team to have visited British shores in search of the Ryder Cup. No doubt it was an ideal situation for United States captain Jackie Burke to have all these golfing superstars available, but the one-sided nature of the competition became a talking point even before the first ball had been struck. The two major Championships won by Tony Jacklin were Britain's only claim to fame, while the American team, in stark contrast, boasted twenty-eight major wins – Nicklaus alone had just achieved his fourteenth by winning the United States PGA Championship at Canterbury Golf Club in Cleveland, Ohio.

This overwhelming feeling of American dominance was further emphasized by the casual way in which the United States team approached the event. Flying from Washington D.C., they arrived in Scotland only two days before the opening day foursomes. Shortly before leaving, Jack Nicklaus had caused something of an uproar by declining to join his team – preferring instead to watch an American football game in Miami. Arriving in Edinburgh only a few hours after his teammates, Lee Trevino joked at the pre-match press conference how he would have liked to have delayed his own journey. It transpired that his wife had just given birth to a baby girl!

The normally reserved British captain Bernard Hunt responded to criticism of his team's ability by saying that most young American professionals had, 'hardly a decent swing amongst them'. Hunt, a clever tactician, then commented on how many up-and-coming tournament winners on the PGA Tour had faded away over the past few years through lack of technique. His own team for Muirfield included three new faces in Eddie Polland, Clive Clark and Tommy Horton. Along with teammates Peter Butler, Maurice Bembridge, Tony Jacklin, Brian Barnes, Christy O'Connor, Bernard Gallacher and Neil Coles, they formed one of the weakest sides in living memory, and for that reason alone had very little to lose.

After all the pre-match doom and gloom, the British team made a spectacular start in the opening foursomes. Watched by a large and enthusiastically patriotic gallery, Lee Trevino and Billy Casper took three putts at the first, to go immediately 1-down to Bernard Gallacher and Brian Barnes. At one point, Casper had amazingly asked Trevino to swap putters with him, but under the rules of golf this was dismissed without argument. Struggling to find their own form, the Americans managed to drag the match back to all square by the sixteenth before losing the next to a fine birdie 4. Now dormie, the fighting Scots drove into a bunker on the final hole and relied on a pressure putt from Barnes to secure the first British point by the narrowest 1-hole margin.

In the second morning foursomes, Weiskopf and Snead had an equally difficult time against the experienced British team of O'Connor and Coles. With the Irishman playing some wonderful recovery shots from sand, they sealed a fine 3 and 2 victory at the sixteenth. This was followed by a dramatic halved game between the strongest home pairing of Oosterhuis and Jacklin against Rodriguez and Graham. With the home team now holding a two-point lead, it was almost inevitable that there would be some disappointment for the large crowds, and it came in the final match of the morning. Eddie Polland and Maurice Bembridge facing the combined might of Nicklaus and Palmer found themselves 5-down at the turn. Never quite able to mount a comeback, they eventually lost by 6 and 5.

A minor change of format saw the first day include a mix of foursomes and fourballs. Once again, Gallacher and Barnes led the way with another valuable win against Aaron and Brewer by 5 and 4. In what proved to be one of the most successful days ever enjoyed by a British Ryder Cup side, further wins for Bembridge and Huggett over Nicklaus and Palmer, and Jacklin and Oosterhuis over Weiskopf and Casper, gave them an unprecedented 4½ point lead at one stage. Late in the day, the British lead was cut by one point after Trevino and Blancas came good against O'Connor and Coles by 2 and 1 – but the home side had good reason to feel optimistic about the matches to come.

Before the match had started, American captain Jackie Burke admitted how difficult it would be for him personally if he were to lose the Ryder Cup twice (the first time was at Lindrick in 1957). With the British team holding a three-point advantage going into the second day, any misgivings he had had before the match looked to be coming true. In the second series of foursomes, Burke put his strongest player Nicklaus out in the first match with Tom Weiskopf. They were scheduled to play against the unbeaten pair of Brian Barnes and Bernard Gallacher, but the night before, Gallacher had suffered a severe attack of food poisoning and was told to rest.

With barely any warning, Peter Butler was called upon to take his place and soon found himself and Barnes 3-down after five holes. The score stayed the same up until the par-3 sixteenth when, to the amazement of everyone, Butler holed his tee-shot for an ace and a win. A further win on the seventeenth with a birdie brought the British pair to the last hole with every chance of pulling off a miraculous escape. However, a par-4 on the long eighteenth gave the American pair the win they wanted and set the pattern for the whole day.

A foursome win for Trevino and Casper against O'Connor and Coles in the final game of the morning was cancelled out by a splendid British victory for Bembridge and Huggett over Palmer and Nicklaus by 3 and 1. Another win for the in-form pairing of Jacklin and Oosterhuis over Weiskopf and Casper meant that by lunch on the second day the Ryder Cup was still in the balance. Sadly for home supporters, things were about to change.

Hunt decided to rest his veteran pairing of O'Connor and Coles in the afternoon fourballs in favour of newcomers Clive Clark and Eddie Polland. Sent out in the third match, they had no more success against Nicklaus and Weiskopf than any of the other three British pairs. Apart from Bembridge and

Below: Even home conditions at windswept Muirfield could not assist an under-equipped Great Britain and Ireland side against a USA team that boasted the number one and two top-ranked players in the world in Jack Nicklaus and Tom Weiskopf.

Above: American professional Tommy Aaron had a woeful record in the Ryder Cup. Having made his debut at Royal Birkdale in 1969, where he lost two matches, won one and halved one, he struggled again four years later at Muirfield, where he failed to register a single point.

Huggett, who battled out a valiant half with Trevino and Blancas, the news from elsewhere on the course was bad. Despite being 1-up after eight, the demoralized team of Barnes and Butler lost by 2-up against Snead and Palmer. This was quickly followed by a surprise 3 and 2 defeat in the third game for Jacklin and Oosterhuis by Brewer and Casper. With the Ryder Cup now all square at eight points each, the result would rest with the sixteen singles to come.

Leading the way for the British side in the singles was the broad-shouldered, pipe-smoking Scotsman Brian Barnes. Playing against the forty-two-year-old Billy Casper, Barnes struggled all the way round and probably would not have broken eighty had they reached the eighteenth. Still aged only twenty-eight, Barnes, who would later struggle against a much-publicized drink problem, complained how tired he felt after playing in all the previous foursomes and fourball matches.

After losing the opening game, better news for the British camp arrived in the reappearance of Barnes's foursomes partner, Bernard Gallacher. Looking pale and drawn and obviously still weak from his ordeal, Gallacher was put out in the second game against Tom Weiskopf. Managing to hold the talented American up to the tenth, Weiskopf took control on the back nine and finished up winner by 3 and 1. A crushing 5 and 4 win for Homero Blancas over Peter Butler in the third match gave the United States the breathing space they needed. Tony Jacklin gave the home side some hope with a fine 3 and 1 victory over reigning Masters Champion Tommy Aaron, but three halves and a further 1-up win for Jesse Snead over O'Connor left the British side with a three point deficit going into the afternoon.

With a Lindrick-style comeback in the singles needed by the British team, Bernard Hunt called upon Brian Huggett to lead the way. There had been some speculation of a rift between the two men, based mainly on the Welsh professional being dropped from the morning singles after having recorded two wins and a half in his previous three games. Matched against the unbeaten Homero Blancas, the tigerish Huggett recovered from being 2-down early on to win by 4 and 2. In the following game, an increasingly frustrated Brian Barnes struggled with his concentration and putting before losing 3 and 1 to Jesse Snead.

The defeat of Barnes brought an avalanche of dropped points, effectively ending any hope the British team had of winning the Ryder Cup. In the next three singles, involving Bernard Gallacher, Tony Jacklin and Neil Coles, there were American wins for Gay Brewer, Billy Casper and Lee Trevino consecutively. Despite late wins for Christy O'Connor (in what was to be his final Ryder Cup singles match) against Tom Weiskopf, and Peter Oosterhuis beating Palmer, this disastrous run of four losses had seen the golden trophy pass once more to the United States.

1975

LAUREL VALLEY GOLF CLUB, LIGONIER, PENNSYLVANIA, USA

19–21 SEPTEMBER

A heavy downpour three days before the Ryder Cup was due to begin had left Laurel Valley with flooded fairways and sodden greens. Further rain meant some of the practice days had to be cut short; even a planned exhibition match involving Arnold Palmer and Bob Hope against Bernard Hunt and singer Perry Como was cancelled. Certainly, after one of the most one-sided matches in the event's history, the British team of which Hunt was non-playing captain must have wished the Ryder Cup had gone the same way.

Now selected straight off the money list instead of qualifying through a complex points system, the British team paled in comparison with their American opponents. Although the top eight players were taken from the top of the money list, the British PGA reserved the right to pick the last four places in case any of the established stars, such as Jacklin and Huggett, failed to make the side. Fortunately for Hunt, both did make it, as did six newcomers to the Ryder Cup matches – Eamonn Darcy, Norman Wood, Tommy Horton, John O'Leary, Guy Hunt and Christy O'Connor, Jr. (nephew of Ryder Cup stalwart Christy O'Connor, Sr.) – and four other experienced professionals Maurice Bembridge, Peter Oosterhuis, Brian Barnes and Peter Townsend. But few experts gave the side any chance of winning.

Even though the British players had a comparatively youthful look about them, the American side could boast seven former US Open Champions, including Hale Irwin, Johnny Miller, Gene Littler and Lou Graham; two Masters winners in Billy Casper and Jack Nicklaus; four PGA titleholders, including Ray Floyd and Lee Trevino; and, most recent of all, the reigning British Open Champion from Carnoustie, Tom Watson. Ably backed up by hardened tour veterans Al Geiberger, Bob Murphy and Jesse Snead, this team was practically unbeatable and everyone knew it, including Bernard Hunt.

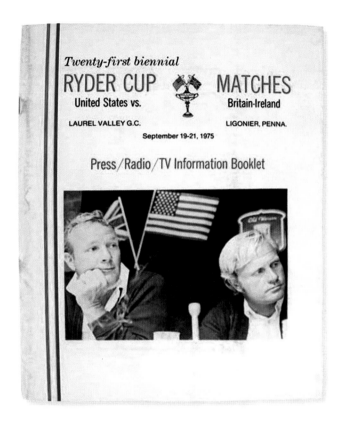

Above: Arnold Palmer and Jack Nicklaus graced the cover of the media guide to the 1971 Ryder Cup. With Arnie as captain and Jack playing, the number of reporters and photographers covering the tournament was double that of previous years.

As always, the only major winner the British side could muster was former British and United States Open Champion Tony Jacklin, but even he was considered a spent force. Not surprisingly, the golfing press billed it as a 'David and Goliath' clash – except this time it was David who would receive a real bashing.

As expected, the opening day foursomes went to the United States. Partnered by Brian Barnes in the first

Below: Lee Trevino made a blistering start to the Ryder Cup at Laurel Valley before falling back down to earth with a bump. Having won morning and afternoon matches on the opening day, Trevino's confidence was somewhat dented when he was 'rested' the next morning by captain Arnold Palmer. Registering just one-half point in his next three games, the gregarious superstar was not smiling for long.

match, Bernard Gallacher, who had combined so well with his fellow Scot at Muirfield two years before, failed to find his putting touch against Nicklaus and Weiskopf and lost by 5 and 4. In a day of bitter disappointment for the British there were further defeats in the morning for Wood and Bembridge, Jacklin and Oosterhuis, and O'Leary and Horton. Finishing in a clean sweep for the United States, the afternoon fourballs offered only crumbs of comfort with a win for Jacklin and Oosterhuis over Casper and Floyd by 2 and 1, followed by a valiant halve for Barnes and Gallacher against Nicklaus and Bob Murphy.

Somewhat as expected, the British side now found itself five points behind going into the second day. In the morning fourballs, Hunt persisted with his two strongest pairings, putting out Jacklin and Oosterhuis first against Casper and Miller, with Gallacher and Barnes following in the third match against Littler and Graham. While his strategy failed to win the day, it did at least slow down the inexorable progress of the Americans for a few hours.

After a half for Jacklin and Oosterhuis in the first match, and another between Darcy and Hunt playing against Floyd and Geiberger in the fourth, Britain had equalled its points tally for the first day. However, this had to be balanced out against losses for Tommy Horton and Norman Wood against Nicklaus and Murphy by 4 and 2, and a surprise 5 and 3 defeat for Gallacher and Barnes by the American team's weakest pairing of Gene Littler and Lou Graham. (Littler had only just made a comeback after surgery for cancer.)

After a few minor adjustments to the pairings by Arnold Palmer, the afternoon foursomes became a matter of business as usual for the United States. With Hunt now having lost confidence in his two 'dream team' pairings of Jacklin and Oosterhuis and Gallacher and Barnes, the British captain also decided to experiment with his line-up. Matching Jacklin with Huggett against Trevino and Murphy in the first match brought immediate success with a 3 and 2 victory to the visitors. Sadly, this was quickly followed by three straight British losses for O'Connor, Jr. and O'Leary against Weiskopf and Miller, Oosterhuis and Bembridge against Irwin and Casper, and Darcy and Hunt against Graham and Geiberger.

It soon became evident that the heavy conditions of the course were taking their toll on the shorter British hitters. Failing to reach even some of the longer 4 holes, the visitors were struggling badly against an American side that often failed to make par themselves. The situation was summed up best by Hale Irwin, who partnered Billy Casper in their 3 and 2 win over Oosterhuis and Bembridge: 'We ought to have been beaten by 6 and 4, but they played worse.'

Palmer, it was said before the match, had an ambition to win at Laurel Valley by a perfect clean sweep of 32–0. While this was no longer possible, his side's three wins against one for the British gave him an almost unbeatable lead going into the final day singles of 12½–3½. The only question that occupied the surprisingly large crowds attending the match was whether the United States could finish the match off before the afternoon singles. Shortly after the first series of eight matches got underway, the simple answer to this question was 'yes'.

After defeats for Jacklin against Murphy, Huggett against Littler, and Darcy against Casper, Tom Weiskopf hammered home the final nail in the British coffin by crushing Guy Hunt by 5 and 4. Unlike in some of the previous games, the giant Weiskopf was six under par for the fourteen holes played against the diminutive Englishman. Peter Oosterhuis also played well in his 2-hole defeat of Johnny Miller, as did Gallacher and Horton in their matches with Trevino and Irwin. Yet perhaps the biggest story of the day was reserved for big Brian Barnes in the final singles match of the morning against the great Jack Nicklaus.

Having recently won his fifth tournament of the year at the World Open in Pinehurst, Jack Nicklaus was probably playing the best golf of his illustrious career. Fortunately for the pipe-smoking Barnes, the 'Golden Bear' appeared more concerned with talking about fishing than playing golf. While this is perhaps an overstatement, Nicklaus certainly struggled to keep his concentration once the Ryder Cup had been lost, eventually losing by 4 and 2 to the elated Scot. To his credit, Barnes never placed a great deal of importance on the morning match, but when the draw was deliberately engineered by Nicklaus to match them together in the afternoon, he knew what to expect.

While fixing the draw was probably against the strict rules of the Ryder Cup, it was certainly in the best traditions of the event. With so little to play for in the afternoon, the overall match was in danger of slipping to an embarrassing conclusion. While there were still seven other matches on the course and a great deal of professional pride to play for, it was the Barnes versus Nicklaus clash that caught the crowd's imagination.

Certainly Nicklaus took the afternoon match a great deal more seriously than he had in the morning. Starting with two birdies, he took an early lead that was eventually clawed back by the determined Scot. Then, with some late birdies, Barnes pulled away to finally win by 2 and 1, and became the first man in Ryder Cup history to beat the great Jack Nicklaus twice in one day.

Above: A draw sheet for the 21st Ryder Cup. With a US victory considered a near certainty even before the match began, the fans turned out to see top American stars like Nicklaus, Weiskopf, Trevino and Billy Casper rather than worrying about the result. No doubt that is why the draw sheet was accompanied by another sheet for autograph collectors.

Adding some respectability to the total match score, the British team won the final afternoon singles by 4½–3½. Apart from Brian Barnes, there was a second win for Oosterhuis against Snead that preserved his unbeaten record in the singles. Previously unbeaten Tommy Horton defeated Lou Graham by 2 and 1, with Norman Wood following up in the penultimate match with a good win over Trevino by the same score. After losses for Jacklin, O'Leary and Bembridge, a halved match between Gallacher and Geiberger left the final score at 21–11 to the United States.

11

Changing Times

1977

ROYAL LYTHAM AND ST ANNES, ST ANNES, LANCASHIRE, ENGLAND

15–17 SEPTEMBER

Of the eleven Ryder Cup matches that had been held in Britain, the one at Royal Lytham and St Annes in 1977 was perhaps the most forgettable. Despite the large crowds that turned up to support the home team, there was an overwhelming feeling among press and public that the match had become too one-sided: the USA had won seventeen matches out of the last twenty-two meetings. The United States PGA had given a commitment to continue competing in the biennial competition, but the very fact they had to be asked was the strongest indication that the Ryder Cup was in trouble.

High-level discussions between the Professional Golfers' Associations of Britain and America following Britain's humiliating defeat at Laurel Valley two years earlier had brought little agreement. Almost two decades after the idea of introducing Commonwealth players had been brought up, the British PGA were still

loathe to bring in changes that might lessen its power. In keeping with past strategies, it deflected further argument by instigating some changes to the playing format in the hope this would make the matches closer. Agreed in time for the Ryder Cup at Lytham, the main change involved reducing the number of points available to be won from thirty-two to twenty. Cutting the games played by roughly a third meant having just five foursomes on the first day, five fourballs on the second and ten singles on the last.

The changes that had been made at Royal Lytham in 1961 and East Lake in 1963 both increased the amount of golf played. The decision made in 1977 to reduce the matches played was a disastrous one. With forty-five-minute intervals between the matches to accommodate television coverage, there was not enough golf for the crowds to watch. With almost four hours between the first match teeing off and the last, the electric atmosphere generated by previous Ryder Cup encounters was sadly missing. Of course, with two sets of matches played morning and afternoon there had been the added pleasure of the hoped-for British comeback after they had lost out in earlier matches. Now if they lost, the crowds would have to wait until the following day. Thankfully for all concerned, it would be the first and last time this format would be used.

With Dow Finsterwald appointed US captain, the visitors had their usual strength in depth. With an average age of thirty-four, the team fielded a number of newcomers, including Lanny Wadkins, Jerry McGee, Ed Sneed, Hubert Green and perhaps one of the greatest golfers to have ever played the game, reigning British Open and United States Masters Champion Tom Watson. Still fresh in the minds of the British golfing public since his historic confrontation with Jack Nicklaus at Turnberry, Watson joined a strong American team that also included Hale Irwin, Ray Floyd, Lou Graham, Dave Hill, Don January, Dave Stockton and, of course, Jack Nicklaus.

Under the captaincy of Brian Huggett, the British team introduced a number of rising young professionals who would ultimately make their mark in future Ryder Cups. At the age of twenty, Nick Faldo was making his debut along with Mark James, Howard Clark, Ken Brown and the only left-hander to have played in the Ryder Cup thus far, Peter Dawson. In what ultimately proved to be the last Great Britain and Ireland team to compete in the event, the remaining seven places were taken by Bernard Gallacher, Tony Jacklin, Brian Barnes, Eamonn Darcy, Peter Oosterhuis, Tommy Horton and Neil Coles. (Coles had actually qualified for the previous match at Laurel Valley but had declined to play because of his aversion to flying.)

Huggett remembered Muirfield and Laurel Valley and the fine partnership forged between the two Scots, Barnes and Gallacher. Unfortunately, sending them out against Hale Irwin and American newcomer Lanny Wadkins in the opening match of the foursomes proved a mistake. With the standard of golf dancing around the par mark, the British pair found themselves 1-up with just five holes left. Then, in a terrible finish, they lost the next four holes in a row to the Americans, to be defeated by 3 and 1.

Above: The Ryder Cup returned to Royal Lytham and St Annes for the second time in sixteen years in 1977. The Lancashire links was to be the last course to see a Great Britain and Ireland team face the USA in a Ryder Cup match.

It had been expected that the experienced partnership of Jacklin and Oosterhuis would lead the way, but Huggett chose to split them up and placed Oosterhuis with Faldo in the third game and Jacklin with Eamonn Darcy in the fourth. In that respect his strategy worked, with a good 2 and 1 win for Oosterhuis and Faldo over Ray Floyd and Graham, and Jacklin contributing well to a good halve against Ed Sneed and Don January.

Down by two points going into the second day fourballs, Huggett decided to make some controversial changes. Keeping three of the pairings intact – Faldo/Oosterhuis, Jacklin/Darcy and Coles/Dawson – the British captain made only one change, dropping Gallacher in favour of Ken Brown. Golfing pundits complained it was nowhere near enough, and after losing by 4–1 to the Americans they felt their view was vindicated.

Once again, the only bright spot of the day was the performance of Nick Faldo in his match against Nicklaus and Floyd. Having been diagnosed the week before as suffering from glandular fever, Faldo was helped along by the experienced Peter Oosterhuis. Using a newly purchased carbon-shafted driver, his long willowy swing consistently drove the ball past both Nicklaus and Floyd. In a close match, Faldo and Oosterhuis took the lead on the second, and despite

Above: Peter Oosterhuis and Nick Faldo combined well in both the fourball and foursome alternate shot matches, winning both against strong opposition. Faldo, who was making his Ryder Cup debut, then crowned a wonderful week by defeating reigning British Open Champion Tom Watson in the singles.

pressure from the Americans, rarely looked like losing it, eventually running out winners by 3 and 1.

With the fourballs going to the United States the match score now stood at 7½–2½, leaving an almost impossible gap of five points between the two sides going into the final day singles. Huggett made the controversial decision to drop Tony Jacklin from his line-up. Incensed at being left out, the double-major winner complained bitterly, but Huggett defended his choice on the grounds that Jacklin had performed badly in both his matches and said that he wanted to give someone else a chance. Huggett was backed up by his opposite number, American captain Dow Finsterwald, who agreed that he would have done the same.

It was an argument that rumbled on throughout the final day, upsetting everyone from Huggett to his embattled team. Having berated the British captain in the press for leaving him out, Jacklin later attacked everything about his style of captaincy, citing his lack of consultation in team selection as one reason why they did not get on. If that was not enough, Huggett had openly criticized Jacklin for waiting until late afternoon to support his teammates out on the course. Though the fiery Welshman later apologized, Jacklin was visibly upset by the incident and refused to talk to his captain for some time afterwards.

It was not the only problem the British team faced that day. Scheduled to play in the sixth match of the singles, Bernard Gallacher had the misfortune of having his putter stolen shortly before his game with Jack Nicklaus and had to rush to the pro-shop to buy another. The incident was typical of everything that had gone on, but in this case there was a happy ending at least. Wielding his newly purchased Ping Anser, the young Scot beat the 'Golden Bear' by 1-up to record the greatest win of his young career. Helping restore a touch of respectability to the overall match score, there were other notable British wins for Peter Dawson against Don January, Brian Barnes against Hale Irwin, Nick Faldo against Tom Watson, and Peter Oosterhuis against Jerry McGee.

Balanced out with American victories for Lanny Wadkins against Howard Clark, Lou Graham against Neil Coles, Dave Hill against Tommy Horton, Hubert Green against Eamonn Darcy, and Ray Floyd against Mark James, the singles were shared 5–5. Never enough to stop the Ryder Cup going once more to the United States, it was uncertain who the 12½–7½ score flattered the most. In the end it hardly mattered, and even though no one knew it at the time, the final putt at Royal Lytham on 17 September 1977 brought the curtain down on over half a century of Ryder Cup history. Over the coming months, a great deal of discussion between the respective British and American PGAs would result in the death of the old Ryder Cup format. No longer would it be the United States versus Great Britain and Ireland. From now on it would be the United States versus Europe, with the first match to be played at The Greenbrier in two years time.

Traditionalists maintained that the Ryder Cup should remain in British hands and be played for among home professionals, but in the end, the decision was made and, as time would prove, it would herald in a bright new era for the matches. More importantly, it would give the Americans the competition they craved.

1979

THE GREENBRIER, WHITE SULPHUR SPRINGS, WEST VIRGINIA, USA

14–16 SEPTEMBER

The Ryder Cup at Royal Lytham in 1977 had proved a watershed in the event's history. After the eighteenth defeat in twenty-two matches, it was obvious that the British team could no longer compete on level terms with the Americans. With the biennial matches now so one-sided in the United States' favour, changes had to be made if the Ryder Cup was going to survive into the next decade. Fortunately, these changes were not long in coming. Nine months after the 1977 match, Don Padgett, President of the United States PGA, announced that, after much negotiation between the American and British Professional Golfers' Associations, it had been decided that the forthcoming match scheduled for The Greenbrier would be the first to involve a European team.

While the decision to include Europeans in the side was wrapped up as a joint decision, it was almost certainly at the instigation of the Americans. It had been suggested over a decade before that players from the Commonwealth like Gary Player and Peter Thompson should be included, but the British PGA had strongly resisted. Feeling that such a fundamental change would compromise its power and influence in the game of golf, the British PGA had resorted over the years to changes in the playing format in the vain hope that it might even up the competition. But the latest decision to reduce the amount of golf played at Royal Lytham had backfired disastrously, and for everyone concerned – especially the American press and public – it was now quite simply a matter of change or die for the Ryder Cup.

Discussions over the future of the Ryder Cup had gone on for more than a decade. It was obvious that while the top five British professionals could probably compete on level terms with the top five Americans, the problem started further down the list. Although the United States could probably field two or three teams with proven tournament winners, the British struggled

gamely to put out one twelve-man team. With the matches now reduced to eighteen holes, rather than the thirty-six hole marathons played prior to 1961, there would always be the chance of an individual upset – like Brian Barnes's two wins in one day over Nicklaus at Laurel Valley, for example. However, with the Ryder Cup matches stretched out over three days, the team that had the greatest strength in depth would always prevail – and that team was America.

Despite the seeming lack of competition, Arnold Palmer was of the opinion that the matches should go on as before. Shortly before the decision was made to include Europeans in the 'British' team, he commented, 'There are occasions even in professional sport when who wins by how much isn't everything, and the Ryder Cup is most certainly one of them. I do not think it should be dropped just because the Americans usually win.'

In contrast, his great rival Jack Nicklaus thought the Ryder Cup needed a complete overhaul. Speaking to the press shortly after the 1977 Ryder Cup, he explained how difficult it was to get 'charged up for the matches themselves'. 'The fact must be faced', he said, 'that British professional golf in recent years simply hasn't developed a sufficient depth of good players to make a true contest out of the event'.

In the weeks and months that followed, the future of the Ryder Cup was discussed at length. Nicklaus felt that a World versus the United States format would make the most sense, and if that was not possible, then the United States versus the English-speaking countries or even the United States versus Europe.

As time would show, his comments proved almost prophetic. The most respected figure in the game, Nicklaus took his involvement in the affairs of the Ryder Cup even further. Though few knew it at the time, he had already approached Lord Derby, President of the British PGA, after the 1977 Ryder Cup at Royal

Lytham to outline the inherent difficulties of continuing such a one-sided contest. Afterwards he confirmed in a letter to Lord Derby that it was 'vital to widen the selection procedures if the Ryder Cup is to continue to enjoy its past prestige'.

As a result Ken Schofield, Executive Director of the fledgling PGA European Tour, met with Lord Derby at his home in Knowlsey. Agreeing that changes were needed, it was decided that Brian Huggett and Peter Butler of the Ryder Cup Committee should travel to

Below: The first continental players ever to take part in the Ryder Cup, Spaniards Antonio Garrido and Seve Ballesteros discuss tactics. Playing a vital role in future matches, Seve would later captain the Europeans at Valderrama in 1997.

Augusta National during the 1978 Masters to discuss exactly what form this new USA versus Europe match would take. But even with the blessing of the British PGA, the idea of opening the Ryder Cup up to 'foreigners' was not universally liked or accepted. In fact, the only reason it was being discussed was that it was preferable to including professionals from the Commonwealth countries – or indeed the 'English-speaking' countries that Nicklaus had also suggested.

The other problem facing the PGA was how the British public would take to this new format. After all, if you include foreign players in the team, it follows that someday you might have to take the Ryder Cup to their country. And while it might be acceptable to take the match to Spain or France, how would people feel about

the match being played in South Africa or even Australia? Then there was the actual team to consider. Currently, there was only a relatively small number of players from the continent that might actually make the twelve-man team and they were all Spanish – Antonio Garrido, Manuel Pinero and the emerging Severiano Ballesteros – whereas an 'English-speaking' team could potentially include players like Gary Player, Bob Charles, Dale Hayes, Hugh Baiocchi, Greg Norman, Graham Marsh, Simon Owen and Bobby Cole. The question no doubt concerning the British PGA was how many British players would actually make the side.

With the decision made to include Europeans, an approach was made to Mrs Joan Ryder-Scarfe, daughter of Sam Ryder, for her permission to change the original Trust Deed. This given, the forthcoming match at The Greenbrier could finally get underway. Having been instrumental in forming the PGA European Tour organization, former Ryder Cup player John Jacobs was given the job of captaining the European team in the first Europe versus United States match. A diplomatic character by nature, Jacobs knew that such a new format would be fraught with difficulty. Yet his main problem at The Greenbrier came not from integrating continental European players into the side but from two professionals much closer to home.

Englishmen Ken Brown and Mark James were newcomers to the Ryder Cup. Almost from the beginning at Heathrow airport, Jacobs struggled to control the independently minded young men. While the rest of their teammates turned up smartly attired in the official team uniform, Ken Brown and Mark James chose to travel to America in more casual dress – Brown, in the words of captain Jacobs, looked 'terrible'. It was the start of what was going to be a difficult week for the three men. Playing alongside Brian Barnes, Bernard Gallacher, Des Smyth, Michael King, Tony Jacklin, Sandy Lyle, Nick Faldo and Peter Oosterhuis, the European element of John Jacobs' side was provided by Antonio Garrido and the highly talented Severiano Ballesteros. Both successful members of the European Tour, they would combine only weeks later to win the World Cup for Spain (Ballesteros retaining the title he had won in partnership with Manuel Pinero in 1976).

The dire format introduced at Lytham had been rightly done away with for the match at The Greenbrier. Two eight-match sessions of fourballs and foursomes were re-introduced, along with twelve singles on the third and final day. While the overall points total was down on previous years, it would be the first time that all twelve team members would play in the singles. To some extent, this new idea brought problems of its own, because some allowance had to be made in case of injury or illness. For the moment, both captains – John Jacobs and Billy Casper – were asked to put the name of one of their players in a sealed envelope so that he could stand down in case the opposition were reduced to eleven men. In such a case, the missing match would then be declared a half.

Apart from this difficult choice, Billy Casper was also faced on the eve of the match with losing his finest young player. Leading American money winner for the past three seasons, Tom Watson, had been called away to attend the birth of his first child (a daughter). As a consequence, Mark Hayes was brought in to join a very young side that already included seven first-time Ryder Cup players: Larry Nelson, Andy Bean, 'Fuzzy' Zoeller, John Mahaffey, Tom Kite, Gil Morgan and the first black professional to take part in the match, Lee Elder. The remaining four places were filled by experienced players Lanny Wadkins, Lee Trevino, Hale Irwin and Hubert Green.

The majestic Greenbrier course was set in 6500 acres of rolling West Virginia woodland. Recognized as perhaps the most luxurious and exclusive inland resort in America, it offered a 650-bedroom hotel with marbled floors and its own shopping arcade. With both teams resident in the hotel, the distractions must have proved a great temptation. Certainly, British players Ken Brown and Mark James were later disciplined for strolling through the shops when they should have been attending a team meeting called by John Jacobs.

The match itself got underway in poor conditions. A sudden downpour drenched the greens and the opening fourball matches were delayed by almost an hour. In keeping with the revolutionary changes made, captain Jacobs put Garrido and Ballesteros out in the first match against Wadkins and Nelson. In what must have appeared a dream start, the two Spaniards won the opening two holes before slipping back to the strong American pairing. Then, behind by the tenth, they went on to lose by 2 and 1.

Somewhat surprisingly, Jacobs paired Ken Brown and Mark James in the second match against Lee Trevino and

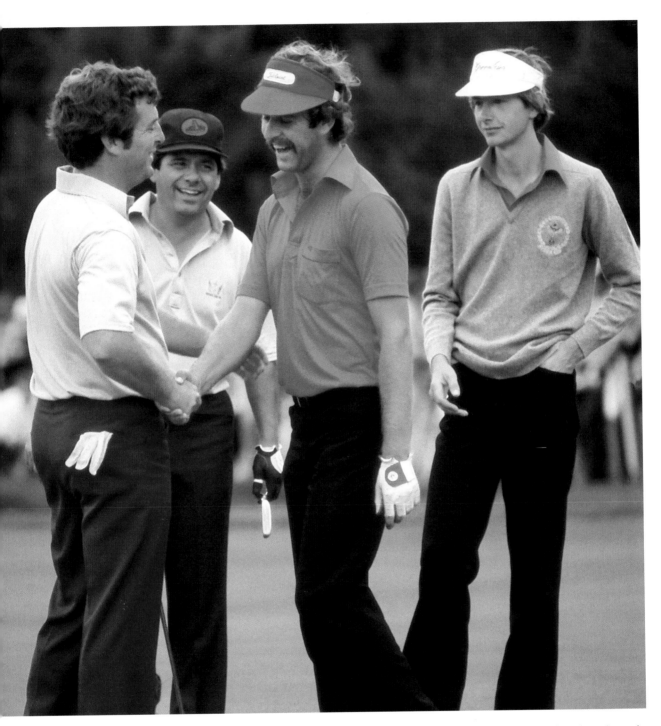

Above: Bad boys Mark James and Ken Brown shake hands with 'Fuzzy' Zoeller and Lee Trevino after the opening rounds of four-balls. Known more for their poor behaviour that week than the quality of their golf, both would later go on to serve with distinction in future Ryder Cup matches.

Francis Urban 'Fuzzy' Zoeller. Close friends and travelling partners on Tour, Brown and James had both displayed a frankly disinterested attitude at the opening flag ceremony the previous day. There had been calls to leave them out altogether, but Jacobs had refused, feeling that their excess energy was better put to use against the Americans. It proved to be a mistake – James, who was carrying a chest-muscle injury, played poorly and the British pair lost by 3 and 2.

Probably the best performance of the opening matches came from Brian Barnes and Bernard Gallacher. With Faldo and Oosterhuis losing 2 and 1 to Elder and Bean in the third match (the Americans were eight-under par at the time of winning), the two Scotsmen played superbly to beat Irwin and Mahaffey by 2 and 1 – and this despite losing three of the first six holes. So, with the home side making their customary fast start, the European team immediately found themselves 3–1 down after the first morning.

The afternoon foursomes also brought problems for John Jacobs. With his erstwhile partner dropping out because of injury, Ken Brown was paired with Irishman Des Smyth in the first game against Hale Irwin and Tom Kite. In what proved to be a petulant and bad-tempered display by Brown towards his partner, it surprised no one when they eventually lost by 7 and 6. Not surprisingly, John Jacobs was obliged to offer apologies all round for his player's conduct. It was a humiliating affair with respected administrator 'Laddie' Lucas describing Brown as 'unpartnerable' and 'uncivil'.

Despite a first win for Ballesteros and Garrido over Zoeller and Green, the Europeans lost the afternoon foursomes by 2½–1½. Having already lost James through injury, Jacobs was faced with having a player in his team – Ken Brown – who was not only unmanageable, but ruining team morale in the process. With three-straight victories for Lyle and Jacklin over Elder and Mahaffey, Faldo and Oosterhuis over Bean and Kite and Barnes and Gallacher against Hayes and Zoeller, the morning foursomes on the second day saw some improvement in European fortunes. With Ken Brown dropped from all the second day matches, Jacobs and his team managed to drag the deficit back to just one point going into the singles – the closest margin in any Ryder Cup match played in the United States.

With all twelve professionals due to compete on the final day, Jacobs decided to lead off with the experienced Bernard Gallacher. However, before either team could play, there was the controversial matter of the name in the envelope. With Mark James unavailable, the rules stated that Billy Casper would leave out one player from his side and call the match a draw – the name being the one he had put in the envelope shortly before the match was due to begin. With everyone expecting Mark Hayes to be nominated player, it had come as some surprise to find Lee Trevino's name in the envelope. After Billy Casper had hurriedly approached Jacobs about the matter, it became obvious that the American captain had misunderstood the situation and had made a dreadful error. To his credit, John Jacobs eventually allowed the Americans to substitute Trevino's name with that of Gil Morgan and the singles finally got underway.

A 3 and 2 win against Lanny Wadkins gave Bernard Gallacher his fourth win in five matches and got the Europeans off to the perfect start. Then, in a collapse that would have done an English cricket side credit, there were successive defeats for Ballesteros, Jacklin, Garrido, King and Barnes against Nelson, Kite, Hayes, Bean and Mahaffey. It was a disastrous run of results, which was only stemmed by a win for Nick Faldo against Lee Elder in the seventh game. More bad news followed with further losses for Smyth, Oosterhuis and Lyle in games eight, nine and eleven against Irwin, Green and Trevino.

With the Ryder Cup lost once more, there was a final sting in the tail for the luckless John Jacobs. After watching the Americans literally overwhelm his team, the rebellious Ken Brown provided him with a 1-up singles victory over 'Fuzzy' Zoeller. While no doubt pleased for the young man, Jacobs must have contemplated the result with a wry smile. 'Laddie' Lucas later wrote, 'The fact that Ken Brown, pursuing his young, idiosyncratic way, was eventually one of only three British and European winners in the singles only compounded the wretchedness of the whole affair.'

No matter what the result, the first Ryder Cup match between Europe and the United States was declared a success. Lee Trevino later commented how close the forthcoming match at Walton Heath in England would be though few appeared to agree with him. Curiously, Mark James would be playing in two years time but neither Seve Ballesteros nor Ken Brown would. Brown would ultimately fail to qualify and, as if taking his place as the 'bad boy' of European golf, Ballesteros would refuse after a long-running feud with the British PGA. It appeared that the new era promised by the introduction of a European team was still some distance away.

1981

WALTON HEATH GOLF CLUB, SURREY, ENGLAND

18–20 SEPTEMBER

For the Europeans, a new decade in Ryder Cup history began in typical controversy. Facing one of the strongest American sides ever to visit Britain, the European Tournament Players Division, who effectively selected the team, omitted two of their best-known players – Seve Ballesteros and Tony Jacklin. If this was not bad enough, it was also proposed that the 1981 match should be played at the new headquarters of the British Professional Golfers' Association – The Belfry.

Designed by Dave Thomas and Peter Alliss, it was an 'American-style' course with water on many holes. Constructed only four years earlier, it was in generally poor condition and, with so few trees, lacked any real definition. The PGA attracted huge condemnation from the press for their choice of venue, and top professionals lined up to voice their criticism of the Midlands

Above: Walton Heath is a classic heath-and-heather course of the type found south of London. Home club of the legendary five-time British Open Champion James Braid, it sensibly replaced the Belfry as the Ryder Cup venue for 1981.

course, which Brian Barnes described as little more than a 'ploughed field'. Eventually good sense prevailed and a new venue was decided upon. Walton Heath was the favoured choice of match sponsors Sun Alliance and its Chairman, Lord Aldington. A fast-running heathland course south of London, Walton Heath had small, unreceptive greens, which, it was thought, might negate the American's strong iron play. While this proved wishful thinking, at least the British PGA had respected the long-standing tradition of the Ryder Cup by staging it on one of England's premier layouts.

Once the choice of golf course had been resolved, the 'Seve' controversy took centre stage. Ten of the twelve players in the team were to be selected straight off the European Order of Merit, but it became increasingly clear that the American-based Spaniard would struggle to qualify through money earnings alone. With two remaining places left to the discretion of a PGA-appointed three-man selection panel, it was confidently expected that Severiano Ballesteros would receive his place via the backdoor. Yet, as the Ryder Cup approached, it was the thorny issue of appearance money that would eventually decide the fate of Europe's most popular golfer.

Seve had followed up his dramatic Open Championship victory at Royal Lytham in 1979 with his first Masters title at Augusta a year later. While American Tom Watson was acknowledged as the world's number one golfer, the dashing young Spaniard was gaining on him fast. A short game genius, Seve was famous for his dramatic escapes and perhaps this more than anything drew large crowds to him on both sides of the Atlantic. Put simply, sponsors wanted him in their tournaments and were willing to pay to ensure his appearance. Though it was accepted practice for top American golfers to be paid large fees to compete in Europe, it was a situation thoroughly frowned upon by the European Tour Division and its newly appointed Secretary, Ken Schofield. The question of appearance money was something that polarized opinion. Team captain John Jacobs wanted the principle to apply to everyone, including American stars, while others, including two-time major winner Tony Jacklin, felt that top professionals deserved to benefit from their fame. Seve's attitude was uncompromising. As someone who added thousands to the gate receipts of any tournament he played in, he was entitled to appearance money. Acting for the European Tour as a whole, Schofield refused to budge on the matter and so almost inevitably it became a matter of principle with the Ryder Cup as the battleground.

In the season leading up to the Ryder Cup, Seve Ballesteros played in only seven events, with most of those relatively minor tournaments on the Continent. In what was seen as an act of petulance, the Spaniard even refused to pay the obligatory £50 membership fee to his home association. With only weeks left before the match at Walton Heath, the situation was becoming intolerable. Hoping to smooth the path to his eventual appearance in the Ryder Cup, John Jacobs rang Seve in America with an olive branch.

With the Carroll's Irish Open at Portmarnock and the Benson and Hedges tournament at Fulford the last two events before team selection was finalized, Jacobs asked Seve to play as a gesture of goodwill. Ballesteros said he would consider it but did not play. This put Jacobs and his fellow selection panel of Bernhard Langer and Neil Coles in an impossible position. With the matter tied at one-all, Langer cast his deciding vote against the Spaniard and in doing so reflected the feelings of the majority of European Tour members; the payment of appearance money would not be tolerated and effectively Ballesteros was out of the Ryder Cup.

Shortly after the Benson and Hedges, the European team was announced. The automatic qualifiers were Sam Torrance, Bernard Gallacher, Des Smyth, Howard Clark, Nick Faldo, Sandy Lyle, Eamonn Darcy, Bernhard Langer, José-Maria Cañizares and Manuel Pinero. Despite being resident in the United States, Peter Oosterhuis was chosen on the strength of his past Ryder Cup record and recent Canadian Open win. The final place was taken, somewhat controversially, by Mark James, who was chosen ahead of the thirty-seven-year-old Tony Jacklin. Understandably upset at being

Above: Former world number-one Tom Watson in singles action against Howard Clark. Watson suffered an unexpected defeat at the hands of the Englishman, who was a surprisingly infrequent player in the Ryder Cup, playing in 1977, 1981, 1983 and 1989.

left out, Jacklin felt he deserved his place on his record alone. In thirty-five matches, he had lost only eight times and only one of those in the singles. It was an enviable record, unlikely ever to be matched, and Jacklin was also the only major winner on the European Tour, apart from Ballesteros, who had since gone on to play full-time in America.

Past record aside, Jacklin had supported the Tour and the Ryder Cup for many years and felt he should have been treated better, especially considering Mark James's disgraceful behaviour at The Greenbrier two years earlier. He then learned that the decision to drop him from the side in favour of James had been unanimous, and despite a phone call from Jacobs informing him of the decision, he felt betrayed and vowed to have nothing to do with the Ryder Cup again. (Ironically, it was Jacklin who had lobbied Lord Derby to re-instate John Jacobs after his failure as captain in the crushing 17–11 defeat in America.)

Arriving in England, the American team could hardly have been stronger or more confident. Captained by Dave Marr, they could boast no less than thirty-six major championships between them, along with hundreds of other lesser titles worldwide. Made up of Jack Nicklaus, Ray Floyd, Jerry Pate, Lee Trevino, Hale Irwin, Ben Crenshaw, Bruce Lietzke, Tom Kite and Johnny Miller, the team was heralded in some quarters of the golfing press as the best American team ever to come to Britain. The evidence was indisputable; it was a side that offered the current Masters Champion, Tom Watson, Current Open Champion, Bill Rogers, and current United States PGA Champion, Larry Nelson. In effect, only Crenshaw, Kite and Lietzke had failed to win a major and only Bruce Lietzke would remain the sole professional not to win one in his career.

In comparison, the European team looked weak and inexperienced. There were four newcomers to the team in Langer, Cañizares, Pinero and Scotsman Sam Torrance. While all four professionals would make significant contributions to the European Ryder Cup cause in the future, at Walton Heath all would struggle. In the opening foursomes match, Langer and Pinero lost by 1 hole to the in-form pairing of Lee Trevino and

Larry Nelson. Yet the first day of the 1981 Ryder Cup offered much hope for the European side. In the morning, the first series of foursomes were halved at two-all, with fine wins for Sandy Lyle and Mark James over Rogers and Lietzke, and Bernard Gallacher and Des Smyth over Irwin and Floyd.

Certainly the most awaited match on that first morning was the titanic clash between the British pairing of Peter Oosterhuis and Nick Faldo and the dream partnership of Tom Watson and Jack Nicklaus. As in the previous matches, both pairings had turned up wearing blue sweaters, but this oversight was soon forgotten as all four players quickly got into their waterproofs in readiness for the rainy day ahead. Nicklaus had already tasted defeat at the hands of Oosterhuis and Faldo four years earlier when partnered by Ray Floyd at Royal Lytham and was obviously in no mood to do so again. After going 2-down after just four holes, the Americans rallied with three birdies in a row from the seventh to take the lead. It was an advantage they never relinquished and they strode out eventual winners by 4 and 3.

Captain John Jacobs responded to the defeat of his strongest pairing by dropping them for the afternoon fourballs. Sending out the successful partnership of Sandy Lyle and Mark James in the second match against Crenshaw and Pate, he surprised everyone by pairing an extremely nervous Cañizares with Des Smyth against Rogers and Lietzke in the opening game. It proved to be an inspired choice. Smyth, still glowing from his morning victory over Irwin and Floyd, played brilliantly as the Spanish/Irish pairing romped to a 6 and 5 victory. Quickly followed by an emphatic 3 and 2 triumph for Lyle and James, a half in the third match between Torrance and Clark against Kite and Miller rounded off a good day for the Europeans. And even with a late 2 and 1 win for Floyd and Irwin over Gallacher and Darcy, the home team would take a one-point advantage going into the second day.

Boosted by the prospect of a European win, the press gathered around American captain Dave Marr for his comments. Coincidentally the cousin of Jack Burke, who had led the United States to defeat at Lindrick in 1957, Marr dealt with the questions in typically witty fashion. While losing had never been considered, he said how a submarine was on standby for the return journey, just in case!

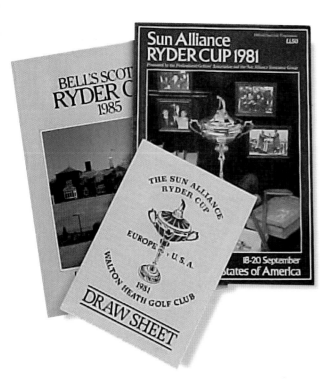

Above: Ryder Cup memorabilia. Commercial sponsors were playing an increasingly vital role in the Ryder Cup and their names were emblazoned on everything from programmes to start sheets, umbrellas to golf bags.

As things turned out, it was not needed. The second day saw the American side take a stranglehold on the match. A 3–1 defeat in the morning fourballs was followed by a 4–0 whitewash in the foursomes, and any hopes for a surprise European victory were completely dashed. The pairing of Nicklaus and Watson added two more wins with victories over Cañizares and Smyth in the morning and Langer and Pinero in the afternoon. (To their credit, Langer and Pinero recorded the European's only point of the day by beating Floyd and Irwin 2 and 1 in the fourballs.)

Moving into the final day series of twelve singles, the match was all but lost. At 10½–5½ in favour of the United States, their victory came fairly early on in the final day. In the opening match, Lee Trevino collected his fourth win in as many matches by beating Sam Torrance. This was followed by further American wins for Kite over Lyle, Nelson over James, Crenshaw over Smyth, Irwin over Cañizares, Floyd over Oosterhuis and Nicklaus over Darcy.

Apart from halves for Gallacher and Langer over Rogers and Lietzke respectively, there was the odd ray of sunshine for members of the European side. The diminutive Spaniard Manuel Pinero defeated past United States Open Champion Jerry Pate in the seventh match out. This welcome victory was quickly followed by a fine 2 and 1 win for the young Englishman Nick Faldo over the legendary Johnny Miller – which once again helped enhance his growing reputation as a player for the big occasion. Another home player to receive an honourable mention was Sandy Lyle; despite losing to the rampant Tom Kite 3 and 2, the amiable Scotsman had been a remarkable six-under par. The bespectacled Kite in contrast was ten-under!

With the final margin of defeat 9½–18½ to the United States, the post-match inquest began almost immediately. Did the absence of Ballesteros, and perhaps in a lesser way Jacklin, make the difference between defeat and victory? Probably not. The British press speculated on why it had been such a heavy defeat. Many reasons were put forward in the following days but it was widely accepted that it was the superiority of the American putting that made the difference. In truth, the difference from tee to green *was* hardly noticeable but in a curious throwback to the early years of the Ryder Cup, it was felt that the Americans were simply better putters from a few feet in.

Above: Considered the strongest pairing in Ryder Cup history, Tom Watson and Jack Nicklaus line up a putt during their demolition of Nick Faldo and Peter Oosterhuis on the opening day. A partnership that dated back to 1977, they were unbeaten in the four matches they played together. Indeed, no opponents ever got past the seventeenth hole against them.

Whether this was true or not is unsure. Certainly, the Americans appeared to hole more pressure putts than their European opponents. But this was something that was about to change. At Walton Heath, the Europeans had developed a team for the future, and while they would have to wait a while longer to taste victory, the tide had certainly turned.

12

Enter Tony Jacklin

1983

PGA NATIONAL GOLF CLUB, PALM BEACH GARDENS, FLORIDA, USA

14–16 OCTOBER

After the defeat at Walton Heath two years earlier, the Europeans made some important changes for the match at PGA National in Florida. Still without a win in America in the entire fifty-six year history of the Ryder Cup, the British team was now selected directly on the Order of Merit. Hoping to avoid the type of embarrassment caused by the omission of Severiano Ballesteros from the last match, it was felt that Europe needed in-form players. Having done away with a three-man selection panel, the important thing now was to find a captain. In what ultimately proved an inspirational choice, Executive Tour Director Ken Schofield felt he knew the right man – two-times major winner, Tony Jacklin.

Approached prior to the first round of the Car Care tournament at Sandmoor the previous May, Tony Jacklin agreed to consider the matter while out playing. After his poor treatment at the hands of the British PGA

when he was not selected for the match at Walton Heath, it must have been a difficult decision. Why he agreed to take the post is unknown; perhaps the opportunity to lead a side against his old rival and newly appointed American captain Jack Nicklaus was too good to resist. Whatever the reason, he was obviously cheered by his round of 65 and his appointment was announced to the press shortly afterwards.

Ever the perfectionist, Jacklin demanded, as part of his agreement, a number of far-reaching changes to be made before the match even started. Knowing the team was coming straight off the money list, he demanded three nominations of his own. Another small but important change involved the players' travelling arrangements to America. No longer would the team arrive drained and shame-faced after flying tourist class from Britain. From now on, the European Ryder Cup team would travel first class, in keeping with their position as sporting ambassadors. 'Too many times in the past', wrote Jacklin some years before, 'the [Ryder] Cup had been run, it seemed, more for the officials than for the players. Priorities had been in the wrong places.'

Aided by a considerable sponsorship package from Bell's Scotch whisky, Tony Jacklin got his way and Concorde was booked for the all-expenses-paid trip to the USA. Yet another concession asked for concerned the players' caddies. Caddies were now an integral part of the golfing scene and European professionals felt more comfortable with their own man standing by giving advice. A place on the plane was secured not only for the bag carriers but for wives and girlfriends as well. The changes wrought by Jacklin made him popular with the players, but like his predecessor John Jacobs, he had one major headache – Seve Ballesteros.

Realizing the importance of having Seve in the team, Tony Jacklin made a personal rather than an official approach to the young Spaniard. After the criticism he had undergone in Europe concerning his stand on receiving appearance money, Ballesteros had dismissed any possibility of playing in the Ryder Cup. Having been left out of the 1981 match at Walton Heath along with Ballesteros, Jacklin had something in common with him. In this light he approached Ballesteros over breakfast in the Prince of Wales Hotel in Southport prior to the Open Championship at Birkdale. In a diplomatic coup, Jacklin persuaded Seve of the changes he was making and two weeks later he agreed to play.

Along with Ballesteros there were four newcomers to the European team: Ian Woosnam, Gordon J. Brand, Paul Way – at twenty, among the youngest professionals to play in the Ryder Cup – and forty-three-year-old Brian Waites, who was among the oldest. They were joined by six members of the previous team: Nick Faldo, Bernard Gallacher, José-Maria Cañizares, Bernhard Langer, Sandy Lyle and Sam Torrance, with Ken Brown making his return after four years.

While strong favourites to retain the Ryder Cup, the United States also fielded a large percentage of newcomers. They included the highly rated Curtis Strange, along with the second black American to play in the event after Lee Elder in 1979, Calvin Peete, plus Jay Haas, Bob Gilder and Craig Stadler. With Tom Watson, Ben Crenshaw and Ray Floyd providing the backbone of the side, Lanny Wadkins, 'Fuzzy' Zoeller,

Above: Tony Jacklin remains one of the most influential figures in Ryder Cup history. A two-time major winner, the Englishman transformed the shambles that was the European team in 1981 into a Ryder Cup winning team four years later at the Belfry. An inspirational figure, he also masterminded the first foreign victory on American soil in 1987.

Gil Morgan and Tom Kite were left to fill the remaining places. In what amounted to a transitory period for the American tour, there was no longer a Nicklaus, Trevino or Miller in the side. Nevertheless, what they had was still considered strong enough to beat their European opponents.

In pre-match interviews, Jack Nicklaus made it clear that he intended to give everyone a game before the singles. (This contrasted starkly with Jacklin, who intended to use his top players as much as possible – even going as far as telling Gordon J. Brand on the plane to America that he would not be playing until the singles!) Deciding to pair players who were close friends rather than rivals, Nicklaus put Watson and Crenshaw out first in the opening foursomes. Greeted by stamina-sapping heat that constantly hovered around the 95°F (35°C) mark, the Americans got off to a flying start against Scotsmen Bernard Gallacher and Sandy Lyle, eventually running out winners by 5 and 4.

Above: Seve Ballesteros shows Ryder Cup rookie Paul Way the right line during their match against Tom Watson and Bob Gilder on the second day. An inspirational pairing, they finished with two wins and a halved point out of the four matches they played together at Palm Springs.

In the second match, Nick Faldo and Bernhard Langer quickly recovered the deficit by defeating the highly competitive pairing of Craig Stadler and Lanny Wadkins by 4 and 2. Driven on by captain Jacklin, who constantly prowled the PGA National course encouraging his players, Cañizares and Torrance sprang the surprise of the day by beating the tough American pairing of Floyd and Gilder by 4 and 3. With the ability to turn defeat into victory, even the 2 and 1 win by Kite and Peete over Ballesteros and Way in the fourth match gave Jacklin something to work on.

Prior to the match, Ballesteros had wanted to be paired with his fellow Spaniard Cañizares and was upset about being matched with the youngster Way.

Proving himself an expert at getting the best out of his players, Jacklin took Seve to one side after their defeat in the foursomes and explained how much the young professional needed the guiding hand of a senior player. That was enough for Ballesteros. Taking Paul Way under his wing, he partnered the twenty-year-old throughout both the foursomes and fourballs, only losing once on that opening day.

Like the morning foursomes, the afternoon fourballs were a close affair, with the Europeans managing to take a one-point lead into the second day. Defeat for Langer and Faldo in the second match against Watson and Haas was sandwiched by wins for Waites and Brown (2 and 1 against Morgan and Zoeller) and Ballesteros and Way (1-up against Floyd and Strange.) With the final match of the day halved between Woosnam and Torrance and Americans Crenshaw and Peete, Jacklin's tactics had started to pay off. However, problems were beginning to pop up concerning some of his players. Shortly before the afternoon fourballs, Bernard Gallacher and Sandy Lyle, who had been paired in the opening match, requested not to play. Fortunately, Brian Waites and Ken Brown, who had been summoned from a few practice holes together, played well in their victory over Morgan and Zoeller. This left Jacklin with a major headache. Two of his most important team members were struggling with their game, and if Europe was to beat America, he needed *everyone* in tip-top form.

The second day brought more of the same hot and humid weather. A Florida thunderstorm on the final practice day had dotted the course with casual water, which forced the Europeans to order extra pairs of golf shoes and absorbent shirts just to counteract the sticky conditions. Using his hotel suite as team headquarters, Jacklin stressed the need for concentration and the task of having to 'do it all again tomorrow'. Yet, as the morning fourballs on the second day began to unfold, he must have felt his words were wasted.

Waites and Brown were sent out first against the hard men of the American team, Craig Stadler and Lanny Wadkins. Having been 3-up early on, they succumbed to a chip-in on the final hole by Stadler to lose by one hole. Just as the result was posted on the giant scoreboard behind the eighteenth green, Jacklin received news that Ballesteros and Way had lost a one-hole lead to go dormie 1-down playing the last. Competing against Gil Morgan and Jay Haas,

Ballesteros rose to the occasion by hitting two woods to the back of the par-five, chipping close and holing the putt for a half. On any other occasion a half would probably have been a disappointment, but the manner in which it was achieved eventually acted as a boost to the European cause.

In the third match, Faldo and Langer played well once more to record their second win of the Ryder Cup against Peete and Crenshaw by 4 and 2. While Torrance and Woosnam lost to an in-form Tom Watson and Bob Gilder in the last match of the morning, Jacklin reflected on how much worse it could have been. In the afternoon foursomes, he resolved to make only one change in the second match out – replacing Woosnam with Cañizares as partner for Sam Torrance.

On reflection it proved to be a mistake, as both men performed poorly in a crushing 7 and 5 defeat by Wadkins and Morgan. Fortunately, the damage was repaired by wins for Faldo and Langer against Kite and Floyd, and Ballesteros and Way against Watson and Gilder. With Brown and Waites suffering their second defeat in three matches at the hands of Haas and Strange, the overall match score was finely balanced at 8-all going into the singles. Handing in his order of play for the singles, Jacklin looked to make a strong start by putting out his strongest players first – Ballesteros, Faldo and Langer. In what proved a fascinating tactical battle between the two captains, Nicklaus placed his best players – Stadler, Wadkins, Floyd and Watson – near the end. So, almost inevitably, the battle for the twenty-fifth Ryder Cup would be decided upon the middle order results.

In the opening game, a half for Ballesteros against 'Fuzzy' Zoeller, and wins for Faldo and Langer over Haas and Morgan respectively gave Jacklin the start he wanted. Now two points ahead, he needed further wins from players like Sandy Lyle, Sam Torrance, Ian Woosnam and Ken Brown to consolidate the lead. Sadly they never came. Starting in the fourth game, three consecutive defeats for Brand, Lyle and Waites against Gilder, Crenshaw and Peete helped tip the balance of the match in favour of the Americans.

A creditable win for Paul Way over Curtis Strange, and a half between Sam Torrance and Tom Kite restored matters slightly – Kite had in fact pitched the ball stone dead out of the rough to snatch a half when Torrance looked favourite to win the hole. Yet, with only four matches left out on the course, the entire tournament was still there to be won or lost. Things looked grim for Jacklin and his team when defeat for Woosnam at the hands of Stadler took them behind once more. Then moments later the news came through that Ken Brown had inflicted a surprise 4 and 2 defeat on past Masters Champion Ray Floyd. Now, with just two matches left out on the course, the pressure was really on both captains.

With Tom Watson leading Bernard Gallacher in the final game, Nicklaus and his team followed Lanny Wadkins down the fairway in his increasingly tense struggle with José-Maria Cañizares. With the evening drawing in and a thunderstorm threatening, the Spanish veteran came to the 578-yard final hole with a 1-up advantage. Playing short of large cross bunkers, both men left themselves with a full pitch to the green with a wedge. Playing first, Cañizares misjudged his shot, coming up fractionally short of the green, then looked on as Wadkins prepared to take his shot. In what must be one of the greatest shots played in Ryder Cup history, the American almost pitched it into the hole for an eagle. Resting only inches away, it was enough to win the hole and halve the match. Nicklaus sank to his knees and actually kissed the spot from which Wadkins had played his shot.

As Lanny Wadkins walked off the final green, Tom Watson and Bernard Gallacher were playing the par-3, seventeenth. After losing the sixteenth to a par, Watson walked onto the tee holding a 1-up lead. Needing only to halve his match to retain the Ryder Cup he, like Gallacher, had missed the green and failed to make the putting surface with the chip. In the gathering gloom and with fraying nerve ends, Bernard Gallacher chipped up to around five feet with Watson a little closer. As his team looked on, the Scot failed to make his short putt for a bogey and the match was effectively over.

After coming so close to victory, Jacklin's reaction was understandable. Commenting after the match he said, 'It was a hell of a let down. We'd done everything right and now we have nothing to show for it.' Nicklaus admitted that a tie would have been a fair result but the final 14½–13½ score-line offered little comfort to the disappointed Europeans. Having been pencilled-in as team captain for the 1985 Ryder Cup at The Belfry, all Jacklin could do was wait and plan for victory in two year's time. As things turned out, it was time well spent.

1985

THE BELFRY, SUTTON COLDFIELD, WEST MIDLANDS, ENGLAND

13–15 SEPTEMBER

Four years earlier the new Belfry golf course on the outskirts of Birmingham had been a controversial choice of Ryder Cup venue. Now, after years of re-seeding, fertilization and extensive tree planting, the Brabazon course offered a formidable test of golf. In addition, there was an impressive on-course hotel, in which both teams would stay for the week. The press criticism that had greeted the choice of The Belfry in 1981 literally melted away over the three days of competition there in 1985. Prior to the match, even European team captain Tony Jacklin had voiced his reservations about the 'American-style' course. Yet as the match progressed to its glorious conclusion, the two-time major winner must have wished that all future Ryder Cups could be played on this patch of Warwickshire countryside.

Re-appointed captain in January 1984, Jacklin set about building the sort of team spirit that had been so evident at the PGA National two years earlier. With nine places taken from the European Order of Merit, he requested three 'picks' in case any of his top players failed to make the side because of commitments on the United States Tour. He chose American-based Nick Faldo and Ken Brown, along with Spanish newcomer José Rivero. The side, which proved to be similar to his first as captain, also included Ian Woosnam, José-Maria Cañizares, Sandy Lyle, Howard Clark, Sam Torrance, Paul Way, Manuel Pinero, Severiano Ballesteros and Bernhard Langer. Jacklin was considerably helped by both Ballesteros and Langer altering their schedules to include more European events.

After facing the possibility of defeat in Florida, the American team had also made some minor changes in their selection process. In 1983 they had been without both Hal Sutton, their PGA Champion, and Larry Nelson, their Open Champion – Sutton because he had not served his probationary period as a professional, and Nelson because he had not accumulated enough merit

points to qualify automatically. Provided they were American citizens, both winners could now be included. The American team, which included Lanny Wadkins, Craig Stadler, Ray Floyd, Tom Kite, Calvin Peete and 'Fuzzy' Zoeller, now also boasted US Open Champion Andy North and PGA winner Hubert Green. There were three other newcomers to the Ryder Cup in Mark O'Meara, Peter Jacobson and Hal Sutton.

The US side was captained by Lee Trevino, renewing a rivalry with Tony Jacklin that went back to the 1970 British Open Championship at Muirfield. Trevino was determined not to become the first American captain to lose the Ryder Cup in twenty-six years, but his cause was weakened by the failure of Tom Watson to make the side. In a team that had few star names, Watson's inclusion would have given the American side a huge psychological boost in what was always going to be a difficult match. (Only a few weeks earlier, Watson had needed to par the final hole in the USPGA Championship to qualify automatically. Then, when requested to play in the final qualifying event, he had declined.)

Certainly, the British public felt the European side had a good chance of winning. Boosted by Bernhard Langer's win at the Masters earlier in the year at Augusta and Sandy Lyle's British Open win at Royal St Georges, record crowds of 25,000 turned up each day at The Belfry to cheer their side on. Indeed, it was their voluble support over the three days that gave much cause for complaint in the American camp. Peter Jacobson later commented, 'All that cheering when we missed shots. I've never known anything like it before, especially from British crowds. You expect so much more from them.' Jacobson's views were later repeated by other members of the American team, but, perhaps more significantly, captain Trevino not only refused to join in the chorus of complaint but even accused his players of being 'cry babies'.

In what proved a tension-packed opening day, the United States took the morning foursomes 3–1, before being pulled back to only a one-point lead after the afternoon foursomes. For the Europeans, the Spanish partnership of Ballesteros and Pinero proved the most fruitful, with a 2 and 1 win over Strange and O'Meara in the foursomes and a victory over North and Jacobson by the same score in the fourballs. Also in the afternoon fourballs, Paul Way joined up with the older and more experienced Ian Woosnam in a repeat of his successful partnership with Seve to inflict a 1-hole win over Zoeller and Green. Despite a close 1-hole loss for Cañizares and Torrance in the final match of the day against Floyd and Wadkins, the Europeans' 2½–1½ comeback in the afternoon had cheered everyone. The Ryder Cup was now truly underway.

After performing heroics on the opening day, including driving the par-4 tenth-hole, Ballesteros played poorly in his morning fourball match against Mark O'Meara and Lanny Wadkins. Still partnered by Manuel Pinero, they had failed to capitalize on two earlier European wins for Torrance and Clark against Kite and North, and Woosnam and Way against Green and Zoeller. Eventually losing by 3 and 2, the American pair had an outward score of 32 and, after quickly racing to a 4-up lead, they were never in any danger of losing. For Tony Jacklin, it was a vital opportunity missed to forge ahead and put real pressure on the Americans. The Spaniards had proved to be Jacklin's most successful pairing, and with the fourth match between Langer and Lyle and Stadler and Strange looking to go the Americans' way, the momentum was seemingly lost. Then, in one of the most dramatic moments in Ryder Cup history, everything changed.

The strong American pair approached the par-5 seventeenth dormie 2-up. On the green, Sandy Lyle holed a huge putt for an eagle to cut the deficit to one and, despite Stadler making birdie, all four men found themselves playing the 474-yard final hole. Langer and Lyle drove well down the fairway along with Stadler, while Curtis Strange found the right-hand bunker. Despite making the green, neither European threatened the hole with their approach; nor, for that matter, did Stadler, who found himself on the lower tier with Lyle. With the hole perched precariously on the middle-tier of this huge three-tier green, Langer found himself a good twenty-foot way with a sloping putt.

With Langer and Lyle effectively assured of par, the pressure was on American Stadler to get down in two for a possible half on the hole and win in the game. He responded with an excellent twenty-yard putt up the severe slope to finish only eighteen inches away. Shortly after the Europeans had missed their birdie putts, all that was left was the formality of Stadler tapping in for a win. Remarkably, this most experienced of professionals pulled it wide and the game was halved. Quite what Stadler was thinking of is unsure but it was enough to make the scores level at six matches all with the momentum running Europe's way.

Above: Craig Stadler of the USA turns in disbelief as he misses a short putt at the eighteenth green, which resulted in Europe's Langer and Lyle halving the match in the day-three fourballs.

The afternoon foursomes saw even more success for the European team. Leading off with the Spanish pairings of Cañizares/Rivero and Ballesteros/Pinero against the Americans Kite/Peete and Stadler/Sutton, the 'home' team raced to a two-point lead. The European surge was halted only momentarily by an unexpected defeat for Way and Woosnam at the hands of Strange and Jacobson before Langer's and Brown's 3 and 2 victory over Floyd and Wadkins restored the balance. After they won the foursomes 3–1, hopes were high for a glorious home win. But first the singles had to be negotiated.

Even with a two-point lead going into the final day, the experienced Tony Jacklin realized that over twelve matches the Americans would be favourites. Unlike two years earlier at the PGA National, he chose to play his best players in the middle and hope his early picks could spring a surprise or two. Manuel Pinero is supposed to have jumped with delight after hearing he was matched in the opening singles against Lanny Wadkins; his attitude summed up the overall team spirit. The match itself was a hard-fought affair, with the Spaniard going down twice early on. A win on the par-3 eighth was quickly followed by birdies on the tenth and eleventh to move Pinero into a 2-up lead. Another at the par-5 fifteenth took him out of range and, suddenly, defeat for one of the United States' strongest players was assured.

A topped bunker shot at the last into the lake by Raymond Floyd gave young Paul Way an unexpected 2-up victory in the third match out. For captain Jacklin – travelling about the course and ever alert on his mobile radio – this win made up for a poor display by Ian Woosnam in his 2 and 1 defeat by Craig Stadler. Now, with a run of singles, which saw his strongest players Ballesteros, Lyle and Langer out against Kite, Jacobson and Sutton respectively, hopes were high.

In the fourth game out, Ballesteros struggled to hold the bespectacled American Kite. Playing sporadically, Seve found himself 2-down at the turn and then 3-down with only five to play. Placed under the sort of pressure that would make most professionals give up, the Spanish maestro holed a monstrous putt for a birdie-two at the fourteenth and another, slightly shorter, for another winning birdie at the fifteenth. On the long seventeenth, Ballesteros was over the green in two and, after a poor chip, managed to hole his putt for a birdie-four to bring his match all square. To his credit, Kite had the better of the final hole after his opponent hit a poor tee-shot, but a halved eighteenth and match was probably a fair result for both men.

Following in the match behind, Sandy Lyle was also struggling with his game in the early stages of the bout with Peter Jacobson. Still managing to score well enough,

Left: Arms aloft, Sam Torrance celebrates his match-winning birdie putt on the eighteenth green. Standing on the tee, the Scot had hit the drive of his life against former US Open Champion Andy North.

he went out in thirty-four strokes and the newly crowned British Open Champion found himself 2-up. Still swinging a little erratically, Lyle hooked out-of-bounds on the par-4 thirteenth and his 2-up lead was halved. A concession by Jacobson on the fifteenth green restored Lyle's lead once more, then a remarkable twenty-five yard putt from off the back of the sixteenth green finally closed out the American Jacobsen by 3 and 2.

After the loud cheers that greeted Lyle's win had died down, the taste of victory was in the air for the Europeans. Further wins for Bernhard Langer and José-Maria Cañizares against Hal Sutton and 'Fuzzy' Zoeller in matches six and eleven appeared to bring it even closer. The Americans slowly began to crumble under the pressure and, despite late defeats for Nick Faldo, José Rivero and Ken Brown, Howard Clark had a short putt in his match against Mark O'Meara to win the Ryder Cup. He missed, but would win his game on the following hole. He paved the way for a dramatic finale on the eighteenth green soon after, but it was his partner, Sam Torrance, who would hit the winning putt.

Level with Andy North, standing on the eighteenth tee, Torrance hit the tee-shot of his life down the final hole. Smashing it over the trees on the testing par-4 hole, his ball came to rest in perfect position in the centre of the fairway. Playing second, and now under immense pressure, the American ballooned his drive into the lake 200 yards from off the tee. Failing to make the green in three, he could only watch in anguish as the Scot hit a superb approach to within 20-foot of the hole. Knowing that it was enough to win the Ryder Cup, Torrance's walk down the final fairway turned into a victory march. Left with two putts to win, he took one and was immediately engulfed by his delighted teammates.

Victors by 16½–11½, the Europeans had beaten America. With champagne corks still popping, Tony Jacklin stepped up to receive the famous trophy. History had been made and it would not be for the last time.

Below: It's all smiles for Europe's inspirational captain Tony Jacklin as he receives the most coveted trophy in team sports.

1987

MUIRFIELD VILLAGE, COLUMBUS, OHIO, USA

25–27 SEPTEMBER

Named after the Scottish course on which Jack Nicklaus had won his first British Open title in 1966, Muirfield Village was to prove a superb Ryder Cup venue. Described in some parts of the media as the 'course that Jack built' and the 'Augusta of the North', it certainly compared favourably with its more illustrious counterpart in Georgia. A tree-lined, arena-style course with water in play on many holes, its slick greens were among the fastest in the United States. With rarely

a blade of grass out of place, Nicklaus's ambitious design was deemed to favour the sort of 'target' golf so common on the United States Tour. Obviously benefiting the style of players like Kite, Strange and Wadkins, this was believed to be an important consideration, with the home side now having to win back the trophy lost two years earlier at The Belfry.

With Lee Trevino standing down, Jack Nicklaus was asked once more to captain the United States Ryder Cup side. The 'Golden Bear' was considered by the USPGA as the person best suited to winning the trophy back. After all, no one knew the course better and, unlike Trevino, Nicklaus had successfully captained his side to victory four years earlier at the PGA National – albeit by the narrow margin of a single point. This broke with the tradition of previous years, when the job of captain was handed around to veteran professionals in recognition of their service to the American Tour.

Despite looking forward to renewing his twenty-year rivalry with European captain Tony Jacklin, Nicklaus was apparently unprepared for the huge media interest in the competition. With the prospect of a truly competitive Ryder Cup on American soil, ABC Television decided to cover the match live for the first time, such was the incredible interest in this fascinating sporting contest. Perhaps not surprisingly, they proposed that the match be extended to four days with an extra series of singles to make it more attractive commercially. With the unofficial backing of the United States PGA, the suggestion was then put to Executive Director of the European PGA, Colin Snape, who in turn discussed it with Tony Jacklin at his new home in Spain.

Left: Deep in concentration, US captain Jack Nicklaus tries to work out a winning strategy. In a rare experience for him, he was on the losing side, with Europe winning 15–13.

Aware of the implications it would have for his team, the European captain rejected the proposal almost immediately. At the 1986 Open Championship at Turnberry, the proposition was formally tabled again by the American PGA. With pressure on him to accept, Tony Jacklin threatened to resign should such important changes to the playing format be pushed through without his consent. Unlike some members of the British PGA, who were keen to see the event extended, Jacklin knew the disastrous consequences that such a move would have on his team's chances of winning.

Even though in Nick Faldo, Seve Ballesteros, Sandy Lyle, Ian Woosnam and Bernhard Langer, he had five of the best players in the world, Jacklin knew that the Americans would always be able to boast greater strength in depth. Having taken part in nine Ryder Cup matches – seven as a player and two as captain – he knew it was in the final series of twelve singles that the Europeans had traditionally struggled. And he knew that, while his lower-order players might have one good day against the Americans in the singles, an extra series of matches would be asking just too much. His threat to resign stood and Nicklaus, not wishing to captain his side under such controversial circumstances, persuaded the American PGA to withdraw the proposal.

Peace had finally been achieved, but the rampant commercialism that had threatened the Ryder Cup a year before resurfaced only days before the European team was due to fly out to the United States on Concorde. With the Scottish company of Glenmuir appointed official suppliers of clothing to the European Ryder Cup side, players like Nick Faldo, Sandy Lyle, Ian Woosnam and Bernhard Langer were all warned they might be in breach of contract with rival clothing manufacturers. Clients of Mark McCormack's International Management Group, all four professionals agreed that while they would wear the official sweaters, shirts, etc., the offending logos would be blacked out. In an event known for its fine sportsmanship and lack of commercialization, the whole matter proved an embarrassing sideline.

Apart from his 'star' names, which included current British Open Champion Nick Faldo, Jacklin also had a selection of established tournament winners in his team. Apart from losing Paul Way and José-Maria Cañizares from the side that had beaten the Americans at The Belfry, his team now included Gordon Brand, Jr. and

Howard Clark, who had both won twice in Europe that season. With José Rivero, Eamonn Darcy and Sam Torrance all recording one win each, and Jacklin's own picks of Ken Brown and the promising Spaniard, José-Maria Olazábal, it was a confident European side that set off for America.

The United States team, in comparison, had a relatively weak look. Apart from Andy Bean and Hal Sutton, it included five newcomers: Payne Stewart, Mark Calcavecchia, Larry Mize, Scott Simpson and Dan Pohl. With past Ryder Cup stalwarts like Tom Watson and Ray Floyd failing to qualify, captain Nicklaus looked to experienced players like Ben Crenshaw, Larry Nelson, Curtis Strange, Tom Kite and Lanny Wadkins to help him win through. Following a typically exuberant display by the Ohio State Marching Band at the opening ceremony, he quietly announced his team in alphabetical order, declaring, 'I couldn't have twelve finer players or twelve finer gentleman.'

After marching down the eighteenth fairway accompanied by the sound of Scottish bagpipes, Jacklin, in contrast, introduced his team by name and country, deliberately leaving the masterful Seve Ballesteros until last. Proving what a popular sporting event the Ryder Cup had become, the European team were accompanied on the trip by more than two thousand highly vocal supporters, who had made the trip in anticipation of the first 'away' victory on American soil in almost sixty years of Ryder Cup history. It is impossible to gauge what impact these supporters, who made their presence felt as early as the first day, had on the final result. What is certain is that after the opening day's play, which saw the Europeans move into a remarkable 6–2 lead, Jack Nicklaus made a widespread appeal for more support from the American fans.

Certainly, the foundation of what was to prove an historic performance by the Europeans came in the first day fourballs. With the morning foursomes shared two-all, Jacklin retained his two successful pairings of Faldo/Woosnam and Ballesteros/Olazábal for the afternoon. Reorganizing his team after a poor display by Torrance and Clark in their 4 and 2 opening match defeat by Strange and Kite, followed by another with Brown and Langer losing to Sutton and Pohl, Jacklin dropped all of them except the German Langer.

In a decision that would surely have drawn criticism from the press had it gone wrong, the inexperienced

Gordon Brand, Jr. and José Rivero were thrown out first against Crenshaw and Simpson. Bernhard Langer was brought back to partner an out-of-form Sandy Lyle in the second match against Mark Calcavecchia and Andy Bean. With Nicklaus persisting with his policy of giving everyone a game as quickly as possible, Jacklin's selection proved an inspirational piece of captaincy. Victories in the opening two games were quickly followed by wins for Faldo and Woosnam over Sutton and Pohl, and for Ballesteros and Olazábal over the strong American pairing of Kite and Strange. Gathering at the end of the day in their sprawling team bungalow close by the final green, the team talked mainly about the first fourball European whitewash on American soil in the event's history. Tony Jacklin's team was buoyant, but, as the captain reminded them, there were still two days to go.

Knowing better than to change a winning team, Tony Jacklin went into the second-day foursomes with the same pairings that had performed so well the previous afternoon. Nicklaus, in comparison, surprised everyone by his choices for the morning foursomes. After conceding that the Europeans had dominated the first day, he persisted with two-time losers Strange and Kite, sending them out first against Rivero and Brand, Jr. Then, in the second match, he paired Sutton and Mize against the strong British partnership of Woosnam and Faldo. It was a risky strategy with points needed early on, but as the morning wore on, his plan looked to have worked.

In the opening foursomes, Brand, Jr. holed a long putt on the first to take the lead, Strange replying with an even longer one on the second green to bring the match back to level. Taking the lead for the first time on the sixth, the Americans lost it again four holes later, reaching the turn 1-down. Then, with the help of three birdies on the back nine, Strange and Kite took command of the match, eventually running out winners by 3 and 1. The first halved match of the Ryder Cup followed moments later after Sutton and Mize won the eighteenth with a par to deny Faldo and Woosnam their third consecutive victory.

Above: Sandy Lyle and Bernhard Langer celebrate a dramatic win over American pair Lanny Wadkins and Larry Nelson late in the day at the eigtheenth by one hole.

Clutching the colourful Stars and Stripes flags given out free to encourage home support, the home crowd's mood was optimistic. With the strongest US pairing of Wadkins and Nelson following up in game three against Lyle and Woosnam, hopes were high for yet another American point. In a highly competitive match, the European pair dashed any hopes of a home win by making an eagle on the eleventh and birdie on the thirteenth to go 2-up. A scrappy win on the fifteenth made the point secure and the visitors drew level in the second series of foursomes with one match left on the course.

Always at his best under pressure, Severiano Ballesteros took second place to his young Spanish partner José-Maria Olazábal in their match against Crenshaw and Stewart. With the help of some fine iron play from the Europeans, they had built a commanding 3-up lead with only five holes left to play. However, a poor drive into a stream by Ballesteros to lose the fourteenth, followed by a splendid approach shot by Crenshaw at seventeen for a birdie, reduced the lead to just one as they walked onto the final tee. With the chance of a morale-boosting halve for the Americans a distinct possibility, Ballesteros left Olazábal with a six-foot putt for a bogey to win the game. To the enormous relief of both Ballesteros and Jacklin, he calmly slotted

the ball home for a 2½–1½ win in the foursomes and a creditable 8½–3½ overall lead.

After the strain of the morning, the European pairings cut loose with some wonderful golf in the afternoon fourballs. Keeping with his successful policy of selecting in-form players, Jacklin made only one change from the morning, dropping José Rivero as Gordon Brand, Jr's partner in favour of Eamonn Darcy. It proved a poor choice, as both were soundly beaten 3 and 2 by Payne Stewart and Andy Bean in the second match out. With defeat in the opening match for Kite and Strange at the hands of Woosnam and Faldo, the second American point came in the third game with a surprise 2 and 1 defeat for Ballesteros and Olazábal by Sutton and Mize.

As the evening light faded, the possibility of a concerted American comeback loomed large for the European team – especially as Wadkins and Nelson were staging a fight back in the last match against Langer and Lyle. Wadkins had birdied both the par-3 sixteenth and par-4 seventeenth to pull back the dormie 3-up lead held by the Europeans. Looking a little shaken on the eighteenth tee, Lyle and Langer followed two excellent drives by their opponents with two of their own. With the American pair longer off the tee, Lyle was left to hit his approach first into the narrow green. Hitting the shot of the day, the ball finished no more than two yards from the hole. Turning to his German partner, Lyle said, 'Get inside that and we'll be alright.' Moments later Langer duly obliged and the Europeans found themselves leading the overall match by 10½–5½.

The record books show that for the sixty-five holes played that afternoon, the Europeans were cumulatively 29 under par against the United States' 22. In the press conference that followed, Nicklaus admitted, 'I've seen the superior golf played by the European team. We fought to the end but our best simply was not good enough today.' Tony Jacklin agreed, saying, 'I never thought I would live to see the day when I would see golf played like this.'

With only four points needed from the remaining twelve singles, the destiny of the Ryder Cup was in European hands. The evening before, Tony Jacklin discussed his order of play with his senior players, including Seve Ballesteros. Nicklaus, it was thought, would put his best in first and hope to get off to a winning start. This meant that the Europeans should save their strongest players – Langer, Lyle and Ballesteros – until later in the day. In the event, the US captain surprised everyone – including his own players – by saving Nelson, Kite, Strange, Sutton and Wadkins right to the end. Also, by choosing to lead off with the inexperienced Andy Bean and Dan Pohl, his highly unusual strategy led to some surprises during the final day. While his tactics would ultimately fail, the small task of achieving four points to win the Ryder Cup proved remarkably difficult for the Europeans.

Ian Woosnam was given the task of leading off against Bean in the first match. Surprising everyone, the past US Open winner led, after taking 34 strokes to the turn. After halving the par-5 fifteenth in birdies, the Welshman missed a putt to square the match on the seventeenth. On the final hole, Bean consulted his captain regarding the approach shot (something allowed in the Ryder Cup) and wisely chose to play to the heart of the green. Despite a good drive, Woosnam could not make better than par and the opening match was lost.

With one of his key players defeated, Jacklin looked to Nick Faldo to restore the balance. As Woosnam walked off the last green, the scoreboard showed Europe down in five of the eleven matches out on the course, with three all square. Playing in the fourth match against Mark Calcavecchia, Faldo struggled throughout, finally losing on the eighteenth green 1-down. With only one win for the Europeans in the first five games out, the crisis that Jacklin feared was beginning to take shape. Grateful for Howard Clark's early win over Dan Pohl in match two, the Ryder Cup would now be decided over matches six to eleven, with Ken Brown and Gordon Brand, Jr. thrown as sacrificial lambs against Lanny Wadkins and Hal Sutton in the final two matches.

In match six, an unlikely hero emerged in the shape of Eamonn Darcy, who was matched against Ben Crenshaw. The difference in their golf swings could not have been more apparent. Compared with the classic, free-flowing Texan, Darcy had a swing with too many moving parts, a loop on the backswing and a restricted follow through. Yet both men were renowned for their sure putting touch, and it was on the slick Muirfield greens that the match would be finally settled.

Under the pressure of the day, Crenshaw was first to crack. Frustrated by a missed putt on the sixth green, he snapped the shaft of his Wilson 8802 blade putter and was forced to improvise for the rest of the match. Using

Above: One of the legendary figures of the Ryder Cup matches, Nick Faldo of Europe punches the air as he birdies the fourteenth during his fourball match with Ian Woosnam against Strange and Kite.

a mixture of bladed sand-irons and de-lofted long-irons, the American amazed everyone by taking the lead with a birdie at the par-3 sixteenth. Boasting one of the poorest records in the Ryder Cup, Darcy squared the match on the seventeenth after Crenshaw had missed the green in three. Now level, playing the final hole, Crenshaw hit his second crooked tee-shot in a row. Hooking the ball left into water, he coaxed his third into a green-side bunker with Darcy in the same place, but for one shot less.

With thousands looking on – and millions more in America and Europe watching the match on television – Crenshaw hit a fine shot, which unfortunately ran on much further than he expected. With his right elbow flying out in trademark fashion, Darcy splashed out to around four feet with his opponent three times the distance from the hole. In keeping with his reputation as a world-class putter, Crenshaw calmly rolled the ball

Above: The great Jack Nicklaus consoles Ben Crenshaw, who snapped his putter early on while playing Eamonn Darcy in the singles and had to putt with his one iron.

into the hole for a bogey-5 using his three-iron. If Darcy was shaken, he certainly did not show it. Stepping up to his twisting downhill putt, he rolled it smoothly into the hole for a vital point for his team and walked off the final green the hero of the hour.

With a halve between Sam Torrance and Larry Mize, followed by further home wins for Payne Stewart against Olazábal, and Scott Simpson against Rivero, the match score was now poised at 13–11 to the Europeans. Darcy's vital win over Crenshaw meant that Europe needed just 1½ points from the final five games, which began with Bernhard Langer's match against Larry Nelson.

In what proved a controversial decision, the two men arrived at the final green all square. Langer was on the green in regulation, while Nelson had to chip and putt for his par. The American played up to around three feet, leaving the German a long putt for a dramatic win. Playing with caution, Langer rolled his putt just inside his opponent's and, almost half-heartedly, called for a half. To everyone's surprise – including his captain's – Nelson agreed. In hindsight, it was a curious decision: the United States team needed all the points it could muster and, with Ballesteros close to beating Curtis Strange, it proved a fatal one. Minutes later, the dashing Spaniard closed out the American on the seventeenth green. After he had shaken hands with his opponent and walked to the back of the green, the news came through that Langer had halved. Raising his arms in salute, it was somehow fitting that Seve should have struck the winning putt – the stroke that had inflicted the first home defeat on the United States in six decades of Ryder Cup history.

In the great celebrations that followed, the last two matches were almost forgotten amid the chaotic scenes around the final green. (Ken Brown eventually lost to Lanny Wadkins and Gordon Brand, Jr. halved with Hal Sutton.) In the post-match interviews Jack Nicklaus was typically gracious in defeat, commenting that 'The Europeans were tougher coming down the last hole today.'

In truth, the finest golfer the world has ever seen had been badly let down by his star names. Curtis Strange, among others, had won more than $700,000 in the season leading up to the Ryder Cup and was billed as the world number-one golfer – a reputation that Ballesteros had taken great pleasure in demolishing.

Above: Fellow countryman José-Maria Olazábal and other European players celebrate with José-Maria Cañizares as he beats 'Fuzzy' Zoeller at the eigtheenth to win the singles match.

The same was true of the man who had been hero of the PGA National four years earlier, Lanny Wadkins. Playing in four matches, Wadkins' solitary point for the United States came in his defeat of Ken Brown.

For European captain Tony Jacklin, the result vindicated his decision to take on the job more than six years earlier. Following on from the bitter disappointment of not being selected to play in the 1981 Ryder Cup at Walton Heath, Jacklin had revolutionized the event in competitive terms. With the help of world-class players such as Ballesteros, Faldo, Langer, Woosnam and Lyle, European golf had undergone a renaissance, with the Ryder Cup acting as the catalyst. Following on from great British captains of the past like J.H. Taylor, Henry Cotton and Dai Rees, Jacklin had achieved what none of his predecessors could have thought possible, beating the Americans in their own backyard. An emotional man at the best of times, Jacklin, not surprisingly, was almost speechless with joy. Joined at the back of the final green by his team, not a little tearful and clutching a well-earned glass of champagne, all he could say was, 'it is the greatest week of my life'. And who would argue?

1989

THE BELFRY, SUTTON COLDFIELD, WEST MIDLANDS, ENGLAND

22–24 SEPTEMBER

Victory two years earlier at Muirfield Village meant the Europeans would start as strong favourites for the twenty-eighth Ryder Cup. With The Belfry acting as venue for the second consecutive occasion, hopes for another dramatic home win saw this billed as the most highly anticipated match in living memory. As at Royal Birkdale two decades ago, huge crowds flocked to the Warwickshire course hopeful of continuing a run that had included two wins in the past six years. Long before the match got underway, media coverage had been intense, with almost a thousand reporters, photographers and television personnel given press accreditation by the British PGA. With viewers as far away as South Africa and Japan, an estimated worldwide television audience of 200 million would tune in as the match approached its climax on the final afternoon. For the vast majority, it was certainly worth waiting for.

Captained again by Tony Jacklin, the European side had an experienced look about it. Compared with the Americans, who had five newcomers to the Ryder Cup, the solitary new face on the European team was Order of Merit winner Ronan Rafferty. The most notable absentee was Sandy Lyle. In what proved to be a dramatic decline in form, the past Masters and Open Championship winner had struggled with his game for some time. After beginning the 1989 season with two seconds and a third on the US Tour, the amiable Scot was considered a certainty to face the Americans. Then, for no apparent reason, he underwent a slide, which included missing the cut nine times in eleven tournaments. While Jacklin kept the door open for him, Lyle had lost his confidence and, by the last qualifying event of the European season in Germany, he had already contacted Jacklin with his decision not to be considered.

For Jacklin himself, the period between the two matches had been a particularly tragic and emotional one. A few months after the match at Muirfield Village, his wife Vivian had died after collapsing at the wheel of her car in Spain. At what must have been a personally distressing time, the question of him carrying on as European captain was raised in the British media, especially by some of the more downmarket tabloid newspapers, which had printed the story of his alleged relationship with a much younger woman. However, in a matter of months, Jacklin had married a Norwegian divorcee, Astrid Kendall, who bravely took over the task of supporting him on and off the course.

On the merit side for the Europeans, Tony Jacklin was now able to include Bernhard Langer in his team. Having suffered from the dreaded putting 'yips' twice in his career, the German had developed a new technique that finally enabled him to benefit from his excellent long game. Finishing just outside the nine automatic places, Langer was one of three 'captain's picks', along with Irishman Christy O'Connor, Jr. and Howard Clark. Both past Ryder Cup performers, they joined a strong team that also included the three Spaniards Severiano Ballesteros, José-Maria Cañizares and José-Marie Olazábal, plus British golf's best in Nick Faldo, Sam Torrance, Mark James, Ian Woosnam and Gordon Brand, Jr.

The United States, in contrast, were talented but inexperienced. Captained by American 'hard-man' Ray Floyd, the team included five debutantes in Paul Azinger, Chip Beck, Fred Couples, Mark McCumber and Ken Green. For the first time in Ryder Cup history, the American PGA had given the captain two selections of his own, which would hopefully strengthen the side. Looking for experience, Floyd went with Lanny Wadkins and five-time British Open Champion Tom Watson. While Jackson's two choices would lead to some criticism in parts of the American press, the in-form Watson had finished well in both the Open at Royal Troon and the United States PGA. Wadkins, however, had missed six cuts in the previous eight tournaments and was struggling to find his long game.

Discarding the low-key approach of the previous two US captains, Lee Trevino and Jack Nicklaus, Raymond Floyd seemed determined to make his point early on. At the pre-match Gala Ball held at the Birmingham Metropole Hotel, he introduced his team as 'the twelve greatest players in the world', in a poor attempt to imitate the words of Ben Hogan some years before. The boast fell flat – especially as Nick Faldo, 1989 US Masters winner, was sitting only a few places away. If it was an attempt at gaining the psychological advantage over the Europeans, it was to be soundly bettered before the end of the night. As the cabaret finished, an impromptu rendition of *Land of Hope and Glory*, struck up by the Band of the Irish Guards, had many of the guests on their feet and the American players and officials hurrying for the door.

Leaden clouds and a heavy mist greeted the opening round of foursomes. Unwittingly breaking with Ryder Cup tradition, Ian Woosnam teed-off first for the Europeans in partnership with Nick Faldo against Tom Kite and Curtis Strange. There had been some speculation that as holders, the home side should play first, and Kite had stepped back to allow the Welshman to play. As the four players set off down the first fairway, it was decided, after some discussion, to stick with tradition and allow the away team the honour on the opening hole. Newly crowned United States PGA Champion Payne Stewart duly teed-off in the next match and the matter was resolved.

In a repeat of the 1985 Ryder Cup, the Americans surprised everyone by taking a 3–1 lead in the morning foursomes. A halved match for Faldo and Woosnam was followed by defeat for Clark and James against Stewart and Wadkins in the next. In the third, Ballesteros and Olazábal looked like recording Europe's first win of the day, being 3-up after ten holes against Beck and Watson. Subsequently, in the space of four holes, two birdie putts by Watson and a poor drive by Ballesteros on the thirteenth brought the match back to all square. Despite regaining the lead two holes later, the Spanish pair lost it at the next and the match finished level.

In the final foursome, the European pairing of Langer and Rafferty went out in 41 and found themselves 3-down to Calcavecchia and Green. After halving

Above: Europe's mercurial Spaniard Seve Ballesteros tries another impossible recovery shot down the left side of the eleventh as the crowd looks on in amazement.

the par-5 fifteenth in seven, they were never quite able to get back into the match, eventually losing by 2 and 1. Without a single win in the morning, the result was a terrible blow to European hopes and there were press calls for wholesale changes in the afternoon fourballs.

Resisting change, Jacklin, in typically independent style, changed only one of the morning pairs, replacing the out-of-form Langer and Rafferty with Torrance and Brand, Jr. As at Muirfield Village two years earlier, it was to prove an inspired piece of captaincy with exactly the same result.

The Europeans showed much greater resolve in the afternoon and achieved a remarkable 4–0 clean sweep. In the opening game, Torrance and Brand, Jr. got their side off to a flying start by defeating Strange and Azinger by the narrow margin of 1 hole. There quickly followed victories for Clark and James, who won 3 and 2 against Couples and Wadkins, Faldo and Woosnam, 1-hole against Calcavecchia and McCumber, and lastly for Ballesteros and Olazábal, 6 and 5 against Watson and O'Meara. With the United States team failing to get ahead in any match, it was a remarkable display by the 'home' side, who went into the second day with a 5–3 lead.

Below: Ireland's Ronan Rafferty raises his arm in triumph as he beats Mark Calcavecchia of the USA by one hole at the eighteenth. Two of the game's most determined competitors, they had already met twice in the earlier foursomes matches.

For the United States team, the second day saw a far more even contest. Sharing the morning foursomes 2–2, there were welcome wins for Beck and Azinger over Brand, Jr. and Torrance, and Green and Calcavecchia over O'Connor and Rafferty. For the Europeans, Jacklin persisted with his two top pairings of Woosnam and Faldo and Ballesteros and Olazábal. Still unbeaten, Woosnam and Faldo brushed away the challenge of Stewart and Wadkins by 3 and 2 in the opening match, while in game four the Spaniards fought out a close match with Kite and Strange. With Europe 3-up after eleven holes, the match looked a certain point, until mistakes at the next two holes brought the Americans back into the match. Struggling to hold onto a slim advantage, Olazábal played two fine green-side bunker shots on seventeen and eighteen, eventually winning by 1-up.

In the opening game of the fourballs, Azinger and Beck played wonderfully to hold a 1-up lead on Woosnam and Faldo. With a better-ball score of 30, further birdies on the par-4 tenth and par-3 eleventh helped build up a lead, which resulted in a victory on the seventeenth by 2 and 1. In what amounted to a minor crisis for Tony Jacklin and his team, Kite and

McCumber inflicted the second consecutive defeat on the European side by beating Cañizares and Langer by 2 and 1. However, Jacklin could take some comfort in the fact that the Americans were jointly 7-under par at the time of winning.

Like Kite and McCumber, Ballesteros and Olazábal were also 7-under par for their 2 and 1 win over Calcavecchia and Green. Bringing in the point that Jacklin so desperately needed, the fourth match took on added significance. Leading 2–1 in the fourballs, the United States relied on the strong pairing of Payne Stewart and Curtis Strange to beat Howard Clark and Mark James and level the overall match score at eight-all. Ahead 1-up with four holes left to play, birdies on the sixteenth and seventeenth by Clark turned the match in favour of Europe. Playing his approach to the eighteenth green, James then hit a superb three-iron from the edge of the fairway bunker to ensure his par and a surprise 1-up win.

Moving into the final day singles with a two-point advantage, the prospect of another famous European victory brought huge crowds flooding into The Belfry. Correctly surmising that Ray Floyd would put his strongest players out last, Jacklin spread his top players throughout the playing order. While keeping Faldo and Woosnam in reserve until matches eleven and twelve, he sent out Ballesteros, Langer and Olazábal in the opening three games in the hope that they would build up a rapid points lead over the Americans. For once, his strategy failed.

Teeing off at 11.30 a.m., Seve Ballesteros took an early 2-up lead against the reigning United States PGA Champion, Paul Azinger. Mistakes by the Spanish maestro, followed by some solid play by the American, saw Azinger take and hold a slender 1-up lead going onto the eighteenth tee. One of the best-known holes in British golf, the testing dogleg had proved particularly generous to the Europeans in the past and it looked so again as Azinger drove into the water off the tee. Forced to take a penalty drop, his opponent had cleared the water hazard, but his drive had run into the shallow fairway bunker to the right of the fairway. Concerned with making the green in two, Ballesteros failed to see the remarkable third shot Azinger played from the rough behind the lake. Fully 250 yards to the green, he smashed a fairway wood into a green-side bunker and now had a good chance of making a

Above: The USA's Curtis Strange shadows his eyes from the sun as he helps teammate Tom Kite line up a putt. A strong pairing, Strange and Kite forced a creditable half with Nick Faldo and Ian Woosnam in the opening match of the 1989 Ryder Cup.

match-winning bogey. Shaken at the result, Seve smothered his second into the lake at the front of the green. Then, despite holing a long downhill putt for a bogey, Paul Azinger splashed out to a few feet and holed the putt for a 1-hole win.

The defeat of Ballesteros was followed by yet another for Bernhard Langer – his third in a row.

Above: Ireland's Christy O'Connor and Ronan Rafferty congratulate each other on winning their respective singles matches for Europe by one hole.

Beaten by Chip Beck, José-Maria Olazábal helped restore the balance by beating Payne Stewart after the American had driven into the water on the last. Now holding just a one-point lead over the Americans, Tony Jacklin was forced to rely on his middle order players to restore the advantage. Starting with Ronan Rafferty's 1-hole win against the recently crowned British Open Champion Mark Calcavecchia, the points he needed to retain the Ryder Cup came flooding in (the Irish player's victory on the final hole coming after Calcavecchia had twice found the water).

Running around the course with his deputy, Bernard Gallacher, Jacklin looked on nervously as Europe recorded four wins in five matches – the only defeat coming in Tom Kite's 8 and 7 win against Howard Clark. Needing only fourteen points to retain the trophy, Christy O'Connor came to the eighteenth all-square with Fred Couples. A halved match looked a real possibility as both professionals found the fairway off the tee. With the hole surrounded by spectators waving flags and cheering for their respective teams, O'Connor had just over 200 yards to the flag with Couples about 50 yards nearer. In a shot that has since gone down in Ryder Cup folklore, the Irish veteran hit a perfect two-iron to around four feet. Obviously shaken, Couples missed the green with his nine-iron approach and failed to make his par. Gesturing to O'Connor to pick up his marker, the European hero was instantly surrounded by friends and teammates in a tearful celebration on the eighteenth green.

Following up behind, it was left to another stalwart of the European Tour to score the point that would retain the Ryder Cup for his side. Playing against Ken Green, José-Maria Cañizares had come to the final green all-square after his opponent had scored five consecutive threes from the turn. With the flag on the middle-tier of three, both players had huge putts for birdie – Green from below the hole and Cañizares from above. Playing first, the Spaniard left his approach above the hole a few feet short. Green followed his effort by hitting a poor approach putt and missing the return. With Jacklin watching from just off the green, and knowing his putt would retain the Ryder Cup, Cañizares calmly rolled the ball into the hole for his par.

The celebrations that followed were somewhat diminished by the failure of either Gordon Brand, Jr., Sam Torrance, Nick Faldo or Ian Woosnam in the remaining four matches to find the single half-point that would have brought overall victory. Faldo had squared his match against Lanny Wadkins on the seventeenth, but had uncharacteristically driven into the water on the final hole to give his American opponent a valuable 1-hole win. Playing in the final match, Ian Woosnam had suffered a similar indignity at the hands of Curtis Strange. Leading 1-up with four to play, the two-time American Open Champion birdied three consecutive holes to lead Woosnam going onto the eighteenth tee. After a drive and glorious two-iron to the last green, Strange left the tigerish Welshman needing a birdie to tie. Sadly, in what proved an anti-climactic finish, Woosnam failed to threaten the flag with an eight-iron approach and the hole was halved in par. The match tied at 14–14; it had been one of the most memorable finishes in Ryder Cup history.

Ray Floyd congratulated his team on their determined fight back and Tony Jacklin predictably announced his retirement from the post of European captain, stating that, 'You have got to know when to quit and this is that moment. It's been an honour and a privilege, but the players now need someone who is closer to their own age.'

Reflecting on three tension-filled Ryder Cup matches, there is no doubt Jacklin meant what he said. He recommended his trusty lieutenant Bernard Gallacher for the post and, within a few weeks of his leaving, the Scot was confirmed as the new European captain.

Quite how difficult a task it would be to follow in Jacklin's footsteps would come as a shock to Gallacher.

Below: This was one of the strongest European sides ever to be assembled for the Ryder Cup matches, boasting among its ranks both past and future major winners. Seve Ballesteros, Bernhard Langer, Nick Faldo, José-Maria Olazabal and Ian Woosnam are all smiles as they join captain Tony Jacklin and the rest of their teammates with the Ryder Cup trophy.

13

The War on the Shore

1991

THE OCEAN COURSE, KIAWAH ISLAND, SOUTH CAROLINA, USA

13–15 SEPTEMBER

The Ryder Cup at Kiawah Island in South Carolina was always going to be a tough match, but few realized just how bloody it would ultimately prove. Played in the aftermath of 'Operation Desert Storm', the 1991 match will long be remembered as the 'War on the Shore' for its unprecedented intensity and battle zone mentality. Held on the newly constructed Ocean Course, the Ryder Cup match began with accusations of cheating, and temperatures remained at boiling point throughout the week. In the end, the result swung on a missed 6-foot putt on the final green of the final match, giving the United States a narrow one-point victory. One local sportswriter summed up the feelings of the partisan American crowd when he wrote: 'We're hot. We're on a roll. Check it out. We thumped Iraq. We whipped Communism. And now, at last, we put Europe in its place.'

The 1991 Ryder Cup began badly for the United States, and especially so for Steve Pate. Shortly after the Grand Opening Gala, he was involved in a car crash that left him with bruised ribs and a damaged hip. This was a major blow to United States captain Dave Stockton: Pate had been in the form of his life and, apart from a brief appearance in the second day fourballs, would miss out almost entirely on his first appearance in the Ryder Cup. Another surprise was the omission of the newly crowned PGA Champion, John Daly. Relying on a wildcard pick from Stockton, the veteran campaigner had gone for Chip Beck and the experienced Ray Floyd instead. On hearing the news, Daly, nicknamed 'Wild Thing', immediately faxed a note through the American team headquarters saying, 'Good luck. Now go kick butt!' It was an attitude the team would adopt for much of the week.

As for European team captain Bernard Gallacher, his problem was the lack of Ryder Cup experience in his side. While he could still boast players with the calibre of Ballesteros, Faldo, Langer, Woosnam and Olazábal, he arrived in South Carolina with five rookies in his line-up – David Gilford, Colin Montgomerie, David Feherty, Paul Broadhurst and Steven Richardson. As the US team had just three newcomers – Wayne Levi, Corey Pavin and Steve Pate – no one was predicting an 'away' win at Kiawah Island that year.

Another problem that faced the Europeans was the overtly nationalistic fervour surrounding the build-up to the contest. Still basking in the success of Operation Desert Storm in Iraq, the American people were on a real high and this was reflected in their attitude to the European team. A good example of this attitude came when a local radio presenter from Charleston started a 'Wake up the Enemy' campaign on the eve of the match, encouraging his moronic listeners to telephone the hotel where the European team was staying. Gallacher responded to one 'obscene' call to Nick

Above: The unmistakable profiles of Europe's Seve Ballesteros and José-Maria Olazábal as they shake hands against a shimmering orange sunset. They had just halved their day two afternoon fourball against Payne Stewart and Fred Couples.

Faldo's wife, Gill, by saying, 'If we get any more, I'm going to phone the FBI about it!'

Not that the American captain helped the situation. After boasting about how much money his team had won collectively, Stockton invited the European players to enjoy a film entitled the *History of the Ryder Cup*. Halfway through, it became obvious that the film should have been subtitled *How We Kicked the Foreigners' Butts at Golf* as it showed little but US victories, US shots and US celebrations. Nick Faldo, among others, was ready to walk out. 'It was unbelievable', he said afterwards. 'You would think players like Seve Ballesteros were there just to make up the numbers.'

By the time the opening foursome matches began on Friday, there was little love lost between the two teams. In the third match of four, Hale Irwin and Lanny

Above: José-Maria Olazábal looks on as his opponent Chip Beck sizes up a putt from the fringe. Olazábal was partnered with Seve Ballesteros and the two Spaniards beat Beck and his partner Paul Azinger twice on the opening day.

Wadkins beat the experimental partnership of Colin Montgomerie and rookie David Gilford by 4 and 2. Ray Floyd and Fred Couples beat Bernhard Langer and Mark James 2 and 1 in game two. Then, in the final match of the morning, Faldo and Woosnam lost to Payne Stewart and Mark Calcavecchia by the narrow margin of 1-up. Already a black day for Europe, it could easily have been 4–0 instead of 3–1. The strong American pairing of Paul Azinger and Chip Beck had

been 3-up after nine holes against Ballesteros and Olazábal, only to lose 2 and 1. Even then the match was not without incident or controversy.

Having demanded a questionable free-drop on the second, Seve Ballesteros accused Paul Azinger of cheating on the tenth. Complaining to the match referee that the Americans had played the wrong ball since the seventh, the Spaniard demanded that action be taken. (Having told each other what make and number of ball they were playing on the first tee, any changes had to be cleared with their opponents, which in Ballesteros's opinion had not been done.) Three down at this point, a 'livid' Azinger thought it was nothing but gamesmanship, but Seve persisted, even after the ruling went in the Americans' favour. If his intention was to put Azinger and Beck off their game, it obviously worked. Clawing their way back into the game, they finally won on the par-3 seventeenth after Seve rolled in a twisting putt for a birdie. Barely able to shake hands, Seve said afterwards that, 'The American team has eleven nice guys and Paul Azinger.'

Effectively setting the tone for the week, it came as no surprise when European captain Bernard Gallacher announced that he would use the Ballesteros/Olazábal pairing in all four matches leading up to the singles. Already trailing by two points, there was better news in the afternoon as the visitors hit back in the fourballs to win by 2½–1½. Once again, it was the Spaniards who led the way, with yet another 2 and 1 victory over Azinger and Beck, which was followed by a magnificent 5 and 4 win for Steven Richardson and Mark James over Corey Pavin and Calcavecchia, and a halved game between David Feherty and Sam Torrance against Lanny Wadkins and Mark O'Meara. The biggest disappointment was the form of Nick Faldo. He was unable to resurrect his previously successful partnership with Ian Woosnam and the English pair were fortunate not to lose by more than the 5 and 3 drubbing they received from Fred Couples and Raymond Floyd. Two defeats in a day were more than enough for Gallacher and he resolved to split them up the following day.

With the United States ahead by one point, Faldo was surprised to find himself paired with Ryder Cup debutante David Gilford, a shy, unassuming character. The result was an absolute disaster as barely a word passed between the two throughout the entire match. After the pair were humiliated 7 and 6 by Azinger and

O'Meara, the British press roundly condemned Faldo for his lack of encouragement and support to the already nervous rookie. Typically, the four-time major winner brushed off any criticism by stating that he should not have been paired with Gilford in the first place! Writing for a Sunday newspaper, respected golf journalist Lauren St John observed, 'Faldo's surliness and Gilford's painful shyness ensured a pairing with less conversation than Trappist monks.'

It was a bad day all round for the Europeans as the United States once again dominated the foursomes. In the first match, Torrance and Feherty lost 4 and 2 to Wadkins and Irwin, while Richardson and James lost 1-up to the in-form Stewart and Calcavecchia. As Bernard Gallacher would later remark, Ballesteros and Olazábal 'kept Europe in the match' with another hard-earned victory, this time over Couples and Floyd by 3 and 2. It was now vital that Europe gain the upper hand in the afternoon fourballs if they were to have any chance of retaining the Ryder Cup. With that in mind, captain Gallacher decided to gamble on two new pairings in Langer and Montgomerie and Woosnam and Broadhurst. Considered one of the lesser lights of the PGA European Tour, Broadhurst had forced his way into the reckoning with some spectacular play in practice. Like Gilford, Richardson and Feherty, it was his first Ryder Cup, but unlike his fellow rookies, the pencil-thin Midlander transferred some of his sparkling form to the match. Chipping and putting brilliantly throughout, he combined well with the experienced Woosnam to beat Azinger and Irwin by 2 and 1. More importantly, his win signalled a complete turnaround in fortunes for his team.

In the second match, the Langer/Montgomerie partnership proved another inspired choice by Gallacher as they concluded a narrow 2 and 1 win over Corey Pavin and Steve Pate. Reducing the gap to just one point, Mark James and Steve Richardson then levelled the match at 7–7 after beating Wayne Levi and Lanny Wadkins 3 and 1. Looking forward to taking an unlikely one-point lead going into the singles, all eyes turned towards the last match out on the course, featuring Seve Ballesteros and José-Maria Olazábal against Payne Stewart and Fred Couples. Amazingly, the hitherto invincible Spaniards had been struggling to keep up with some exceptional play by the Americans, especially Couples. Battling back from 2-down with six

Above: The USA's controversial Corey Pavin celebrates victory at the sixteenth green in his singles match against Steve Richardson. It was a key match, in which the out-of-form American transformed his game to beat the rookie English professional.

to play, Olazábal was left with a six-foot putt on the eighteenth just for a half. Thankfully for his teammates standing around the green in the gathering gloom, he made the putt and Europe could breathe again.

With the match score level going into the final day, the tension could be cut with a knife. Steve Pate's injury forced Gallacher to drop one of his own players and concede a half point to both sides. This meant that the player nominated by Gallacher at the beginning of the

Above: Fred Couples and Ray Floyd – a formidable US partnership – ponder the line of a putt during the day one afternoon fourballs.

week had to sit out the singles. The name that had been secretly placed in a sealed envelope was that of David Gilford, and, as Gallacher later admitted, 'Telling David he wasn't playing was one of the toughest things I have ever had to do in my career.'

Away from the heartbreak of team selection, the singles began brightly for Europe. In the opening match, Faldo got off to a fast start and won the first three holes against Ray Floyd. Playing in the match behind, David Feherty was also getting the better of Payne Stewart, winning the first two holes while Ballesteros was up on Wayne Levi. Then the United States hit back with Mark Calcavecchia. Standing 5-up after nine holes on Colin Montgomerie, it looked a certain point for the home team, as did Couples against Sam Torrance. For a time it was impossible to know who was going to win as the matches went first Europe's way, then America's, then Europe's once more, and finally back to the United States.

Ray Floyd fought back but eventually lost by 2-down to Faldo, while Stewart was unable to catch Feherty and lost 2 and 1. Meanwhile, Mark Calcavecchia, overcome by nerves, lost it completely and was fortunate to halve with Colin Montgomerie in the end. Woosnam, who looked in such good form the previous afternoon, lost to Chip Beck; Pavin also narrowly beat Richardson 2 and 1. With the match all square, Ballesteros and Broadhurst then made it 'Advantage Europe' by beating Levi and O'Meara respectively.

As expected, the Americans hit back with wins for Fred Couples over Sam Torrance, Lanny Wadkins over Mark James and Azinger over Olazábal. Suddenly, the Americans were one up with only one game left out on the course. As Dave Stockton and his team stood behind the eighteenth green, the simplest mathematics now told them that a half between Bernhard Langer and Hale Irwin would be enough to win the Ryder Cup for the United States. For Gallacher and Europe, only a win would be good enough.

Proceeding almost unnoticed, as the crowds concentrated on the glamour clashes between Nick Faldo and Ray Floyd, and Olazábal and Azinger, Irwin had the upper hand early on. However, as the match reached its climax, the German seemed to gain the advantage. After fourteen holes played, the American was 2-up and seemingly in control. Then Langer won the fifteenth, holed a six-footer for a half at the next, and the world held its breath as Irwin three-putted the penultimate hole from 30 feet to lose another. He was visibly shaken and the parallel between him and Calcavecchia's collapse earlier in the day was hard to dismiss.

The apprehension as both players teed off at the last was tangible. Brilliant under pressure, Langer played a great tee shot down the middle while Irwin pulled his left into the crowd. Then, almost inexplicably, the ball appeared in prime position in the fairway. A good bounce? A helping hand from the partisan American gallery? Whatever the truth, Langer was too interested in his own ball to care.

Playing first, Irwin missed the green, chipped horrendously and was never going to do better than a bogey-5. In contrast, the ice-cool Langer was on in regulation about 30 feet away and looked to have two putts to win the game, the match and the Ryder Cup. Then it all went wrong. Langer's first putt, attacking the hole, rolled six feet past. Meanwhile, Irwin bravely two-putted for bogey and the world once again held its breath. Langer was left with a mere six feet between him and victory, while the American team clustered behind the hole, willing the German to miss. Meanwhile, Payne Stewart had his arm around the shoulders of Calcavecchia, who was still in tears. Standing 4-up with four to play on Montgomerie, it was his halved point that had brought the Ryder Cup to this conclusion and the strain on his face was visible.

Then came the fateful moment. Lining up the putt with his oh-so-ugly putting method, Langer missed, and the American team erupted. The German blamed a spike mark for deflecting the ball off its path: 'I saw two spike marks on my line', he said. 'I talked to my caddie [Peter Coleman]. He said. "Hit it left-centre and firm to avoid the spike marks." That is what I tried to do. It did not go in.' Aware just how important the putt

was, Langer later admitted, 'It's going to stick with me for a lifetime, that putt. I will never forget it.'

Someone else who would never forget it was Hale Irwin, commenting, 'There is no way I would ever wish what happened on the last hole to anyone.' Seve agreed: 'Nobody could have holed that putt, not Nicklaus in his prime, not me. The pressure was just unbelievable.' Reflecting back on a dramatic 14½–13½ loss to the US, he consoled the tearful Langer, saying, 'Don't worry, we will win it back next time at The Belfry.'

The problem was that the 1993 match was exactly two years away and that was a long time to wait for every European player, especially Seve Ballesteros.

Below: A devastated Bernhard Langer reacts to missing his putt – and losing Europe the Ryder Cup – on the final green. Michael Bollanack later described it as the 'greatest pressure putt in golf'.

14

Building Bridges

1993

THE BELFRY, SUTTON COLDFIELD, WEST MIDLANDS, ENGLAND

26–28 SEPTEMBER

After the controversial 'War on the Shore' at Kiawah Island in 1991, it was hoped that good sense would prevail for the forthcoming match at The Belfry. Golf had worked extremely hard to maintain a long-standing reputation of fairness and good sportsmanship and now was in danger of going the same way as many other sports. Everyone agreed that something had gone badly wrong. As one British journalist said, 'American professionals sporting army fatigues, unruly crowds influencing the play and accusations of gamesmanship have no place in the Ryder Cup. What next? Arm wrestling to decide who has the honour on each tee.'

With feuds reported between individual players, measures had to be taken to stem the tide of criticism. Incidents like those seen in North Carolina during the final stages of the crucial Langer/Irwin singles, where the American's ball was thrown back into the fairway,

could not be tolerated. If they were, the future of the Ryder Cup itself would be thrown into doubt. With the support of top players like Nick Faldo and Tom Watson, the British and American PGAs thrashed out a series of proposals aimed at future matches. Crowd numbers would be strictly limited and restrictions would be placed on the number of people walking inside the ropes, which had been a constant source of irritation to the galleries that attended the match at The Belfry four years earlier. As for the professionals themselves, guidelines were set on the sort of inflammatory press statements that had so raised the temperature at Kiawah. Two years on, approaching The Belfry match,

Right: A winning pairing was created for Europe by good friends Peter Baker and Ian Woosnam, here on the tenth green on day two playing against the USA's Fred Couples and Paul Azinger.

it was hoped that such controversy was a thing of the past. Unfortunately for the United States team, this was not to be the case.

In keeping with the tradition of appointing on a one-off basis, Tom Watson was given the job of captaining the American side in 1993. After having made his Ryder Cup debut at Royal Lytham in 1977 – coincidentally the last match played between the United States and a Great Britain and Ireland team – the five-time Open Champion had made no secret of his desire for the job. Shortly after being appointed, he referred back to the opening ceremony almost two decades earlier:

> Dow Finsterwald was our captain and he talked about what it meant to be part of the Ryder Cup, about all the great players who had taken part and how honoured he was to follow in the footsteps of all the captains who had come before him. I just stood there with shivers running down my back thinking, I want to do that someday.

After Kiawah Island, Tom Watson was considered the perfect choice. A highly popular figure with British golf fans since his glory days in the late 1970s and early 1980s, he had expressed a desire to captain an American Ryder Cup team in Britain, saying how 'winning at home just wasn't quite the same challenge'. This challenge of winning 'away from home' proved a strong motivation for the Kansas-born professional, who seemed to thrive on this pressure throughout his whole career. An eight-time Major winner, Watson had seemingly lost direction in recent years. The birth of his son Michael in 1982 had effectively signalled a downturn in his desire for major titles and by 1991 he had ceased to be a dominant force in golf. As such, the Ryder Cup captaincy could not have come at a more propitious time and, like past British captain Tony Jacklin, he grabbed the opportunity with both hands.

Like millions of armchair golfers in the United States, Watson had viewed the one-point victory at Kiawah with a mixture of joy and dismay. Like Ben Crenshaw, he was a great traditionalist, who valued the spirit of friendship and camaraderie that had been fostered in previous Ryder Cup encounters. As part of his intense preparation, he contacted Nick Faldo and discussed at length the problems that had arisen between the two sides. Faldo himself cited an incident at the gala dinner in 1989 when Raymond Floyd had echoed the words of Ben Hogan and introduced his team as 'the twelve best golfers in the world'. Somewhat slighted, the European team had called upon Tony Jacklin to introduce Seve Ballesteros – probably the best player in the world at the time – as 'the thirteenth best player in the world'. Despite the obvious temptation, it was a request he diplomatically refused.

The controversy did not end there. At a pre-match dinner arranged for players and guests in 1991 , part of the entertainment had included a forty-minute film on the history of the Ryder Cup. As the United States contingent whooped and hollered at each holed putt, the Europeans looked on in stony silence as the film barely mentioned anything other than American victories. Knowing the film was made at the behest of the United States PGA, it was taken as an insult and consequently set the tone for the entire week. Listening to Faldo, Watson agreed the importance of bringing an element of good feeling back into the event. Shortly before leaving for Britain, he resolved to put matters right by giving his thoughts on the forthcoming match:

> This isn't war, this is golf. We're going over there and try like hell to kick their butts. And they're going to try like hell to kick ours. That's as it should be. But when it's over, we should be able to go off together, lift a glass and toast one another. That's what the Ryder Cup is all about.

After playing most of his golf in the United States throughout 1993, Faldo himself looked for some time as though he would require a captain's pick to make the European side for The Belfry. Fortunately for Bernard Gallacher, in his second Ryder Cup as captain, the past Open and Masters Champion played well enough in the majors and on his few trips back to Europe to qualify on merit. This effectively left the Scot with the three selections that his predecessor, Tony Jacklin, had negotiated back in 1985. The first two were simple enough – Seve Ballesteros and José-Maria Olazábal – both of whom, like Faldo, were playing much of their golf on the United States tour. Gallacher's third choice – the young Swedish professional, Joakim Haeggman – came as more of a surprise.

The first Swede to play in the Ryder Cup, Haeggman was included over more experienced players such as Eamonn Darcy and José-Maria Cañizares and his selection was openly questioned in the golfing press.

Gallacher, to his credit, stood firm, insisting that the twenty-six-year-old was just the first of many Scandinavians that would be challenging for future Ryder Cup places. His inclusion, Gallacher reasoned, would inspire them to work even harder, which in the long term could only benefit European golf. (Indeed, the golfing world has since seen the emergence of many top-class Swedish players, including Per-Ulrik Johannson, Jesper Parnevik and Anders Forsbrand.)

Having refused to continue the job as captain after Europe's defeat at Kiawah, Bernard Gallacher was persuaded by players and PGA officials to try again. Yet he must have recognized the size of the task against what looked to be a strong American side. After the success of the past decade, the European team had a distinctly weak look about it. Even with stars like Faldo, Ballesteros, Olazábal, Langer and Woosnam in his team, the feeling was that many had reached their playing peaks under Jacklin. And, while ably supported by Ryder Cup veterans Mark James, Sam Torrance and Colin Montgomerie, the side also included three untested rookies in Peter Baker, Barry Lane and the Italian Costantino Rocca.

While Bernard Gallacher was defending his team, Tom Watson's own preparation for the post of captain was exhaustive. Having witnessed the crushing disappointment of his great friend and rival Jack Nicklaus in captaining a losing side at Muirfield Village in 1987, he resolved to leave nothing to chance. Knowing that a tie would be enough to retain the trophy for the United States, he decided to immerse himself in the psychology of the event – surely an easy enough task for a psychology major from Stamford University. With this in mind, he sought out head basketball coach, Roy Williams, at nearby Kansas University. Talking from first-hand experience about the last Ryder Cup at The Belfry in 1989, Watson expressed his deep concern about the failure of his teammates to respond to the pressure on the final day.

From a winning position, player after player had been overhauled down the stretch in the singles, resulting in a halved match overall – a score that meant that Europe retained the trophy. Watson remembered the constant roars that had gone up around the course that day in celebration of each European win and how much this had affected his American teammates. Recognizing his concerns, Williams responded with

Above: Caddy Bruce Edwards helps his man, Lanny Wadkins, from a bunker during his fourball match with Corey Pavin against Bernhard Langer and Barry Lane on the afternoon of day two.

some sage advice – advice that would prove invaluable to Watson in the heat of battle. 'We always tell our players that there's nothing better than quieting the crowd', Williams said. 'I tell them to listen for the silence, because you never hear anything sweeter, and to be sure to look up at the end and watch the stands empty when we're ahead.'

Tom Watson's next task was to pick a team. With ten of the twelve coming straight off the American money list, he was left with two captain's picks. While the media speculated feverishly on the possibility of having the big-hitting John Daly in the side, Watson himself had other ideas. He wanted two players who would not buckle under the intense pressure of a Ryder Cup. Hardened tour professionals who, unlike Daly, would not give up at the first sign of difficulty. Professionals like Ray Floyd and Lanny Wadkins.

Both good friends and experienced Ryder Cup campaigners, Floyd and Wadkins would be used by Watson to bolster up a United States side that included four untested rookies – Lee Janzen, Davis Love III, Jim Gallagher, Jr. and John Cook. With the United States PGA tournament in August the last qualifying event, they would be joined on the trip to Britain by Payne Stewart, Paul Azinger, Chip Beck, Corey Pavin, Tom Kite and Fred Couples. All had experienced Ryder Cup disappointment at The Belfry four years earlier and had

worked hard during the qualification period for the chance of revenge.

Despite the fact that the team had eight past and future major winners in its number, press and public reaction to the side was surprisingly lukewarm. Perhaps too many of them had cracked under pressure in the past. Players like Couples, Love III, Stewart, Cook and even Paul Azinger had all lost winning positions in major tournaments before, and question marks had arisen about their ability to perform under extreme pressure. With only days left before they were due to leave, Watson must have welcomed the chance to escape, yet even before they stepped foot on Concorde, the biggest storm of controversy was yet to hit. It was described in the tabloid press as 'Clintongate'.

Scheduled to fly out of Dulles Airport in Washington D.C., the United States team was invited at short notice to the White House to meet President Bill Clinton. A keen golfer himself, newly elected Clinton had expressed a desire to meet the players and wish them well for the coming match. Unfortunately, it soon became obvious that not all the players wanted to meet him. Reasons varied from differing political beliefs to outright hostility to his proposal to raise taxes on the nation's highest dollar earners (including top professional golfers). Whatever the truth, the story quickly became headline news on both sides of the Atlantic.

Not surprisingly, criticism rained down on the heads of the Ryder Cup players. Whatever their opinions, the fact remained that a representative team from the United States of America had refused an invitation from their president. To a basically patriotic nation this was unforgivable. Worse still, here was a group of very rich young men complaining about the high taxes they would have to pay under his administration and refusing point blank to meet with him. As the debate widened, the damage to the image of golf was growing.

Looking to put an end to the matter, captain Tom Watson stepped in and quickly made the decision to go. After all, he commented, 'It doesn't matter who the president is, if you're invited to the White House you go.' Then, after describing Bill Clinton as the 'country's

Left: The irrepressible Corey Pavin celebrates a vital win in partnership with Jim Gallagher, Jr. against the European pairing of Mark James and Constantino Rocca. A gritty Ryder Cup competitor, Pavin was instrumental in the narrow USA victory at the Belfry.

First Golfer', Watson thought long and hard about what he would say – the comments made by some of his players were both critical and, in some cases, highly personal. Strolling on the White House lawn just as the president arrived back from his morning jog, surrounded by secret servicemen, Watson shook his hand and informally introduced his team.

Tactfully ignoring Paul Azinger's comment 'Okay. I've seen enough', Watson gave a carefully rehearsed speech about the similarities between the golf grip and politics, hoping to put Bill Clinton at ease. 'You know, Mr President', he said, 'If you hold the club too far to the right, you're going to get in trouble on the left. If you hold it too far to the left, you're going to have trouble on the right. But if you hold it in the middle...'

'You'll get it just right', Clinton answered, finishing off the Watson story with a smile. It was a moment of genuine humour that broke the ice and settled the nerves of those players unsure as to the reception they would receive from the most powerful man in the world. With politics forgotten, the time passed quickly. Even Paul Azinger, who had cancelled his subscription to his hometown newspaper because it had endorsed Clinton in the election, seemed genuinely at ease discussing golf. Indeed, even the 'Bill and Hillary' masks he had worn to the player's dinner the night before at the Sheraton-Carlton Hotel were now a thing of the past. In common with the rest of his teammates, the most important thing on his mind now was how to retain the Ryder Cup.

Greeted by heavy, rain-leaden clouds at Birmingham airport on the Monday before the competition, the American team – like the Europeans – established their base at the on-course Belfry Hotel. Watson looked at different pairings during the practice days while also keeping a close eye on the form of John Cook and Chip Beck, both of whom had struggled with their game in recent weeks. Knowing the damage the finishing hole at The Belfry had done to the American side four years earlier, he spent hours meticulously measuring the landing area for the tee-shot.

A sharp dog-leg left with water snaking all the way down the left-hand side of the hole, it had proved a formidable test in the previous two Ryder Cups held here. Almost 470 yards long, the carry off the tee was over 200 yards. Not considered a problem to any of the big-hitting American team, even against the wind, the shallow bunker, which swallowed up the straight 'safe' drive, was. With the second shot over water to a lengthy, three-level green, any tee-shot that found the sand just off the right side of the fairway automatically risked losing the hole. With a high draw nominated by Watson as the ideal shot, he gathered his team around him to discuss the hole on numerous occasions during the week. If they were going to lose, thought Watson, it was not going to be because of lack of preparation.

By preparing a timetable for his players with detailed information on practice schedules, eating times, team meetings, laundry details, etc., Watson attempted to leave his players free to concentrate on the matches themselves. Unfortunately, these regulations included a weeklong ban on all autograph signings until the trophy presentation dinner scheduled for the Sunday night. So that his players should not be distracted by such trivialities, Watson gave notice that the ban would be enforced during the important Wednesday night gala held at the nearby Metropole Hotel. Following so quickly on the heels of the 'Clintongate' controversy, it was to prove a bad move on Watson's part.

Traditionally a formal occasion, the gala dinner usually involves dinner for the two teams, lengthy speeches and some light cabaret. With the majority of guests paying £150 each to attend, the players patiently spend the later part of the evening, which rarely ends before midnight, signing autographs and making sociable small talk. It has also been the long-standing tradition that professionals from the two sides sign each other's menus as keepsakes. Consequently, when Sam Torrance was asked to send his menu to the American team room to be signed later in the week, it caused a great deal of resentment. Somewhat foolishly, Tom Watson reasoned that after politely turning down a long line of autograph hunters all evening, he could not agree to the Scotsman's request. Not surprisingly, Torrance was incensed and waved away any attempt by the American captain to explain the situation.

From a relatively small affair, the whole 'autograph' incident splashed onto the front pages of the tabloids the next day. 'Fork Off!' ran one headline, while another called the American captain 'a disgrace!' Everything that Watson had tried to avoid – the controversy and bad feeling of previous Ryder Cup matches – was now dogging his every footstep. He later commented: 'It did shake me up. I know how the tabloids are over here, but

Above: Europe's Colin Montgomerie and Nick Faldo beat the USA's hard nuts Lanny Wadkins and Corey Pavin 3 and 2 at the sixteenth green, which left them with 2½ points from 4.

some of the things that were said by people hurt. It was exactly what I didn't want to happen.'

The following day (Thursday) Watson apologized to anyone – including Sam Torrance – who had been upset by his decision. Hoping it would be the end of the matter, he warmly applauded Bernard Gallacher's response to the question as to whether or not the European team had had their evening ruined by the incident. 'Well', said the smiling Scot, 'Seve did struggle a bit with his *fromage*.'

No doubt under orders from his captain, Sam Torrance sensibly told the awaiting press that he would let his golf do the talking. Attending the flag-raising

ceremony later that day, Watson introduced his team, before ending with the comment, 'Gentlemen, I cannot tell you how proud I am to be your captain.' Perhaps reflecting on a similar ceremony at Royal Lytham some years before, it was obviously a poignant moment for him. Yet, more importantly, controversy was now put behind the American team and the real business of the Ryder Cup could begin.

Looking for a fast start, Bernard Gallacher put out his strongest pairings in the opening day foursomes. With play delayed two hours because of a heavy mist, the Brabazon course, already playing long after a wet summer, was set to play even longer. Keeping faith with the partnerships that had done so well in previous Ryder Cups, he sent out the experienced Torrance and James in match one (against Pavin and Wadkins), Ballesteros and Olazábal (against Kite and Love III), Langer and

Woosnam (against Couples and Floyd), and finally Montgomerie and Faldo (against Azinger and Stewart).

Described by the American press as 'alternate ball', the morning was shared two matches all. For the Europeans, the surprise of the day came with a defeat for the near-invincible Spanish duo of Ballesteros and Olazábal. Having reached the turn 1-down, an out-of-sorts Seve played safe on the short, par-4 tenth with an iron. Hardly able to believe his eyes, Tom Kite took full advantage by drilling a solid three-wood into the heart of the green, leaving an uphill putt for eagle. After Olazábal had wedged into ten feet – still outside the Americans – Ballesteros calmly slotted home the putt and visibly challenged Davis Love III to do the same. Hole it he did, and then followed it with another on the penultimate green to win by 2-up.

Looking to break the deadlock, Tom Watson called up two of his rookies for the afternoon fourballs. In what amounted to major surgery, he brought in Gallagher and Janzen as a pair and dropped Payne Stewart and Ray Floyd, before matching up Azinger with Couples. Pavin and Wadkins played well to win again, but Love III and Kite met a storm of birdies from the revenge-seeking pair of Ballesteros and Olazábal, eventually losing on the fifteenth. Gallagher and Janzen lost a close game on the final hole to Woosnam and the in-form Peter Baker. (A local boy, Baker holed a twenty-five-foot putt on the eighteenth to close out the Americans. It would prove to be the first of many that week.)

As the dark clouds rolled in, play in the final match out between Azinger/ Couples and Faldo/Montgomerie was suspended. A Faldo birdie on seventeen had pulled the match back to level, and after some discussion on the final tee, it was agreed to resume at 8.00 the following morning. Walking up the final fairway in the dark, Azinger said, 'It's gonna be a long night waiting to play one hole.' With the scoreboards showing the match score at 4–3 to the Europeans, nobody would disagree.

The uncertainty surrounding the delayed match made for an unsettled night for the Americans. In addition, seven-months pregnant Robin Love, wife of Davis, was thought to have gone into premature labour. A local doctor determined that the baby had dropped down in the womb but confirmed that the danger was minimal. Davis Love III was ordered to rest and Linda Watson stayed the night with her recovering friend. For the time being, the crisis was over.

Early next morning, the four players were ferried back to the eighteenth tee to conclude their match. It was still overcast and cold, but crowds already lined the fairways hoping that Europe could win the hole and take a two-point advantage into the second day. Poor drives by Monty and Couples effectively left Azinger and Faldo to fight out the hole alone. Renewing a tense rivalry stretching back to the 1987 British Open at Muirfield, Azinger followed Faldo onto the green with a well struck eight-iron from 163 yards. With tension mounting, Faldo left his uphill approach putt from sixty feet over eight-foot short, leaving his opponent a difficult decision. Only twenty feet from the hole and putting for birdie, it must have crossed Azinger's mind that two putts would be enough if Faldo were to miss.

By now his teammates had finished the morning warm-up and were gathered at the back of the green, as were many of the European side. As he looked at the putt from every angle, Tom Watson heard the crackle of a television microphone from next to the grandstand. Barking out the order to turn it down, he resumed his intense gaze on Azinger's putt. As it slid close by the hole, the American snapped his head back in frustration and let out a deep sigh of anguish.

Tapping in for a par, Azinger somehow knew that Faldo would not miss. Sure enough, the experience of countless major tournaments had hardened the Englishman to the pressure and the ball dropped into the cup dead centre. Leaving the green to loud cheers and the congratulations of his teammates, Faldo called out 'What's for breakfast?' before stumbling in a mock feint. Knowing he would be teeing off shortly, Faldo had little time to prepare himself for the morning foursomes, let alone breakfast. Yet, even as the weather gradually improved during the morning, he had struck an apparently significant blow for the Europeans that far outweighed the 4½–3½ score-line.

The rest of the morning proved a major disappointment for the United States team. Spurred on by Nick Faldo's earlier heroics, the Europeans won three of the four matches. Leading 7½–4½, the home side had taken command of the match and Watson needed something extraordinary to happen in the afternoon. Calling up the out-of-form pairing of John Cook and Chip Beck, he threw them in against none other than Nick Faldo and Colin Montgomerie. As Cook was heard to remark on the practice ground after being given the news,

'Nothing like skipping the frying pan and going straight into the fire, huh?'

Going out in the final match, Faldo started where he had left off in the morning by holing a birdie putt on the par-4 first. Significantly, Cook followed him in for a half, which set the tone for the entire match. With very little in it either way, Beck chipped and putted from off the green at twelve, thirteen and fourteen for hole-saving pars. Holding onto a slim advantage, he then did the same from a green-side bunker on the par-5 fifteenth for yet another halve in birdie. Walking the final tee 1-up, he glanced at the scoreboard, which showed the United States up in three matches and down in one. While Woosnam and Baker were demolishing Couples and Azinger – eventually running out 7 and 5 winners – the other two matches showed leads for Pavin/Gallagher against James/Rocca and Stewart/Floyd over Olazábal/Haeggman (Seve Ballesteros having asked to be rested).

More than ten hours after the Azinger/Couples match, Faldo and Montgomerie stepped onto the final tee. Once again, Monty failed to make a contribution, leaving his partner with yet another nerve-jangling eight-foot birdie for a possible win on the hole. Sadly for Faldo, he missed, leaving John Cook two putts from an even shorter distance for a 2-up win. Then, even before Cook could replace his marker, Faldo had stretched out his hand to concede. This unexpected result gave the Americans a 3–1 afternoon win and reduced the overall lead to just two points. Perhaps more importantly, it had restored their confidence. As Azinger later said, 'If I were a betting man, I'd have bet all I had on us right then. John and Chip just turned the whole thing around.'

Going into the final day, trailing by only a single point, the mood of the American camp had turned full circle. Confidence was now soaring and everyone was looking forward to the challenge of the singles – a series of matches in which the United States had traditionally proved stronger. While Couples and Azinger were not exactly on top form, the forgotten men of Thursday, John Cook and Chip Beck, had performed well under pressure and proved themselves worthy of a place in the team. However, returning from the captain's meeting on Saturday evening, Tom Watson had been presented with a dilemma. It seemed that Sam Torrance was likely to withdraw because of an infected toe and, according to the rules, Watson was required to leave out one of his own players.

Walking into the team room, Watson explained the situation. As in 1991, when American Steve Pate sat out the singles after being injured in a car accident en route to the gala dinner, Watson had to put the name inside an envelope. This would then be handed over to the opposing captain should it be required. It was, and, after volunteering his own name, Lanny Wadkins was the player dropped from the singles. Wadkins was scheduled to play Ballesteros – a player he was quite capable of beating – and Watson still had to be convinced that he could do without someone with Wadkins' record in the Ryder Cup – he had won twenty matches out of thirty-three played. There were at least five other players Watson would have sacrificed ahead of his close friend, but Wadkins was persistent and Watson reluctantly accepted. Applauding the gesture, the United States captain later said:

> Lanny made a very difficult situation a lot easier for me. The more he talked, the more I realized it was the right thing to do. I think the other guys understood the sacrifice he was making, because no one wanted to play more than Lanny. It was one of the greatest gestures I've ever seen anyone make.

Apart from the injury to Sam Torrance, the European camp had a far more serious problem with Peter Baker. On the same evening, his eleven month-old daughter had been rushed to Birmingham Hospital with what appeared to be spinal meningitis. Then, dressed in his Ryder Cup uniform and pacing the hospital corridors, Baker received the happy news in the early hours of the morning that his daughter had nothing more than a severe ear infection and was in no danger. Returning to the Belfry Hotel, he was asked by Gallacher if he was fit to play. Baker smiled and told his captain that, after hearing his daughter was fine, he was willing to take on anybody.

As the day of the singles dawned, Bernard Gallacher thanked Davis Love III for the thoughtful gesture of sending a note on behalf of his team concerning the health of Peter Baker's daughter. It had also occurred to the European captain that had Baker been unable to play in the singles, the Americans were quite within the rules to have claimed the match. While it had been discussed, many of the players considered such an action to be unthinkable, and even Ray Floyd had offered to drop out should it be required.

Once again the weather was overcast and threatening rain. Needing a minimum of six points to tie the Ryder Cup at 14–14, Watson sent his team out with one final message: 'If you start to feel down do two things. Think about Lanny and how much he wanted to play and don't stop smiling whether you're 4-up or 4-down.'

In what proved to be a roller-coaster ride of emotions for both teams, this was good advice. Woosnam, leading off for Europe against Couples, lost a 2-up lead with six holes left to give the USA an unexpected half in the opening game. The next game saw another American fight back when Chip Beck clawed back a three-hole deficit to Barry Lane to win on the final green. (Lane had been leading with five holes left when Beck won the fourteenth, eagled the fifteenth, won the sixteenth, before making a par on the eighteenth to win 1-up.)

After trailing by two points, the teams were now level at 9½–9½. Then Europe hit back again by winning in the next three matches – Colin Montgomerie over Lee Janzen, Peter Baker completing a remarkable twenty-four hours by beating Corey Pavin, and Joakim Haeggman defeating John Cook on the final hole after the American had found water with his second. Having restored a European lead, Gallacher roamed the course with a walkie-talkie at his ear, desperate for updated news. His team was close to winning the Ryder Cup, but the remaining matches were so finely balanced that any result was possible, especially with Payne Stewart on the verge of beating Mark James and Tom Kite holding a strong lead over Bernhard Langer. Further down the list, Jim Gallagher was playing well enough to beat a very out-of-form Seve Ballesteros, and with these three matches going America's way, Europe was struggling to reach the 14½ points that would bring them victory.

As expected, the United States made the match level at 12½–12½, but the drama did not end there. With just three matches left out on the course, Rocca was beating Love III with two holes left, Ray Floyd was beating Olazábal with four holes left and Faldo was getting the best of Paul Azinger with seven holes remaining. Inevitably, the spotlight fell on the ex-factory worker from Italy, Costantino Rocca. He was holding a 1-up advantage, and if he could just shut out Davis Love III, the Ryder Cup would surely stay in Europe.

A virtual unknown outside of Europe, Rocca had proved himself a wonderful striker of irons but had a suspect reputation on the greens. Approaching the seventeenth green, Rocca was 1-up with two holes to play and, like Davis Love III, was now putting for birdie. With the American not really threatening the hole for a birdie, Rocca looked to have two-putts for a par and a relatively safe half in five. Putting downhill from twenty-five feet, it looked for a moment as though he had holed it. Then, just as the ball slid past the hole, it inexplicably kept running. Rocca, who had walked after the putt, suddenly halted in amazement as it came to rest at least four-foot past the hole. Looking on, Davis Love III later commented that it was the first time he had seen fear in his opponent's eyes.

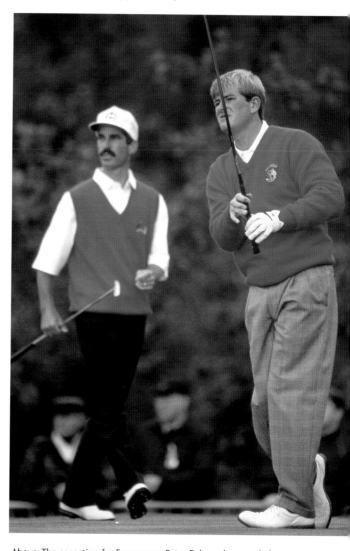

Above: The sensation for Europe was Peter Baker, who rounded off his Ryder cup debut with victory over Corey Pavin of the USA in the singles by two holes.

Obviously looking to hole for a birdie and a clean win, Love III's approach putt also slipped past the hole but stayed within tap-in range. Conceded moments later, the barrel-chested Italian surveyed his own putt with obvious trepidation as his teammates gathered at the back of the green. Stalking back and forth around the hole before taking his stance, Rocca drew the putter head slowly back and almost inevitably missed it on the right. Gasps of horror from the home crowd mixed with cheers of support for Love III. Lanny Wadkins' caddie, Bruce Edwards, was jumping up and down shouting, 'You're gonna win Davis. You're gonna win.' With Faldo and Azinger still four holes back, Rocca and Love III were level.

As Rocca stormed off towards the eighteenth tee, Davis Love III delayed for a few minutes hitting a few practice putts. Hardly aware of the shouts of support, he knew there would be a delay teeing off and the last place he wanted to be was hanging around on possibly the hardest finishing hole in golf. Leaving the penultimate green, it had occurred to Love III that his opponent might miss – indeed he had whispered it to his caddie, Frank Williams, while waiting for Rocca to take his putt. Now it actually crossed his mind that he might be the player that would lose the Ryder Cup for the United States. Standing on the tee, Davis Love III discussed with his captain, Tom Watson, what club to take. With the wind slightly from the right, it came down to a simple choice – three wood or one iron? It was approaching 5.00 p.m. and the temperature had

Below: Constantino Rocca reacts to losing his singles match against Davis Love. The scoreboard behind reveals how close the match was at that moment.

plummeted in the past hour. Rocca was looking nervous and Love III wanted to ram home any advantage he may have by drilling a wood shot down the middle, so three wood it was. Later describing it as one of the best pressure shots he had ever hit, his drive split the fairway well past the fairway bunker.

After the cheers of the visiting fans had died down, Costantino Rocca stepped up to his ball in what can only be described as a cathedral hush. Taking a deep breath, he settled over the ball with his driver and prepared to swing. Suddenly a huge roar came from the Faldo/Azinger match several holes back and he was forced to pull away. Coming off the last green, the scoreboards showed the final pair level, but as the cheers hung in the air for several minutes, something extraordinary had obviously happened. Faldo had just aced the par-3 fourteenth to take the lead. The pressure was now squarely on Rocca.

At last there was quiet. Rocca went through his pre-shot routine and hit his drive. A poor contact, it cleared the water without too much difficulty but left a second shot well over 200 yards out of semi-rough. With Davis Love III left with little more than a short iron to the flag, Rocca knew he had to get his ball on or near the green to salvage a half. A physically powerful man, he launched himself at a long iron with only one thought in mind – to clear the water that guarded the front of the green. He managed it – just. To the delight of the home supporters, the ball flew low and hard, managing to scramble up the grassy bank in front of the green. It would leave a long 50-yard chip up the green, but at least he had given himself a chance.

From just under 150 yards, Davis Love III hit a nervy approach shot into the green, aware that his opponent would struggle to make par. His nine-iron shot was under-hit and, spinning back from the middle shelf of three, finished 50 feet under the hole. Any advantage that had been gained off the tee had certainly been lost with the second shot. As the ball finally came to a stop within a few paces of Rocca's shot, Love III tried desperately to gather his thoughts as he walked across the wooden bridge that connected the fairway and green. His team was still cheering him on, but how could he ever explain losing from the position he was in.

After the deafening noise that greeted both players had died down, Rocca took his stance. Coming out low and a little thin, the Italian's chip fizzed up the green

Above: Davis Love III secures the winning point at the eighteenth green for the USA in his match against Costantino Rocca. A crucial match in many ways, it was a real turning point in European fortunes at the Belfry.

and for a moment looked good enough to go in. Yet, like his putt on the previous hole, it raced on, only coming to rest twenty feet above the hole. Standing behind the hole, Love III could see what a treacherously slick putt Rocca had left himself and resolved to try and leave his approach below the hole. He did, just six feet short of the hole. Walking up the green, the normally laid-back American chided himself for not hitting it hard enough. It was an unforgivable mistake that could have disastrous results. As in a tactical chess match, Rocca knew that if only he could hole his putt, the pressure on Davis Love III would be enormous. Sadly, he was unable to hold his nerve long enough to do so. Looking on dejectedly, his first putt trickled two-foot past, accompanied by disappointed murmurs from the packed grandstands. Immediately after it had stopped rolling, the high-pitched screams of the American players' wives – including those of his now-recovered wife, Robin – could be heard encouraging their man on.

Costantino Rocca's miss appeared to lift some of the weight that had rested on Love III's shoulders since his own putt minutes earlier. Then, somewhat generously, Davis Love III conceded it and set about looking at his own putt from every conceivable angle. Straight up the

hill with a little break from the right was the accepted line. After clearing his mind of all negative thoughts, he went through the pre-shot ritual he had worked out with sports psychologist Bob Rotella, taking a deep breath before striking the putt, which never looked like missing. Rolling dead centre, it was greeted by a moment of shocked silence from the partisan crowd. Then, as the American team broke ranks from behind the green, Davis Love III was suddenly engulfed in a mass of excited teammates. Even Lanny Wadkins was heard shouting, 'The cup is on the Concorde. The cup is coming home with us.'

Below: Having sat out the final day singles after his opponent Sam Torrance was retired due to injury, Lanny Wadkins of the United States embraces his captain, Tom Watson, after victory over Europe 15– 13.

In the pandemonium that followed, Costantino Rocca had waited to shake his opponent's hand, but in the celebrations that followed he slumped quietly off the green and was heading towards the clubhouse. Catching up with him, Love III tapped him on the shoulder only to find tears in the eyes of the amiable Italian. The two men shook hands and hugged. Then, feeling his despair, Love III said, 'I hope you're proud of the way you played. And I hope your country is proud of you. It should be.' Moments later news came through that Ray Floyd had moved 3-up with three to play on Olazábal and the match was effectively over. As Wadkins had predicted, the Ryder Cup would be going back to the United States on Concorde.

After retaining the trophy, Tom Watson and his team now wanted to 'win' the actual match. As they headed out to the course, news came through that José-Maria Olazábal had pulled two holes back and was about to play the eighteenth. With Faldo still leading Azinger, it was now possible that the Europeans could pull off an unlikely halve at 14–14. Sadly for the European team, the drama was short-lived. Olazábal hooked his drive into the water, Floyd made the green in regulation and the game and match was effectively over. Minutes later, Azinger putted out on the same green for a half against Faldo, leaving the overall match score at 15–13 to the United States.

As the evening closed in, Tom Watson gratefully accepted the Ryder Cup on behalf of his team. The controversy leading up to the match forgotten, he dignified the occasion by reading out a short speech made by past United States president, Theodore Roosevelt. Telling how it summed up everything he wanted to say about the competition, he read:

It is not the critic who counts, nor the one who points out how the strong man stumbled or how the doer of deeds might have done them better. The credit belongs to the man who is actually in the arena whose face is marred with sweat and blood. Who strives valiantly, who errs and comes short again and again. Who knows the great enthusiasms, the great devotions and spends himself in a worthy cause and who, if he fails, at least fails while bearing greatly so that his place shall never be with those cold and timid who knew neither victory or defeat.

When he was finished, Watson turned to his players and repeated what he had said at the opening ceremony on Thursday, 'Gentlemen, I cannot tell you how proud I am to be your captain.'

Walking back to the clubhouse, Davis Love III asked him, 'Can you hear it?'

'Hear what?', asked Watson.

'The silence', replied Love III, looking up at the empty grandstands.

Watson smiled at the thought. 'That is as sweet a sound as I have ever heard.'

Below: One of the true legends of the modern golf era, US captain Tom Watson proudly holds the Ryder Cup trophy after his team's triumph over Europe. He can add this to his long list of golfing achievements, among which lie five British Opens, one US Open and one US Masters.

15

From Oak Hill to Choke Hill for the USA

1995

OAK HILL COUNTRY CLUB, ROCHESTER, NEW YORK, USA

22–24 SEPTEMBER

After conceding second best to Europe in the late 1980s, the United States had bounced back with two consecutive victories in 1991 and 1993. Now, with the Ryder Cup to be played on home turf, they were hot favourites to make it three in a row, and that had the American media predicting the type of domination last seen in the 1960s and '70s. Forgetting that only three points had separated the two teams since the 1983 match at PGA National, their overwhelming feeling was that Europe was past its best. Faldo and Ballesteros, for example, had not won a major in years, while Langer and Woosnam also looked to be 'over the hill' in golfing terms. Questioning the future competitiveness of the Ryder Cup, they hinted that it was vital that Europe win and win soon, just to keep interest in the competition alive. At Oak Hill they got their wish, whether they *really* wanted it or not.

One thing the American media were right about was the higher than average age of the Europeans. Captained by Bernard Gallacher, who was hoping to make it 'third time lucky' after consecutive defeats at Kiawah Island and The Belfry, the European team had seven players aged over thirty-seven and only one under thirty (Per-Ulrik Johansson). That said, they boasted thirteen major championships between them compared with just six for the USA. But as the match at Oak Hill would show, Ryder Cup points are won by guts and skill and not by statistics or record books. (Interestingly, the US team had five forty-year-olds in its line-up, but no one saw fit to mention that.)

Another problem Gallacher had in the run-up to the match was his choice of 'wild-card' players. In previous Ryder Cups, nine players qualified automatically for Europe, with the captain selecting three others. Now the rules had been changed to allow Europe just two picks, bringing them into line with the United States. Limiting his choice quite considerably, the rule raised the alarming possibility that he might have to choose just two players from a talented group that included Nick Faldo, Ian Woosnam, José-Maria Olazábal and Mark James. Faldo, not surprisingly, thought the new system favoured the Americans and lost little time in outlining his views at the Buick Open in August. Playing most of his golf on the PGA Tour in America, he called for a return to three picks instead of two, saying, 'They should move the goalposts for the good of the Ryder Cup. We must have our best guys. Simple as that.'

In the end, Faldo need not have worried. Along with other 'wild-card' pick Ian Woosnam, he was selected to make a record-tying tenth successive appearance in the Ryder Cup. Sadly, the problems did not end there. With the match less than a fortnight away, the five-time major champion was forced to withdraw from the Lancôme Trophy in Paris with a niggling wrist injury. Playing in his last tournament before Oak Hill, he had jarred his right hand while participating in an exhibition match in Germany a few days before. Rumours quickly began to circulate about a substitute being brought in to replace him, but a spokesman for Faldo said that his withdrawal was merely precautionary. 'There is nothing to panic about', he assured the waiting press. Faldo would be practising all next week in Florida with his coach David Leadbetter.

As it turned out, Faldo was not the only player with health problems. Having lost José-Maria Olazábal, who had a long-standing toe injury, Gallacher also had injury doubts about Bernhard Langer, Seve Ballesteros and David Gilford, all of whom complained of back problems. Like Faldo's damaged wrist, their injuries would all turn out to be fairly minor, but they were of major concern to Gallacher leading up to the match.

Like his rival captain, Lanny Wadkins had his own problems. While Europe had five players with a positive record in the Ryder Cup – winning more matches than they had lost – he had one only – Jay Haas. As such, he had gone out on a limb by selecting Fred Couples and Curtis Strange as his 'wild-card' choices. Both major winners, they had a good record in the Ryder Cup, and with five rookies in his side – Brad Faxon, Phil Mickelson, Tom Lehman, Jeff Maggert and Loren Roberts – he desperately needed players he could rely on. The only problem was their recent record. Strange had not won a PGA Tour event in six years, while Couples' form was equally suspect. The American press speculated that Wadkins had chosen them because they were friends, but with Oak Hill deliberately set up like a US Open course, he knew he needed professionals who could cope with that type of golf.

Below: Howard Clark holes in one at the par-3 eleventh versus Peter Jacobson in their singles match. Clark went on to win the match for Europe by one hole.

It was a gamble that looked to have paid off as the United States raced into two-point lead going into the singles. Winning both sets of fourball matches 3–1, it was only their ineptness in the foursomes that stopped them from establishing a formidable lead. With Europe trailing 9–7 going into the final day, Nick Faldo looked to redeem what had been a fairly poor week by his standards. He had resumed his partnership with Colin Montgomerie, but any magic they had had two years earlier at The Belfry had disappeared as both

players struggled to find some form. Slipping to defeat twice on the opening day, the pressure on them was perhaps best summed up by an incident in their morning foursome match against Tom Lehman and Corey Pavin. As early as the second hole, Faldo berated Lehman for tapping in his winning par putt after it had already been conceded. 'When I say it's good', barked an annoyed Faldo, 'it's good!'

Lehman got the message, but was not going to be intimidated by his more famous opponent. 'I told him to speak clearly', he recalled afterwards. 'He claims he said a couple of times that my putt was good. I wasn't going to put up with any crap, especially after he stretches his arm out as if to say, "Put the ball in your pocket, you idiot!" I was hot.' Eventually winning the match on the final green, the American pair knew just how important beating Faldo and Montgomerie had been. As Lehman said later, it was 'a statement that Europe's best team could be beaten'.

Losing in the afternoon to Fred Couples and Davis Love III, Gallacher persisted with the Faldo/Montgomerie pairing in the opening foursomes on the second day. In truth, he had little choice. Trailing 5–3 after day one, he could not afford too many more mistakes and needed his top players to perform at their best if Europe were going to win. Nicknamed 'Snooty and the Blowfish' by some US golf writers after their ill-tempered display the day before, Faldo and Montgomerie rewarded their captain's decision to keep them together with a solid 4 and 2 win over former Wake Forest University pals, Curtis Strange and Jay Haas. Helping Europe to a 3–1 victory in the foursomes, Gallacher hoped for even more success in the afternoon; but it was not to be. With just the final round of fourballs left to play, he amazed everyone by sending out four completely new partnerships to face the United States – Montgomerie with Torrance, Woosnam and Rocca, Ballesteros and Gilford, and Faldo with Bernhard Langer.

Whatever strategy Gallacher had planned, it certainly did not work. Large defeats for Torrance and Monty (4 and 2) and Ballesteros and Gilford (3 and 2) were only slightly eased by a win by Woosnam and

Left: Ian Woosnam nearly comes to grief in trying to lift his teammate Constantino Rocca as they celebrate their unlikely victory over the USA 14½ to 13½.

Rocca over Love and Crenshaw. After that, things went from bad to worse. With one match left on the course, the Pavin/Roberts versus Faldo/Langer match came to the eighteenth hole all square. At least it was until Corey Pavin chipped in for a spectacular birdie from just off the green to secure the vital point that made it 3–1 to the USA. A huge blow to European hopes, it gave them an unexpected 1-hole victory and extended the overall match score to 9–7.

Two points clear with just the singles to play – something that usually favoured the home side – the press now speculated on a victory by at least five clear points. They were not alone. 'Phone it in mates', said Ian Woosnam to a group of British reporters. 'It's time to catch the Concorde home.' Not surprisingly, United States team captain Lanny Wadkins was elated at Saturday evening's press conference but still found time to add a note of caution. 'Yeah, I'm real confident,' he said. 'I have twelve guys playing well, but this is golf and a two-point lead is not big enough.'

Wadkins was right to be cautious. If the history of the Ryder Cup revealed anything, it was that nothing could be taken for granted. That was certainly the case at Oak Hill Country Club that Sunday afternoon as the tide finally turned in Europe's favour. With Bernard Gallacher packing the middle order with his most experienced players, Faldo found himself up against his old rival, Curtis Strange. They knew each other well. In times past the American had scored a considerable psychological blow after beating Faldo in a play-off to win the 1988 United States Open at Brookline.

A tense battle between two of golf's greatest tacticians, it was never going to be a classic but it was no less absorbing for that. Chipping in from twenty-foot, Strange nudged ahead for the first time at the par-5 sixth. Faldo hit back straight away, winning the next with a par. Having levelled the match, Faldo fell behind again at the par-3 eleventh but was unable to make inroads into his narrow one-up lead. The match ploughed on in similar fashion until they reached the seventeenth. You could cut the tension with a knife as both men wrestled desperately for control.

By now, the atmosphere of the match had changed considerably, along with its importance to the overall result. Over the past two hours, European fortunes had picked up considerably with wins for Howard Clark, Mark James, David Gilford and Colin Montgomerie.

Above: Bernhard Langer splashes out of a fairway bunker at the eighth during his morning foursomes match on day two with teammate David Gilford versus Corey Pavin and Tom Lehman.

Above: An emotional Nick Faldo wipes a tear from his eye as he secures victory by 1 hole over Curtis Strange at the eighteenth hole in their singles match.

With the score now level at 11½–11½, the Faldo versus Strange match took on massive importance, and it was probably no exaggeration to say that the destiny of the Ryder Cup lay in their hands.

Playing his second to the 458-yard, par-4 seventeenth, Strange was the first to crack. Accompanied by frenzied shouts of 'fore right!', his approach sailed wide of the green, handing the advantage to Faldo. Sadly for Europe, their hopes were short-lived as Faldo hit an equally poor shot that found the front left bunker. Like the end of a gruelling heavyweight boxing contest, the players swapped shots like tentative jabs, hoping all the while not to make the one fatal mistake that would let their opponent in for victory. A good example came on the penultimate green. On in three, the American was still eight feet away putting uphill for par while Faldo was a foot nearer on the same line. Strange, on the type of putt he would normally have holed nine times out of ten, made a nervous prod at the ball and missed. He presented Faldo, who did not need asking twice, with the chance to win the hole with a par. The match was now level with just one left to play.

Stepping onto the tee, Faldo did not feel confident about playing the testing 450-yard, par-4 eighteenth. Twice he had reached this point in a match only to lose out, and after pulling his drive into the left-hand rough it looked like history was repeating itself. Forced to chip out within pitching wedge distance of the hole, his ball ran through the fairway into the first cut of rough. His problems were building by the second, and with Strange assessing his options from the centre of the fairway after a wonderful drive, things could not have been much worse. 'I was trying not to think whether my match was going to be the turning point, but I could sense it', Faldo said later. 'You really have to play from the heart.'

Watching from the edge of the fairway, US captain Wadkins, walkie-talkie in hand, must have been congratulating himself on his inspired choice of wild card. A few minutes later, however, his dreams were in tatters as Strange failed to find the green with his approach shot. Hitting the worst three-iron of his career, his ball pitched short and left him an impossible chip to a raised green out of ankle-high rough. Looking at the two, it was hard to know who had the more difficult shot. Lining up his shot from 94 yards out, Faldo hit the most exquisite pitching wedge shot. Landing on the firm green, it bounced twice before finally coming to a halt just six-foot from the hole. Considering the enormous pressure he was under at the time, it was a magnificent stroke – and how his opponent must have cursed him for it. Yet Curtis Strange is not a two-time major winner for nothing. With the pressure firmly back on his shoulders, he scrambled it onto the green and somehow managed to stop it within eight-foot. The applause both men received stepping onto the green was well deserved that day.

The end, when it came, was typical Faldo. Unable to watch as his opponent lined up his putt, it was the loud gasp from the partisan crowd that told him that Strange had missed. Now it was his turn. While it was not the actual putt that won the Ryder Cup, it might as well have been. Left with a hugely quick, right-breaking putt to win, the Englishman had never felt such pressure. 'Everything was shaking', he said later. 'Everything except the putter.'

Faldo now had to capitalize on the golden opportunity he had carved out for himself. Stepping up to the ball, he fought hard to dismiss all the negative thoughts that were currently racing around in the back of his mind. What if I miss? What if the ball rolls past the hole and keeps on rolling or I three-putt? In the end he did neither. Slotting it right into the heart of the cup, he stood arms aloft in victory. Faldo, five-time major winner, the greatest pressure-player of his generation, had done it again. 'That was the greatest scrambling par of my life', he admitted afterwards. 'It was as good as Muirfield in '87. Actually, it was tougher, because if I miss, it goes four feet past and I have to start negotiating with Curtis.'

Below: In a match that swung one way then the other, Nick Faldo plays an awkward swinging putt for a vital win over Curtis Strange at the eighteenth green.

Above: Winning point and jubilation for Philip Walton of Ireland as he is stormed by his captain Bernard Gallacher and his teammates on the eighteenth. He beat Jay Haas by one hole.

After three exhausting days of intense competition, the tide had finally turned in Europe's favour. Faldo beating Strange by the narrow margin of 1-up took the visitors ahead by 13½–12½. Talking about the match, Faldo said, 'When everything was churning inside me going into those last two holes, when I had to fight to keep my legs still, when I knew how important it was for me to win, I wondered – can I still do it?'

The answer was a resounding, 'yes!'. Faldo's victory now meant the Americans needed to win the Mickelson versus Johansson match and halve the Haas versus

Walton match just to keep the Ryder Cup hopes alive. And with Haas 2-down with two to play, that looked unlikely, and so it proved.

For the record books, it was Philip Walton who officially gave Europe a 14½–13½ victory after shutting out Jay Haas on the last hole of their match, but everyone knew it was Nick Faldo who had made the difference. 'When Nick put that putt in at seventeen, then won at the last,' said a delighted Ian Woosnam, 'I knew then we had won the Ryder Cup.'

As the European team celebrated long into the night, the relief on each face – especially that of Bernard Gallacher – told its own story. In ten Ryder Cups – eight as a player, two as captain – Bernard Gallacher had experienced ten defeats. Two days into his eleventh, it looked as though it would be the same story, with the British press criticizing everything from his team tactics to the individual pairings. His reputation was in tatters, yet against all the odds Europe had accomplished one of the greatest comebacks in Ryder Cup history. Winning 7 of the remaining 12 singles, they took the match by a single point and made it 'third time lucky' for captain Gallacher.

In six decades of Ryder Cup competition, the United States had lost only six times and only twice on home soil. Many experts blamed the defeat on the PGA Tour and its emphasis on winning prize money over winning tournaments. Placing a question mark over their competitive nerve, the American press lambasted the players and their seemingly lacklustre attitude. Without mentioning players like Faxon, Haas and Maggert by name, none of whom had won a Tour event in the last two years, they suggested that players had become 'lazy', picking up huge cheques every week for very little effort. Harsh criticism indeed. But perhaps the harshest of all was reserved for Lanny Wadkins' two wild-card picks, Fred Couples and Curtis Strange. Ignoring strong claims from both Lee Janzen and Jim Gallagher, Jr. – both of whom won two PGA Tour events in 1995 – Wadkins chose experience over youth and paid the price. Having picked up just 2½ points from a possible 7, Wadkins would find that the blame would fall squarely on his shoulders over the coming days and weeks.

'America lost the [Ryder] Cup in a week Nick Faldo made two birdies, Seve Ballesteros hit three fairways, and the European captain forgot Ian Woosnam existed', wrote one frustrated journalist. A lot of his American colleagues agreed with him, as they did about the folly of picking Curtis Strange as a wild card. Keeping his dignity throughout, the two-time US Open winner had come within one putt of being hailed as a national hero. Now he was depicted as the man who lost the Ryder Cup! 'It's a frightening thought,' he said in the post-match press conference, 'how I'm going to feel when I wake up and realize we didn't win.'

If Strange wanted some idea of how the country felt about his defeat, it came at the Honda Classic the following March when a heckler shouted at him 'Bogey, bogey, bogey. Ryder Cup choker.' The proud American, who coincidentally was partnered by Nick Faldo, did his best to ignore the interruption. But the Englishman

Above: The sweet smell of success at last for Europe's captain Bernard Gallacher, who until now had been a losing captain – or playing on the losing side – in the Ryder Cup.

was having none of it. Pointing out the heckler to a tournament marshal, he demanded that he be removed from the course. 'It was the worst thing I've seen in almost twenty years of playing professional golf', said an angry Faldo. 'He has no idea of the pressure of playing at the top of a sport.' Sadly it would not be the last time that a Ryder Cup player would face such abuse from so-called fans.

16

Seve Reigns in Spain

1997

VALDERRAMA GOLF CLUB, SOTOGRANDE, SPAIN

26–28 SEPTEMBER 1997

After Captain Bernard came Captain Seve. With the Ryder Cup scheduled for southern Spain, Severiano Ballesteros was the natural, perhaps only, choice for leader. Asked to captain the European side shortly after Bernard Gallacher's swan song performance at Oak Hill in 1995, he had hoped to make the team on merit, but a slump in form helped change his mind. Yet for many of the 1997 European team, the only thing Seve didn't do was actually hit the shots at Valderrama. In three days of intense competition, he planned the tactics, chose the pairings and even picked the colours his team would wear on the final day! Stalking the course like a nervous mother hen, he would offer advice to his men when it was called for, and even when it wasn't. An inspirational figure throughout the match, he showed the indomitable style that had brought him five majors in his career. And even with the much-vaunted Tiger Woods in the USA side for the first time, the visitors had very little answer to the determination showed by the Seve-inspired Europeans.

The biggest problem facing Ballesteros in the run-up to the match, which was played on the continent for the first time, was team selection. Like Gallacher before him, he was allowed just two wild-card picks and had three top-class players in Nick Faldo, José-Maria Olazábal and Jesper Parnevik to choose from. It was an intolerable situation, but even here Seve was able to work his magic. Proving that three into two does go, he selected Faldo and Parnevik, then set about making room for his long-time Ryder Cup partner Olazábal.

Miguel Angel Martin, a self-taught professional who emerged via the caddie ranks in Madrid, had qualified automatically for the team. Putting together a good run of form, he had virtually had his place secured, long before the August deadline, after a win in the Heineken Classic in Australia. Martin was looking forward to making his Ryder Cup debut in his home country, but his season was unexpectedly curtailed shortly before the Open in July when he sustained a wrist injury that was serious enough to require surgery. He arrived at Valderrama without having played a competitive tournament in weeks. Reasoning that he would be strong enough to play, Martin brushed aside all questions concerning his lack of competitive practice. After all, he had earned the right to play and who could argue with that? Seve Ballesteros, for one.

Determined to have Olazábal in his team, Ballesteros insisted that Martin take a fitness test on his injured wrist. Martin refused and was deselected. Inevitably, it was never going to end there: the desperately upset Spaniard threatened legal redress. A compromise was finally reached whereby Martin was officially recognized as a Ryder Cup player for the 1997 match, taking part in team photographs etc., but could not actually play! It left a bitter taste in the mouth of everyone concerned. Yet by the time the match began at the end of September, Martin was out, Olazábal was in and Seve had the team he wanted. Interestingly, it would also be the first time in the history of the event that less than half of the team were British – with two Swedes, two Spaniards, a German, a Dane and an Italian.

In contrast, the American team practically picked itself. Boasting six major champions in Justin Leonard, Lee Janzen, Tom Lehman, Fred Couples, Davis Love III and Tiger Woods, the USA looked a good bet to make it three wins in the last four Ryder Cups. Captained by 1992 US Open winner Tom Kite, they were hot favourites to win back the trophy they lost at Oak Hill. Worse still for Europe, they all looked in good form in the weeks before Valderrama, leading some members of the American press to predict a victory by at least five clear points. 'To think Europe will win the Ryder Cup', said one journalist, 'is to think the moon is made of cheese and Mickey Mouse will make it to the White House one day'.

Not surprisingly, the Europeans were upset at being written off even before a shot had been hit in anger.

Below: Europe's genius captain Seve Ballesteros takes a rare moment of quiet time to think as he waits on his buggy at the seventeenth for his next pairing to arrive to receive instructions.

Overleaf: A general view of the notorious par-5 seventeenth at Valderrama. Its difficulty lies in the severity of the slope from the top of the green down to the water.

Rising to the bait, Colin Montgomerie caused uproar when he unwittingly suggested that Brad Faxon's well-publicized marital difficulties might prevent him from playing well. Seve in turn went out of his way to exploit the relative inexperience of Tiger Woods by saying, 'I think any of my golfers can play against Tiger Woods

Below: So far, Tiger Wood's impact on the outcome of the Ryder Cup matches he has played has not been as great as that he has made on the rest of golf's great championships.

and beat Tiger Woods.' Even the media-allergic Nick Faldo added his comments to the growing furore by pointing out that 'since 1985, the European team has a better record in the Ryder Cup than the American team'.

Another problematic issue was the golf course, and notably the 511-yard, par-5 seventeenth. Remodelled by Seve Ballesteros some months earlier, the hole, like the entire Valderrama layout, was specifically designed to blunt the superior firepower of the American team. With fairways narrowed at exactly the distance big-hitting players like Tiger Woods were expected to drive, it forced them to either lay-up or risk leaving their ball in the rough. And with the small, awkward greens unreceptive to anything other than a perfectly struck shot from the tightly mown fairways, complaints began as early as the opening practice round. 'I'm not a fan of rough in the middle of the fairway', complained Phil Mickelson about the penultimate hole, where the fairway had been deliberately split into two sections and bordered by ankle-high rough. His colleague Tom Lehman was equally upset with the hole, saying, 'I never much cared for a par-5 where you hit driver, sand wedge, sand wedge'.

In many ways it was a relief when the match finally got underway on Friday morning after a two-hour delay. With a heavy downpour threatening to wash out play completely, the greens staff pulled off a minor miracle in getting the match started at all. Mopping away gallons of water from the rain-soaked fairways and putting greens, they, like everyone else, were rewarded with some excellent play from both sides in what would prove a typically tight encounter.

In a break from tradition, the first two days of the Ryder Cup saw fourballs in the morning and foursomes in the afternoon instead of the other way round. Having predicted 'some very close matches', Fred Couples provided the first point for the United States as early as the second game. Partnering Brad Faxon to victory against the experimental pairing of Nick Faldo and Lee Westwood, it was his much-maligned colleague that holed a five-footer on the last to shut out the English pair. 'Sinking this one', said an elated Faxon, 'helped all of us believe things will be different this time.'

He was wrong. Just one of seven games that made it to the eighteenth over the first two days, the closeness of the matches tested the Americans resolve to the absolute limit and they were found wanting. Having shared the opening fourballs 2–2, the American team wilted under the pressure. Picking up just 3½ points from the remaining foursome and fourball matches (12 points), it was exactly the type of desperate performance that had drawn so much criticism at Oak Hill.

With the match score 10½–5½ to the Europeans going into the singles, the inquest began early. With players like Tiger Woods (1½ points from a possible 4) and Justin Leonard (½ point from a possible 3) lambasted for not getting to grips with the Spanish course, the US press also blamed the team's lamentable putting under pressure. Time after time, they either gave away holes to the Europeans or failed to win them when they should have. As one frustrated American journalist observed, 'The way the US players putted, they couldn't hit the Mediterranean from the Rock of Gibraltar.'

Harsh criticism, but only half right. Gelling as a team, the Europeans had picked up from where they had left off two years earlier. Showing a remarkable desire to better their opponents on every shot, every hole, every match, they never gave the American players a moment's rest from the first tee to the final green. With Seve Ballesteros flitting from match to match on his captain's buggy, rarely did any player put less than 100 per cent into each shot. Spurred on by excellent performances from Faldo and Westwood, Langer and Montgomerie, Olazábal and Rocca, Parnevik and Garrido, the home team took control early on and never looked back. One point ahead after the opening day, they had simply demolished the United States on day two. Winning the morning fourballs by 3½–½, they confirmed their growing dominance by winning the afternoon foursomes by 2½–1½.

Five points clear with only twelve singles left to play, nobody gave the United States a prayer of turning things around. Revealing how desperate he was for inspiration, heavenly or otherwise, Tom Kite turned to former US president George Bush for help. In Spain to watch the action, he was asked to give his beleaguered team a much-needed pep talk on Saturday evening, which he gladly agreed to do. As he said afterwards:

Being able to pass on a word of encouragement was easy for me since I have been in tough situations in sports and in politics', said Bush afterwards. 'There's no reason to get down on something. You just bounce back and these guys are

doing that now. Whether we can pull it out at the end, I don't know, but I am so proud of them – those who win and those who lose.

As things turned out, his speech had a positive effect on his countrymen. Stating that it was 'not so much what he said but the fact that he took the trouble to come and see us', an inspired Tom Kite came up with a do-or-die plan to win back the Ryder Cup. Deciding to put his big guns out first, the American captain reasoned that if

Above: Former US President George Bush acknowledges the crowd during the opening ceremony. Seated over to his right is HRH Prince Andrew representing European interests.

he was going to claw his way back into the match, he needed points on the board as quickly as possible. Putting his big guns out early was a risky plan, but one that looked to have paid off as the singles got underway. Inspired by an 8 and 7 thrashing of Ian Woosnam by Fred Couples in the opening game, the American team fought back strongly with wins for Phil Mickelson (2 and 1) over Darren Clarke, Mark O'Meara (5 and 4) over Jesper Parnevik, Lee Janzen (1-hole) over José-Maria Olazábal, Jeff Maggert (3 and 2) over Lee Westwood, Jim Furyk (3 and 2) over Nick Faldo, and Tom Lehman (7 and 6) over Ignacio Garrido. He had closed the gap to almost nothing, and the worried look on Seve's face as he flitted from match to match told the whole story.

Not that it was all one-way traffic. Balanced against the American onslaught were unexpected victories for Per-Ulrik Johansson (3 and 2) over new PGA Champion

Davis Love III, Bernhard Langer (2 and 1) over Brad Faxon, and perhaps most remarkably, Costantino Rocca (4 and 2) over the disappointing Tiger Woods. And while he only halved his match with Justin Leonard, Thomas Björn had pulled out all the stops to recover from being 4-down after four holes played! In the end it would prove crucial as the Ryder Cup headed towards yet another dramatic finish on the final afternoon.

The players were driven on by Ballesteros, but needed little encouragement from their captain. Indeed, having the hyper-tense Spaniard hanging around was becoming a positive distraction. Keen to discuss club selection with his players, whether they wanted to or not, he openly admonished them for hitting poor shots – or in Thomas Björn's case, for three-putting the second green. By now the pressure was bad enough and the last thing many of them wanted was Seve offering help. 'He's a damned nuisance', admitted one player. 'He was like a head-master peering over your shoulder all the time.'

With the result now in the balance, it all came down to the final match left on the course – Colin Montgomerie versus Scott Hoch. A desperately tight affair, Montgomerie found himself 2-down early on before levelling the match with a par on the fourteenth.

Below: US captain Tom Kite shows the strain of leadership as he wonders what to plan next against Seve Ballesteros' zig-zagging of the course and its matches.

With the score boards at Valderrama a mass of red numbers signifying an American comeback, the big Scot became increasingly aware of the importance of his match. Describing the final nine holes as a 'nerve wracking experience', he finally took the lead on the sixteenth after Hoch made bogey. Informed on the tee that Europe had already gained the 14½ points they needed for victory – mistakenly as things turned out – he did well to keep his concentration. 'It was right after a big roar', said Monty. 'But the official said he heard it [the news] over the earphones.'

With heavy rain making the course play every inch of its 6734 yards, both players were forced to lay-up on the treacherous seventeenth. Then almost without warning, Hoch pitched up to within twelve inches of the hole for a certain birdie. Unable to match it, Montgomerie barely glanced at his teammates gathered around the back of the green as he headed for the eighteenth all square. In practice, Seve had forced his players to play the hole over and over again, convinced from the outset that it would be crucial.

Standing on the final tee Montgomerie could only guess at what the next few minutes held for him. After all the drama, the hype, the destiny of the Ryder Cup would now be decided in the space of one hole. The mathematics was simple. After three days of intense competition, Monty needed a half at the last and Europe would win. If he lost, the Ryder Cup would be shared and, while the trophy would stay on this side of the Atlantic, the moral victory would almost certainly go to the United States.

The closing hole at Valderrama presented its own special problems for the European number one. Having built a highly successful career on a low fade, he knew better than anyone that the ideal shot on this occasion was a high draw avoiding the trees on the left. So, as he viewed the exacting 440-yard hole, twisting its way through a forest of cork, he knew that the tee-shot would prove not only a test of skill and nerve but also one of character. In fact, the only comfort he could take from the situation was that his opponent faced exactly the same problem. It was pure theatre and the record books show what happened.

Montgomerie hit the tee-shot of his life and Hoch didn't. Montgomerie found the green in regulation and Hoch didn't. Montgomerie two-putted for the half point he needed and, having done so, generously

conceded Hoch's twelve-foot putt for par. Still shaking long after his match had ended, Monty admitted, 'Before the Ryder Cup I said that I wouldn't mind being in a position when it all came down to me. Well, I've changed my mind, I can tell you. I don't want to do that again. It wasn't fun out there.'

With Europe beating the United States by 14½–13½, the European celebrations that followed were well deserved. They had won by a single point and even a heavy Spanish downpour during the presentation failed to dampen Colin Mongomerie's celebrations or those of his teammates. Standing on the clubhouse steps holding the trophy aloft, he explained how 'it felt just like winning a major'.

After the match, Tom Kite attempted to console his defeated players as the European team paraded triumphantly with the trophy. Hardly noticed as they slumped off towards their team hotel at San Roque, the American players had bitter disappointment etched on their faces. Reflecting on the defeat, Kite blamed the weather and just about anything else he could think of. Talking to the press, he said that he believed that his team was better from tee to green but lacked the local knowledge to read the putts. 'It's a golf course that requires as much local knowledge as any I've ever seen, with the exception of Augusta National. The only reason we got beat was they knew the golf course and the weather conditions better than us.'

Like Kite, Seve Ballesteros revealed that he would not captain the next Ryder Cup team at the Country Club in Brookline, Massachusetts, in 1999. He stated his wish to 'recover' his game and actually play in the match. The Americans could have been forgiven for thinking that he *had* played in this one!

17

The Battle of Brookline and Beyond

1999

THE COUNTRY CLUB, BROOKLINE, BOSTON, MASSACHUSETTS, USA

24–26 SEPTEMBER

As the dust settled on Valderrama, the American press debated long and hard on the reasons for defeat. In the end they decided that it was not just golfing skill that had won the match, or even local knowledge as captain Tom Kite had stated. Rather it was the huge passion and commitment shown by the Europeans that had proved the deciding factor. Led by an inspirational captain, they had shown an overwhelming self-belief that anything was possible. As Ballesteros said afterwards, 'My players played with their hearts, and that is why we won.'

In short, they wanted to win more than the United States did, and if Europe was going to be stopped from making it three in a row in Boston in 1999, something had to change. In the weeks and months that followed, a 'win-at-all-costs' attitude would pervade the American golfing psyche. Two years later at Brookline it reached its peak. Perhaps the most controversial day in Ryder

Cup history, the final round of singles matches would live in infamy. Making the so-called 'War on the Shore' at Kiawah Island look like a mere garden party, it was a day where fairness and sportsmanship were replaced by hostility and blame. Some would say it was the day that the true spirit of the Ryder Cup was lost forever.

Everything had begun so well. Shortly before stepping onto Concorde for the trip to Boston, Mark James expressed his pride at captaining the European side for the first time. A popular choice with the players, James refused to be drawn into the row concerning some American players' demand that they should be paid to play in the Ryder Cup. Focusing on the positive aspects of the event, he said to the waiting press, 'I am sure this latest chapter will be equally spellbinding and that the twenty-four players and two captains will be richer for the experience.'

Appointed ahead of his old friend Sam Torrance, he had already courted controversy by omitting Nick Faldo, Ian Woosnam and Bernhard Langer from his twelve-man team. Preferring youth over experience, he went instead for Jesper Parnevik (thirty-four) and Andrew Coltart (twenty-nine) as his two wild-card selections. Added to a team that already included Sergio Garcia (nineteen) and Lee Westwood (twenty-six), it was the youngest side to play in the Ryder Cup in decades. 'In my experience', said the Manchester-born James, 'experience is overrated.'

It was a decision that would come back to haunt him. But even without Faldo, Langer et al, Europe could boast quality players like Colin Montgomerie, Darren Clarke, José-Maria Olazábal, Jarmo Sandelin, Miguel-Angel Jiménez and Padraig Harrington in their line-up. Add to them the newly crowned British Open winner Paul Lawrie and runner-up at Carnoustie Jean Van de Velde, and you had the makings of a real upset. Certainly not overawed at taking on an incredibly strong American team, which included the number one and number two ranked players in the world, Tiger Woods and David Duval, Mark James kept insisting in the run-up to the match that his team would acquit themselves well, and for the opening two days at Brookline he was proved right.

Racing to a 6–2 lead after the first day, the Europeans maintained their advantage by ending the second day 10–6 up. The Americans had no answer to the brilliant performance inspired by the pairings of Garcia and Parnevik (winners of 3½ points from a possible 4) and Montgomerie and Paul Lawrie (2½ from 4). Woods, for example, played in all four matches and only won one point! 'No matter what we do, they do us one better,' said Davis Love III who failed to win any of his three matches prior to the singles.

As the American public digested what had happened, the pressure was really on US captain Ben Crenshaw to pull a rabbit out of the hat. Trailing by four points going into the singles, he knew that only five teams in the history of the Ryder Cup had trailed going into the final day of singles matches and won, and even fewer had ever come back from such a large deficit. Despite this, the two-time Masters winner appeared strangely unperturbed. Convinced that his errant superstars could turn things around, he warned the media not to write off him or his team. Speaking on

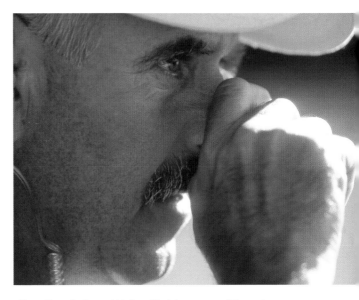

Above: 'Into the bear pit' is how Mark James, one of Europe's most disappointing Ryder Cup captains, described his experiences during the matches at Brookline.

Saturday evening, it was an enigmatic Crenshaw who told reporters that he was 'a big believer in fate'. He went on to add, 'I have a good feeling about this. That's all I'm going to tell you.'

Crenshaw enlisted the help of Texas Governor, George W. Bush, and his team spent part of Saturday night listening to Bush read from the memoirs of a soldier who was at the siege of the Alamo. As players choked back the tears, it obviously had the right effect. 'Ben kept saying, "We can do this. I've got a good feeling about this"', said Davis Love III. 'I kept thinking, "Golly, I hope this doesn't come back to haunt him." But he kept saying it so many times. He got us going.'

'It's not too big of a hole', said a determined Hal Sutton afterwards. 'We've got twelve great players on this team. We've shown a lot of fight this week, and we've got a lot of fight left in us.'

The next day they *all* came out like tigers ready to devour their hapless opponents. And, like the Coliseum in Rome, it would be achieved against a background of excited onlookers all baying for European blood. Needing the points, captain Crenshaw sent his best six players out first, hoping to create some momentum. It was a strategy that worked remarkably well as Tom Lehman beat Lee Westwood 3 and 2 in the opening

Above: Anguish for Europe's Jesper Parnevik as he misses a putt at the seventh during his fourball match with Sergio Garcia against Davis Love III and David Duval on day two.

game. Wins followed for Hal Sutton (4 and 2) over Darren Clarke, Phil Mickelson (5 and 3) over Jarmo Sandelin, Davis Love III (6 and 5) over Jean Van de Velde, Tiger Woods (3 and 2) over Andrew Coltart and David Duval (5 and 4) over Jesper Parnevik. The USA now had the lead for the first time in the match. 'I've never seen such firepower going out in the first six groups,' admitted Crenshaw later. 'It ignited everybody.'

It certainly did 'ignite everybody', including the crowd. As cheers of 'U-S-A! U-S-A!' echoed throughout the course, enthusiastic cheering slowly

Right: The colourful Payne Stewart of the USA punches the air as his approach shot at the first settles by the pin during his singles match against Colin Montgomerie. The sadly missed player was killed in a plane crash only a month later.

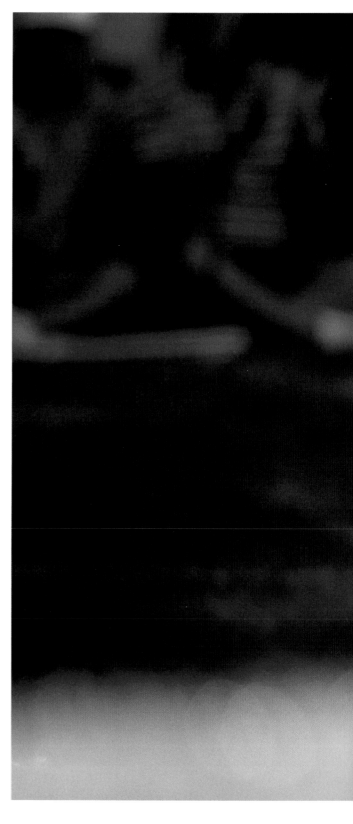

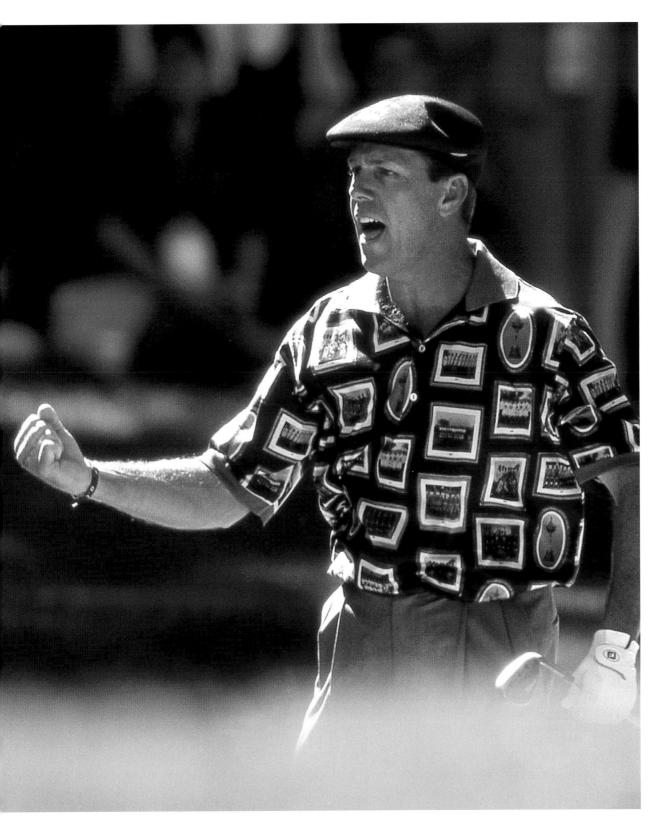

Above: Sergio Garcia of Spain lips his putt out of the hole at the seventh as he and his partner Jesper Parnevik go to halve their match against Davis Love III and David Duval in the afternoon fourballs on day two.

turned into frenzied screams as the home team got nearer and nearer to achieving their target of 14½ points. At times it got nasty, especially when Montgomerie was involved. The day before in the foursomes, the big Scot was forced to back off putts three times because of the crowd noise. Accusing his opponents Hal Sutton and Jeff Maggert of stirring them, he said afterwards, 'They need pumping up because they're losing, and they're losing heavily. You know we've won [when] it's silent and that's the best thing we can do – silence the crowd by outplaying them.'

As Montgomerie and the rest of his team found out, silencing this highly partisan crowd would not be easy. Worse still, you could sense the fight slowly ebbing out of the European players as the scoreboard became a mass of red figures signifying more and more US victories. Astounded by the turn around in fortunes, Mark James looked a worried man. Having taken the decision to play his best players all week, his faltering side looked either worn out or, in some cases, ring rusty. Seven players had played seventy-two holes already while three others – Van de Velde, Sandelin and Coltart – had played none, and now Europe was paying the price. Europe needed only four points from a possible twelve to retain the Ryder Cup, but the question now was where were they going to come from? The evening before, James had said, 'We're under no illusions. The USA is going to fight back hard tomorrow.' The problem was, he did not realize how hard.

Halfway through the afternoon, the match looked all but lost. Then came a faint glimmer of hope after Irish rookie Padraig Harrington made par at the last to beat the out-of-form Mark O'Meara by 1-up. And with Miguel-Angel Jiménez involved in a tight match with Steve Pate, Colin Montgomerie holding a slim advantage over Payne Stewart, and José-Maria Olazábal up on Justin Leonard, it looked for a brief moment as though Europe might escape with an unexpected draw. Then it all started to go wrong once more. Despite Paul Lawrie beating Jeff Maggert 4 and 3, fellow Spaniards Miguel-Angel Jiménez and Sergio Garcia both lost. All eyes now turned to the penultimate green and the match between Olazábal and Leonard.

A fantastic run by the twenty-four-year-old American of par-par-birdie-birdie had been enough to bring his match level with two holes remaining. Knowing that his USA side needed only half a point to win, it was now his job to get it. Both on the green in two, Leonard would putt first from 45 feet – twice the distance of Olazábal. Leonard had little on his mind other than leaving it close enough for a tap-in. At least that was the plan. As the putt was struck, a few solitary shouts went up, but from that distance nobody ever expected it to go in – but it did! After a seemingly tortuous journey up the green, the ball rattled into the hole and the whole world went mad. As Leonard charged off the green in delight, his fellow players, wives and caddies raced across the green to celebrate his triumph. Everything was chaos. Local marshals, partisan in their behaviour throughout the week, failed once more to keep order. Indeed, they looked on smiling as camera crews trampled over the immaculate putting surface to get a view of the action – some close enough to Olazábal's line to create a torrent of concern from the European players.

Whatever Olazábal might have been feeling, his captain Mark James was furious. Not only was he extremely upset at the behaviour of the American, but he was also angry at the abusive comments that he and his players received while the Spaniard prepared to take his own putt. As he said later:

> If I had been playing myself, I might have lost my temper completely. Cheering when you miss putts or hit into bunkers is one thing. But personal abuse is something different. We are going to get into a situation where fights will break out if we don't stop this type of thing now.

In contrast with everyone around him, the Spaniard maintained a dignified silence. A dark and occasionally brooding figure, Olazábal still had a putt for a half and needed to concentrate, but it would prove an almost impossible task, especially after his first attempt to line-up was broken by further shouts of 'U-S-A! U-S-A!' from the crowd. It was an intolerable situation and despite running his putt within inches of the hole, Olazábal could not stop Leonard from wining the hole to go 1-up. A guaranteed half point, even though he managed to halve the match by winning the last with a birdie, he could not stop the United States from winning their first Ryder Cup in six years.

Below: One of the most controversial moments in Ryder Cup history as American players rush across the seventeenth green to celebrate Jason Leonard's outrageous birdie putt.

In the days following the thirty-third Ryder Cup at Brookline recriminations started in earnest. Many watching on television – especially in Europe – thought the disgraceful scenes played out around the seventeenth green were inexcusable. Enthusiasm is fine, they said, commendable even, but the sight of Americans running across the green was against the spirit of the game. Of course, apologies from the American camp were not long in arriving. In a press conference a few days later, Ben Crenshaw described how bad his team felt at behaving that way. 'Still,' he said in their defence, 'the Europeans got pretty heated up when they beat us last time out.'

Then, as he left a few moments later clutching the golden chalice to his chest, he turned and said, 'We are just looking forward to The Belfry in 2001 and retaining this beautiful thing.' For one person at least, the passion for the Ryder Cup was undiminished.

No one would deny that it was a remarkable fight back by the Americans, perhaps the greatest ever in Ryder Cup history. Winning eight matches, halving one and losing just three, it had been a truly wonderful effort

Above: Hal Sutton hugs his teammate and fellow Texan as the euphoric USA team celebrate victory over Europe in the epic that was the 'Battle of Brookline'.

Below: Sporting a golf shirt showing previous US victories in the Ryder Cup, Tiger Woods is in full voice as his arms go up in victory. Cheerleader wife Amy Mickelson is singing along too.

by Crenshaw and his team. Yet the brilliance of their golf will be forever overshadowed by the boorish behaviour of their players and crowd. In the end the United States enjoyed winning back the trophy a little too much.

As victory got ever closer on that dramatic final day, they simply lost the plot, with fair play and comradeship replaced by clenched fist salutes, high-octane aggression and barely transparent gamesmanship. The question everyone wanted answered – especially Mark James and his European team – was how was it allowed to go so far? They were not alone. In the aftermath of the event the British press expressed the sense of outrage felt by many non-Americans. As the *Daily Telegraph* reported, the Americans, 'not only indulged in the worst excesses of triumphalism during and after the match, but also turned in a repulsive display of bad manners', no doubt referring to the incident on the seventeenth green. Michael Bonallack, Secretary of the Royal and Ancient Golf Club of St Andrews, the guardian of golfing tradition, likened the atmosphere at Brookline to 'a bear pit'! 'I felt embarrassed for golf', he said afterwards. 'It went way beyond the decency you associate with proper golf. I love the Ryder Cup and I don't want to see it degenerate into a mob demonstration every time we play it.'

Having watched part of the match on television, Nick Faldo also voiced his concern. 'It has become too much life and death', he said:

> Let's get back to the bottom line. This is twenty-four guys going out and playing golf. Sure, you are going to play really as hard as you can on the golf course. But when you come off, the goal is you can sit at the bar and talk about, 'Hey, the three-wood you hit was an awesome shot.' If we get back to that level, then, great.

While many people applauded the sentiment, few could ever remember a time when Faldo sat in a bar and said to a fellow competitor, 'Hey, the three-wood you hit was an awesome shot.'

Someone who was taking things very seriously was Mark James, whose wife was actually spat on by a spectator. He believed the American victory had been thoroughly tainted by the behaviour of the players and their so-called supporters, and not surprisingly his wife agreed with him. 'It was just awful,' she said. 'There were lots of incidents of people telling us to go home.'

Blaming drunken fans for part of the problem, James urged the PGAs of both Europe and the United States to crack down on such behaviour in future. (Colin Montgomerie's father had also left the course early, unable to withstand the abuse his son was receiving during his match against Payne Stewart.) Calling for a complete ban on the sale of alcohol, James even raised the possibility that some of Europe's top stars might avoid playing tournaments in America entirely. 'A lot of players will not be bothered competing in America again', said James on his return to Britain. 'Certainly that is the case with me. It's not something I look forward to. We don't need to be treated like this.'

It was a point of view that he expressed in his book *Into the Bear Pit* some months later. Adding fuel to the Brookline fire, the release of extracts from the book in May 2000 caused a firestorm of their own. Blasting the American team for their behaviour, James condemned the rabble-rousing antics of the players and the part they played in stoking up the hostile atmosphere. Yet it was a relatively minor incident that created most headlines. Accusing Nick Faldo of undermining team morale in the run up to the match over an incident concerning Colin Montgomerie, James described in the book how he had thrown away a good luck note from the six-time major winner on the eve of the match. Faldo was incensed. Accusing the Ryder Cup captain of bringing the Ryder Cup and European Tour into disrepute, he demanded that disciplinary action be taken and after months of acrimony, finally got his way. James was removed from his position on the Tournament Players Committee and Faldo had his pound of flesh.

With Sam Torrance appointed European Captain for the 2001 match at The Belfry (subsequently postponed until 2002), it is hoped that the 'Battle of Brookline' will be as quickly forgotten as the 'War on the Shore' was a decade earlier. For the spirit of the Ryder Cup to survive, not only must the governing bodies of the game lend a hand, but so, too, must the players. Like most great sporting events of the modern era, the biennial matches can only prosper if the match remains, in the words of its founder Sam Ryder, 'a game for gentlemen'.

Whether it does or not, only time will tell. For the sake of everyone who enjoys the passion and pride engendered by the Ryder Cup, let us hope it does.

18

Strange gets the Belfry Blues

2002

THE BELFRY, SUTTON COLDFIELD, WEST MIDLANDS, ENGLAND

27–29 SEPTEMBER

No sporting event was affected by the events of September 11, 2001 quite as profoundly as the Ryder Cup. As the world struggled to come to terms with the terrorist attack on the World Trade Center in New York, the PGA of America and PGA of Europe were forced to decide whether the biennial match that was scheduled for The Belfry just two weeks later on September 28–30 should be cancelled or not. The decision was fraught with difficulty, and opinion was understandably split between those who said 'Golf must not give way to the terrorists' and those who believed that playing an international sporting event so soon after thousands of people had lost their lives in such horrific circumstances was completely unthinkable.

A disturbing silence descended on both organisations, leaving the media to speculate wildly on the final outcome. If the match was cancelled, should it be merely

Above: The flag shows 2001 but, as we all know, the devastating events of September 11, 2001 not only changed the thinking of the world but also resulted in the postponement of the Ryder Cup matches that year.

put off for a year or expunged from the record books entirely? And what about those players who had fought so hard to qualify? Should they be asked to qualify again? Both teams already had a significant number of out-of-form players and, should the qualification door be reopened, the final twelve would alter considerably, bringing the possibility of legal action from those left out. For example, Justin Leonard, hero of the 1999 victory at Brookline, came into form just too late to qualify automatically but looked a far better bet on paper than wild-card pick Paul Azinger, who was suffering with recurring back problems. Europe, which had young guns Ian Poulter and Justin Rose waiting on the sidelines, boasted more than its fair share of struggling players in Welshman Phillip Price, Swede Jesper Parnevik and even the injury-threatened Lee Westwood.

The permutations were endless and it came as a relief to all concerned when the decision was made to postpone the 34th Ryder Cup for twelve months to September 2002. From this point on, the biennial match would be played on even years and not odd as had happened since 1927. Both teams would remain the same as already selected and, in recognition of this, all signage at the Belfry would stay the same, proclaiming this to be the '2001 Ryder Cup'.

Above: A solemn Tiger Woods reflects on the tragedy of 9–11 during the opening ceremonies of the 2002 Ryder Cup matches. Once again, there were questions over his lack of enthusiasm for the whole event, but, like his hero Jack Nicklaus, Woods' determination to improve his playing record has grown with each match.

'I think keeping the two teams was the right thing to do', said Sergio Garcia, shortly after the decision was announced. 'Those players deserved to play in the Ryder Cup whatever anyone says.'

Tiger Woods also agreed that both teams should stay the same: 'I think that's the way it should be. You have to understand that it's probably not the two best teams we could have assembled, but then again who cares? After September 11, it puts things in perspective real quick for you.'

When the match finally went ahead, staged at The Belfry for the fourth time since 1985, security was of paramount concern, with more than 1000 volunteer stewards patrolling the course alongside large numbers of heavily armed police. Curtis Strange set a solemn and respectful tone at the opening ceremony. Gesturing toward the many flags that flew nearby he acknowledged the victims of '9/11', saying, 'Every country represented here lost citizens that day.'

Speaking to the press a short time later, Sam Torrance echoed his fellow captain's sentiment. 'I don't think we will ever forget why the matches were postponed but I've always said once the tee goes in the ground Friday morning, we're going to have a competitive match in the best traditions of the game. That is what makes golf special.' With both camps determined that the Ryder Cup would be as competitive as possible given the circumstances, the *Daily Telegraph* ran an eve-of-match headline saying: 'Let's say this at full volume, there is no link between the Ryder Cup or any golf tournament and Sept. 11th.'

Even with all the diplomatic sentiment expressed by the two team captains, the Ryder Cup would not be the Ryder Cup without its share of pre-match controversy. Media attention was focused squarely on world number one, Tiger Woods, and his every utterance made back-page news, especially when he suggested that he would rather win the American Express Championship in Ireland two weeks earlier than the Ryder Cup. Then, adding fuel to the fire, he described just how much his practice routine was affected by the number of social functions he and his fellow team members were expected to attend at the Cup. No surprises there either, but his words still made the headlines. Controversy was to dog the 26-year-old American star all week. Preferring to start his practice rounds at 6.30 a.m. – some two hours before the gates were opened to the paying public – he was portrayed as aloof and even unpatriotic. (The fact that he had cleared it with Curtis Strange and his fellow team members was never reported.)

Whether the pre-match publicity affected Woods' concentration is open to question, but, at the end of day one, his failure to win a single point had the press pack on both sides of the Atlantic baying for his blood. With veteran Paul Azinger as his partner in the opening fourball match on a dank autumn Friday morning, Woods' approach to the first found a greenside bunker after being disturbed by an errant camera shutter. Setting the tone for the day, his narrow 1-down defeat at the hands of Darren Clarke and Thomas Bjorn seem to unsettle him and his team. Woods found the afternoon foursomes equally gruelling and his 2 and 1 defeat at the hands of Sergio Garcia and a resurgent Lee Westwood left him and his partner Mark Calcavecchia scurrying back to the practice ground before night fell.

Tiger Woods was acknowledged as the greatest player of his generation, but his record in the event was woeful; he had registered just three points in twelve Ryder Cup matches. Not that Woods shouldered all the blame. Defeats for Davis Love and David Duval (4 and 3 against Westwood and Garcia) and Scott Hoch and Jim Furyk (4 and 3 against Montgomerie and Langer)

Left: Europe's Darren Clarke holes a monster putt at the par-5 seventeenth during the opening day's morning foursomes. This took him and teammate Thomas Bjorn 1-up, and they held on to beat Tiger Woods and Paul Azinger by that margin.

left the USA facing their worst start in more than three decades. Had it not been for a last-hole victory for Phil Mickelson and David Toms (1-up against the new pairing of Harrington and Fasth) then the pre-event favourites would have failed to register a single point.

Perhaps out of desperation, Strange decided to make wholesale changes to his afternoon foursome's line-up, with only Mickelson and Toms surviving the cull. Desperate to bounce back, the American team finally got into the match with wins for Hal Sutton and Ryder Cup wild card Sott Verplank (2 and 1 against Clarke and Bjorn) and Stewart Cink and Furyk (3 and 2 over the Irish pairing of Harrington and McGinley). With Mickelson and Toms managing to come back from three holes down with four to play against Montgomerie and Langer for a remarkable half, the USA shaded the afternoon foursomes 2½–1½. Uncle Sam was back with a vengeance.

Seeking to beat a US side that included six of the world's top-ranked golfers, Europe approached the

Above: Young guns Sergio Garcia and Lee Westwood take an early lead in their match against Tiger Woods and Davis Love III. Despite firing six birdies at the powerful American pair, they lost on the final green after the young Englishman missed a short putt to claim a half.

weekend with growing confidence but only managed a 2–2 draw in the morning foursomes. Garcia and Westwood beat Cink and Furyk 2 and 1, while Montgomerie and Langer shaded Verplank and Hoch by 1-up. Garcia described it as 'probably the worst Ryder Cup match in history'.

The signs were encouraging, but America was proving hard to nail down. Partnered by Davis Love III and no doubt inspired by the visit of former US president George Bush, Snr., Woods finally kicked into gear to defeat Clarke and Bjorn 4 and 3. He put his first point on the board, where it joined that of Mickelson and Toms, who were steadiness personified in their defeat of Ryder Cup rookies Pierre Fulke and Phillip Price.

Hoping to build on their narrow one-point lead, Europe could barely contain a resurgent US side in the afternoon fourballs. With the scoreboard going first one way then another, three of the four matches would be settled on the final green in front of the massed ranks of increasingly nervous home supporters. Lee Westwood, unrecognisable from the player who had tumbled from 4th to 148th in the world rankings, collected six birdies in his match against Woods and Love, but it was still not good enough to beat the world number one. With the match level going up the last, it would be his missed putt from four feet that handed the point to the Americans with Woods round in an estimated 64. 'It was a great match', said an exhausted Tiger Woods afterward. 'We all played well today.'

The same could be said about the indomitable Colin Montgomerie. The stalwart of the European side, he kept up his winning form, partnering Padraig Harrington in a 2 and 1 win over the previously undefeated Mickelson and Toms. Winning four successive holes from the second to race into a three-up lead, they survived a late onslaught from the two Americans, leaving Montgomerie with an enviable record of 3½ points from a possible 4. 'I've never played better than that', said the delighted Scot. 'And it had to be so because we were playing the second and sixth ranked players in the world.'

Another pair that raced into an early lead only to be pulled back were Swedish star Jesper Parnevik and his fellow countryman Niclas Fasth in their match against Calcavecchia and Duval. The out-of-form Parnevik had cut a forlorn figure on the practice ground throughout the week. He had been less than a mile away from the Twin Towers on September 11, and in the early hours of the Tuesday morning before the Cup he had woken up fearing that a terrorist attack had taken place – in fact, the rumbling he heard was a localised earthquake powerful enough to shake his Belfry hotel room. It was hardly the best preparation for a Ryder Cup; the normally flamboyant player relished the opportunity to get a match under his belt before the singles but was unable to stop the Americans winning 1-up on the eighteenth green.

Slowly but surely the momentum was swinging America's way. But in the last match left out on the course, McGinley and Clarke battled back from 2-down with four holes to play to earn a well-deserved half against Hoch and Furyk. In the gathering gloom that encircled the final green, McGinley won the hole by sinking a vital putt for par to ensure that Europe went into the singles level with the USA. Taking the applause of the patriotic gallery that filled the grandstands and the congratulations of his playing partner, he could have no idea that he would putt in exactly the same position twenty-four hours later.

As the crowds milled away from The Belfry, the overwhelming opinion in the media centre was that Europe had played well but failed to capitalise on their 3–1 lead on the first morning. Of course, they were still level on points, but momentum is everything in the Ryder Cup and it was the Americans who were in celebratory mood going into dinner that night. They had played poorly by their high standards but had not lost any ground on their rivals. Now all they needed was 6 points from 12 singles matches and old Sam's trophy would be heading back Stateside.

On paper, the result strongly favoured the Americans – they had a far superior record in the head-to-head matches, winning all but five of the singles series since the Ryder Cup began in 1927. This seemed to be reflected in the faces of the exhausted European team as they trooped in one by one to face the press. As with Clarke and McGinley, the pressure of the last few days was etched into their faces, despite the best efforts of captain Sam Torrance and his deputies to lift their spirits.

European hopes desperately needed a boost of inspiration, and thankfully for Torrance and his team, it was not long in coming. At Saturday evening's press conference, both captains were invited to read out their singles line-up for the following day. Taking his place next to Strange on the raised platform, Torrance took out the sheet of paper on which he had written his selection. Momentarily shielding his eyes from the spotlight of television cameras and photographers' flashes, he began with the name 'Monty'. Moments later Strange offered the name Hoch in reply. Then it went on: Garcia versus Toms, Clarke versus Duval, Langer versus Sutton, Harrington versus Calcavecchia, Bjorn versus Cink, Westwood versus Verplank.

By now there were audible gasps from the American journalists, with the smile on Sam's face growing wider by the moment. Every match seemed to favour Europe, but where was Tiger? The order of play continued on in agonising fashion with Fasth versus Azinger. Slowly the smile on Curtis Strange's face turned into a taut grin at the realisation that Torrance had outfoxed him. And still the list went on: Fulke versus Love, Price versus Mickelson, and, finally, Parnevik versus Woods.

By now the packed room was buzzing with fevered speculation. Not only had Torrance followed Ben Crenshaw's example of three years earlier by sending out his best players first, Strange had saved his biggest guns – Mickleson and Woods – for the final two matches. Of course, if the match went down to the wire – as Ryder Cup matches at The Belfry had a habit of doing – then his tactics were hard to argue against. But what if the match went Europe's way early on, effectively rendering his two biggest stars obsolete?

Looking like a contestant on the television show *Mastermind*, Strange shuffled uncomfortably in his black leather armchair. Surprised at the animosity in some of the questioning, the amiable American struggled to justify his selection to his increasingly sceptical countrymen. What he did not say is that the running order had been agreed with his team less than thirty minutes earlier with barely a dissenting voice – or that Woods was suffering with a high fever. 'I think Sam has thrown me a real curve ball', said Strange, and no one disagreed.

The huge roar that greeted Colin Montgomerie's appearance on the first tee gave a taste of the high drama to come. He won the first hole to take the lead, and neither he nor his team looked back all day as the scoreboards turned deepest European blue. Indeed, from the time Monty teed off at 11.15 a.m. it took an hour and twenty-one minutes before *any* American led in any match!

For the USA it was a timetable to disaster.

1.55 p.m. Monty secures Europe's first point after crushing veteran Scott Hoch 5 and 4. Europe leads 9–8.
2.22 p.m. David Toms takes a one-hole advantage over Sergio Garcia, giving the USA their first red number on the scoreboard.
2.44 p.m. Padraig Harrington defeats Mark Calcavecchia by 5 and 4 to extend Europe's advantage to 10–8.
2.54 p.m. Bernhard Langer, refreshed from not having played in the Saturday afternoon fourballs, completes a wonderful week by beating Hal Sutton by 4 and 3. Europe leads 11–8.

Above: The indomitable Bernhard Langer signals victory by 4 and 3 over the USA's Hal Sutton by birding the par-5 fifth. The two players would end up as opposing captains in the 2004 matches.

3.00 p.m. A consistent performer all week, PGA champion David Toms beats Garcia by 1-up after the Spaniard drove into water at the last. Europe leads 11–9.
3.16 p.m. Bravely holing out from eight-foot on the final green, David Duval secures a half point with Darren Clarke. Europe leads 11½ –9½.
3.38 p.m. With Jesper Parnevik level with Tiger Woods after 11 holes and Philip Price 3-up on Phil Mickelson after 12, Thomas Bjorn beats Stewart Cink to extend Europe's lead to 12½–9½.
4.09 p.m. Ryder Cup wild card Scott Verplank beats Lee Westwood by 2 and 1 to reduce the gap to 12½–10½.

Above: An unexpected point from the unlikely and quiet Welshman Phil Price as he beats Phil Mickelson of the USA 3 and 2 by birding the sixteenth par 4. Mickelson, as you might expect, looked bedazzled.

4.27 p.m. Niclas Fasth heads to the eighteenth tee holding a slender 1-up advantage on Paul Azinger. The US leads in just one match from the five remaining games left out on the course. Europe needs just two points to win the trophy but has four Ryder Cup rookies in play plus the out-of-form Parnevik. In contrast, the USA has four of the world's top-ten ranked golfers plus former PGA champion Azinger.

4.38 p.m. Phillip Price pulls off one of the greatest upsets in Ryder Cup history, defeating Phil Mickelson on the sixteenth green and bringing his team within one point of victory. Europe leads 13½–10½.

4.42 p.m. The winning point looks assured when Azinger bunkers his approach shot to the last. Fasth finds the edge of the green and looks certain of making par. Incredibly, Azinger holes out from the sand for a birdie and, with Fasth unable to hole his putt, secures an unlikely halved match! Europe leads 14–11 but the three remaining singles left out on the course are level.

4.48 p.m. Paul McGinley and Jim Furyk are all-square coming to the eighteenth. Having missed the green long and left, the Irishman chips up to nine-foot attempting to save par while Furyk sizes up exactly the bunker shot Azinger holed only minutes before.

4.52 p.m. In a heart-stopping moment for Sam Torrance and many of the European team gathered by the side of the green, Furyk comes within inches of repeating Azinger's miracle sand shot.

4.54 p.m. Facing a tricky side-hill putt, McGinley holes out to win the 34th Ryder Cup. With scenes reminiscent of Brookline, the Europeans rush to embrace the hero as the vast majority of the 35,000 crowd goes wild. Europe have secured a winning advantage of 14½–11½.

5.00 p.m. Amid scenes of wild celebration and popping champagne corks, a disconsolate Davis Love III expresses his displeasure at watching Garcia run all the way down the eighteenth fairway to tell Pierre Fulke the good news. With the green awash with players, the American, who is leading at the time, decides to concede the hole and offer his opponent a half. Europe leads 15–12.

5.18 p.m. Cutting a disconsolate figure, Tiger Woods concedes a five-putt on the final green to give Jesper Parnevik a deserved half point.

Final score: Europe 15½ – USA 12½.

Torrance's ploy of sending his best players out early proved to be a masterstroke. Europe won four of the first five matches and got a half in the remaining one. With Europe taking an early stranglehold this way, world number one Tiger Woods was left stranded in a dead contest that finished long after the European celebrations had started.

'What a team', a champagne-drinking Torrance told anyone who would listen. 'I led them to the water and they drank copiously.' As McGinley's teammates threw him into the lake fronting the eighteenth green, Torrance praised the parts that Montgomerie and Langer had played throughout the week: 'Monty was king of the castle. I have never seen him like that in any event. He's always been a great team man but this week he was incredible. The same can be said of Bernhard. He has so much experience that it makes it a very easy job to be his captain.'

Curtis Strange agreed: 'Seve was their leader for a long time – now it's Colin.' Then, in a sideswipe at some of his more senior players, he continued, 'Every team needs a leader, not only for their play but also for the way they handle themselves. He led by example and the others took their cue from him. He certainly did not disappoint this week.'

A dignified figure to the last, knowing the barrage of criticism that awaited any losing captain back in the United States, Strange congratulated Sam Torrance and his 'twelve lions', concluding, 'It was disappointing to lose but that certainly did not spoil the occasion for me. I feel sorry for the [American] players but you have to perform and we didn't. We didn't get the job done and that was that. The European team played the better golf so what more can I say.'

Considering the tragic circumstances that forced the cancellation of the 2001 Ryder Cup, this was a truly classic match. Played with intensity, passion and skill, it confirmed the Ryder Cup's position as one of *the* great sporting occasions.

Below: The Belfry crowd rises as Paul McGinley leaps with joy after sinking his birdie putt to secure a ½ point against Jim Furyk and thus victory over the USA.

Above: Paul McGinley is in the middle as the European team plus wives, caddies et al flood the eighteenth green after he sank his putt for the winning ½ point against Jim Furyk of the USA.

19

Europe Slays the Monster at Oakland Hills

2004

OAKLAND HILLS COUNTRY CLUB, BLOOMFIELD TOWNSHIP, MICHIGAN, USA

14–19 SEPTEMBER

It may not have been the 'War on the Shore' at Kiawah Island in 1991 or the 'Battle of Brookline' eight years later, but there was definitely an edge to the 34th Ryder Cup at Oakland Hills.

The mood was upbeat and the skies bright blue as Captain Hal Sutton introduced the American team at the Hollywood-style opening ceremony. With a team boasting seven players in the top fifteen of the world rankings, the Louisiana native welcomed Bernhard Langer and his European side with typical Southern courtesy, but he left no one in any doubt about which side he thought was the stronger that week. After all, he did have Tiger.

'Right now, I would settle for a win', he had said during the weeks leading up to the match, but as the fateful first day approached, Sutton proved surprisingly bullish. 'We're going in there on a mission',

declared the 1983 PGA champion, 'and we're not going to settle for second best'. At the pre-match conference he continued on the same theme. Dismissing the suggestion that Europe should be considered favourites after winning three of the last four encounters, the ebullient Sutton went straight on the attack:

> Everybody always speculates as to why the Europeans fight above their weight and why the Americans look like heavyweights and fight like featherweights. They add up the world ranking, and when you look at the US versus Europe, it's pretty lopsided, but one great thing about the game of golf is that David beats Goliath sometimes.

On paper, the American side was certainly among the most powerful ever put out. Phil Mickelson had answered his critics with a splendid victory in the

Masters in April and he was joined by Davis Love III, Jim Furyk, David Toms and Tiger Woods as the only major winners on either side. The remaining players were all PGA Tour winners, and even Stewart Cink, captain's pick along with Jay Haas, had won the week after he was selected at the NEC Invitational.

One question remained: how would Captain Hal get the best out of his most gifted player, Tiger Woods? The scale of the problem was obvious. Despite his last victory coming in the WGC World Match Play event more than seven months earlier in California, Tiger had shown himself almost unbeatable in the final stages of every tournament for which he was in contention. Yet in the Ryder Cup his record was a woeful 5–8–2. Like Nicklaus before him, he had been described as emotionally unsuited to the demands of team golf and his disappointing displays in previous fourball and foursome matches seemingly bore this out. And there was another difficulty: an eight-time major winner, Woods had been through the same number of partners in his previous 12 matches. This had become such a problem that it was widely known as the 'Tiger issue'.

Not surprisingly, Hal Sutton was determined to find a solution. Within weeks of being appointed captain, he asked for a face-to-face meeting with Tiger, at which he challenged him to live up to his billing as the top golfer in the world. In turn, said Sutton, he would provide a playing partner that would complement Woods' talents, along with an off-course itinerary that would not cut into the practice time that Tiger felt was essential for him to perform at his peak. As for who that partner would be, Sutton kept it secret right up until the very last moment.

On the eve of the match at Oakland Hills, Sutton felt strongly that home support would also weigh heavily in favour of his team. Noting that in the 77-year history of the Ryder Cup the USA had lost just twice on American soil – once at Muirfield Village in 1987 and then again at Oak Hill in 1995 – he called for a strong vocal showing from the expected 30,000 strong crowd. As for the individual games, he believed that most would be won or lost on the treacherously contoured greens of a course Ben Hogan once described as the 'monster' after his US Open victory there in 1951. 'The skill was to keep the ball below the hole', said Mickelson in support of his skipper before describing the entire American team as 'incredible putters'.

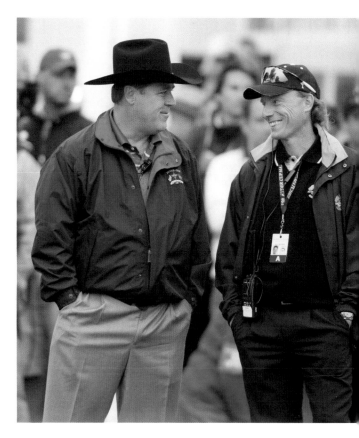

Above: Having played against each other in the 2002 singles, Hal Sutton (USA) and Bernhard Langer (Europe) face the ultimate challenge – captaincy! From day one, it all went wrong for Stetson-toting captain Sutton.

Whether his team were incredible putters or not, Bernard Langer had his own selection difficulties in the run-up to the Ryder Cup. He was unable to call upon players of the calibre of José Maria Olazábal, Nick Faldo, Ian Woosnam and Thomas Björn – all were unable to play because of injury or lack of form – and the Europeans had a distinctly inexperienced look about them with no major winners in the team for the first time since 1981.

Like Hal Sutton, the German had just two captain's picks available to him, and he was forced to choose between two talented young professionals, Luke Donald and Fredrik Jacobson. The place finally went to Donald, who rewarded him the following week with victory in the European Masters in Switzerland. Adding to his fast-growing reputation, this was Donald's second victory in Europe in two months

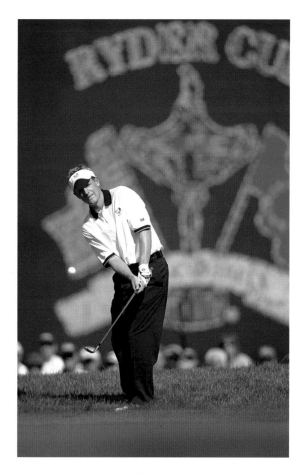

Above: Debutant Luke Donald of Europe chips onto the eighteenth green in his match against Chad Campbell. Known for his ice-cool demeanour, the talented young English professional looks set to play his part in the Ryder Cup for years to come.

following his win at the Scandinavian Masters at the end of July. The twenty-six-year-old Englishman, who now plied his trade on the PGA Tour, knew how to win and that would prove invaluable under the type of pressure exerted at the Ryder Cup.

Colin Montgomerie was also someone who knew how to win, but his selection was in question right up until the last moment. The problem was form, or lack of it. He came a lowly twenty-seventh in the European Order of Merit when the final two places were chosen at the BMW International in Germany. Rarely will a captain go down the list beyond twelfth or thirteenth place, and then only in exceptional circumstances. But as Langer was to prove at Oakland Hills a month later, he was no ordinary captain, and Monty was definitely

no ordinary wild card. The big Scot was pencilled in to make his seventh consecutive Ryder Cup appearance and Montgomerie would later say how his inclusion in the team literally saved his career.

How the news was greeted in the Sutton household is impossible to know. Certainly, no professional had scored more points than the fearsome 'Monty' over the past six matches and certainly no player was as intimidating to play against – especially if you happened to be an American! Many observers felt that his inclusion would make the simple difference between winning or losing – and how right they were.

Arriving at Detroit Metro Airport, the European team bristled with youthful confidence. In addition to the in-form Donald (twenty-six), the team included Sergio Garcia (twenty-four), who was a two-time winner on the PGA Tour, and fellow Spaniard Miguel Angel Jiménez, a four-time victor back in Europe. Even Ryder Cup first-timer Thomas Levet had won the Scottish Open in spectacular style in July before finishing in the top five in the British Open at Royal Troon a week later. As they gathered on the practice ground to have their photograph taken with Sam Ryder's golden chalice, the sound of laughter was never very far away.

Contrast this with American team members. Taking turns to be photographed with Captain Hal and the trophy, many grasped it tight, as if it was the nearest they would come to it that week. For many it was, as accusations of poor preparation began to emerge in the American media.

On Wednesday, for example, Tiger Woods went out so early that only Chris DiMarco was available to play with him. Later the same day, Phil Mickelson decided he wouldn't play a practice round at all, having already done the unthinkable and changed his equipment barely two weeks before the event! Then on Thursday, the day before the Ryder Cup was to be played, Mickelson was seen practising on the neighbouring North Course at Oakland Hills with only his caddie for company! If Sutton had a game plan, it was certainly not obvious from his players' preparations that week. 'It's a convoluted mess basically', he admitted, when asked about matching up players who used different make of golf balls. 'So I'm going to pair everyone I think personally and game-wise match up. They have to work it out between them.'

Bernhard Langer, by contrast, revealed the type of organisational expertise he had brought to his own career. Arranging his team into specific pairings for the practice rounds, he would often change partners around after nine holes as they practised both alternate shot and fourball. He also suggested that they ignore pre-tournament instructions not to fraternise with the paying public. Realising the last thing he wanted was a hostile Michigan crowd baying for his team's blood, he agreed that polite requests for autographs would be granted, as would the odd photograph, as long as they did not interfere with the flow of the game. In hindsight this was an absolute masterstroke.

As for being 'David' to the American team's 'Goliath', Langer appeared unconcerned, as did his team. 'We're completely happy being the underdogs', said a confident Lee Westwood. 'But if you look at the results week in and week out, we do as well as the Americans. Things have changed. As a European team, we now expect to go to the Ryder Cup and win it.' It was a theme eagerly taken up by Sergio Garcia. 'They have always been the favourites. But it's all about

coming together and playing good golf. And we've been able to raise our bar for that week the last several years.'

Then came the pairings themselves. Awarded the job of captain more than eighteen months earlier, Sutton had decided, on leaving the PGA of America offices, that he would pair Woods and Mickelson together in the opening match of the Ryder Cup. It was exactly the type of bold, instinctive move that was expected of him, but the huge risk involved in throwing together two such contrasting players – no matter how good they were – was obvious. Captain Hal, however, was convinced he had pulled off a masterstroke of his own and, as he said at the opening ceremony, 'history demands it'.

Not surprisingly, the opening fourball match between Woods and Mickelson against Montgomerie

Below: Colin Montgomerie, despite personal difficulties, sweeps his drive away off the first tee as Tiger Woods looks on. Setting the tone for the entire Ryder Cup match, he and Padraig Harrington would beat the 'dream team' pairing of Woods and Mickelson in the morning and afternoon of the opening day.

and Harrington was among the most eagerly anticipated games in Ryder Cup history. Setting the tone for the entire series, the players were only too aware of what was at stake as they set off down the opening hole at the 7,077-yard, par-70 South Course at Oakland Hills. If the 'Big Dog' American pairing steamrollered the formidable Europeans it could start a tidal wave that would be hard to hold back. But, as Sutton found throughout his own Ryder Cup career, some carefully laid plans have a way of going badly wrong. This was certainly the case that fateful Friday.

Admitting that the match against world number two Tiger Woods and world number four Phil Mickelson was really 'worth two points', Monty made a dream start against America's dream team. Having found the right-hand fairway trap with his drive, he clipped a

Below: Lee Westwood and Sergio Garcia came into the match at Oakland Hills as two of Europe's most experienced Ryder Cup competitors, despite their young age. Reprising their successful partnership of two years earlier, they helped provide the platform for an impressive win over a strong American team on home soil.

superb approach to six feet before holing the putt for a birdie-three. Following this with another at the short third after Harrington put his tee shot three feet away meant that Europe were now 2-up, and it would prove an unassailable lead.

It would be a difficult morning all round for Sutton. Sporting a huge black cowboy hat given to him by his team's caddies, he looked on in absolute frustration as it took eighty minutes of competitive play before any of his players won a hole! Dominating the action, Darren Clarke (partnered by Miguel Angel Jiménez) holed a four-foot putt on fourteen to beat Love and Chad Campbell to clinch the first point for Europe. Minutes later, Montgomerie stole the limelight from his Irish partner as he holed the winning putt to beat Woods and Mickelson 2 and 1. After Toms and Furyk lost 5 and 3 to the charismatic partnership of Garcia and Westwood, a halved match between Riley and Cink against McGinley and Donald was seen almost as a victory by the American camp.

Moving into the afternoon with a 3-point advantage, Europe picked up where they left off, taking early leads

in the first two matches. With Woods and Mickelson locking horns with the experienced pairing of Clarke and Westwood in the third of the foursomes, it was hoped they could produce some fireworks to help lift the almost silent crowd. Rising to the challenge, Tiger hit a superb approach at the par-5 second as the American pair finally took the lead. It was the first time that the Stars and Stripes had appeared on the leaderboard in more than six-and-a-half hours!

Not long after, they recorded their first point when DiMarco and Haas wrapped up victory at sixteen, beating Jimenez and Levet by 3 and 2. Sadly, the celebrations were short-lived as Love and Funk lost 4 and 2 to Montgomerie and Harrington. It was turning into a rout. The home team desperately needed something to go their way, and after Woods and Mickelson won the penultimate hole to go all-square, it finally looked like it might. What happened next was a microcosm of the entire Ryder Cup. Stepping onto the final tee, Mickelson contrived to carve his ball almost out-of-bounds down the left. Standing just feet away, Woods stared blankly into the distance. The resulting penalty drop effectively meant the match was lost and, as they shook hands on the home green, the golden pair were barely able to look at each other.

With Perry and Cink losing 2 and 1 to Garcia and Donald, the margin was now USA 1½–6½ Europe. It had been a disastrous day and Hal Sutton's 'shock-and-awe' tactics of partnering Woods and Mickelson together had backfired spectacularly. Lack of communication, different styles of play, even the type of golf ball they used were all cited as reasons for failure – especially when it was revealed that Mickelson had been practising on the North Course on Wednesday with Tiger's make of ball rather than playing together with him during the practice rounds on the much faster South Course greens. (As Lee Westwood said, somewhat prophetically, 'As a team, we tend to perform all the way through, and not just rely on any one individual.')

After just one day, the American media were out for blood but sensibly held back in case there was a distinct improvement on day two. There wasn't, and after setting a victory target of five clear points, the 'vast improvement' demanded by Hal Sutton proved as elusive as a John Daly veggie burger as Europe lost by a single point in the morning fourball matches.

Above: Having been defeated twice on the opening day, paired with greatest rival Phil Mickelson, Tiger Woods here enjoys a rare moment of success after he makes an eagle putt against Paul Casey of Europe in the final day singles. It was a struggle for both players as neither played well at all.

Urging his players to forget about Friday's success and focus on the job in hand, Langer must have been delighted by the way in which his team handled what was a potentially tricky morning. Unlike Hal Sutton, who had played all twelve members of his team, the European skipper didn't hesitate to leave three players – Paul Casey, Ian Poulter and David Howell – on the sideline. Supporting their fellow team members every step of the way, they would all be playing on day two.

With chants of 'U-S-A, U-S-A' ringing round the course after some early American success, the Europeans were put under the severest pressure yet. Perhaps this was the comeback Sutton had promised, but in the end Langer and his team managed to hold their collective nerve to come through relatively unscathed. Even victory for Tiger and Ryder Cup rookie Chris Riley over Clarke and Poulter by 4 and 3 and defeat for Monty and Harrington at the hands of Love and Cink failed to dent their confidence. Certainly the most gutsy win came from rookies Howell and Casey, who won the last two holes against Campbell and Furyk for a 1-up victory that sent a surge of confidence through their team. 'It changed everything', said Langer.

They had come through the eye of the storm and were now hot favourites to retain the trophy as the massive electronic scoreboard near the eighteenth green spelled out USA 4–8 Europe. Exhausted after his sterling effort, Montgomerie asked Langer to be rested for the afternoon alternate shot matches and the captain was happy to oblige. More surprisingly, Chris Riley cited the same mental exhaustion after his efforts in the morning and, inexplicably, Sutton agreed to his request, saying that his rookie was 'emotionally and physically drained'. The gasp from the US Press corps must have been audible in Captain Hal's home in Louisiana!

Any momentum the US team may have generated from winning the morning fourballs quickly disappeared. Setting the tone for the afternoon, Clarke and Westwood inflicted a heavy 5 and 4 defeat on Haas and DiMarco. Followed by wins for Garcia and Donald over Furyk and Funk and Harrington and McGinley over Woods and his latest partner, Davis Love III, the Ryder Cup was practically on the plane to Europe. Somewhat curiously, the only American win came after Mickelson and Toms defeated Jiménez and Levet by a margin of 4 and 3. Having personally bogeyed four out of six holes in the middle of the match turning victory into defeat, quite how Tiger received the news never made it beyond the secrecy of the American team room.

By Saturday evening, Captain Hal cut a defiant figure as he addressed the media. It was now USA 5–11 Europe with twelve singles to play. Ignominious defeat was staring him in the face and still he insisted that his preparation earlier that week had not been flawed. Asked if he thought his team should have practised more foursomes and fourball play rather than preparing as individuals, the way they would in the week of a major, he repeated the same answer he had given the night before: 'No!' 'I pushed them as hard as I could', he said in his own defence. 'We almost responded this morning and we lost energy after that.'

Perhaps the same could be said about the US captain as he prepared his team for one last effort on Sunday. In typical style, Sutton sent out his players in the order they qualified: Tiger Woods at number one, Mickelson at number two and Love III at number three. With Stewart Cink given the anchor role as last man out, Sutton's tactics were put under the microscope once more, but there was very little else he could do. He needed to get points on the scoreboard early, but as Woods, Mickelson and Love III had earned only one point each so far and Furyk and Campbell none, he had long since run out of options. Asked if he thought team USA could still win, he replied, 'I believe in my heart that they can. Whether they will or not is another story.'

Needing only three points to retain the Ryder Cup, Langer was asked how he felt about seeing Woods, Mickelson and Love III at the top of the line-up? 'I'm not scared at all', he said. 'I'm actually pretty sure and convinced that out of the first three matches, I'd be very surprised if we don't get two points.'

In the end he got 1½ points as Garcia toppled Mickelson 3 and 2. Clarke fought out an amiable half with his close pal Davis Love III and Paul Casey lost to a smiling Tiger Woods, also by 3 and 2. It was now only a matter of time as Europe edged closer and closer to victory. Easy victories for Jim Furyk and Chad Campbell over David Howell (6 and 4) and Luke Donald (5 and 4) respectively delayed the inevitable, but only for a matter of minutes as Lee Westwood closed out Kenny Perry by 1-up to retain the Ryder Cup.

Fittingly, it would be Colin Montgomerie – the man who almost missed out on Ryder Cup selection after a nightmare year – who finally clinched the historic European win. Arriving at the final green with a one-hole advantage against 2001 PGA champion David Toms, Monty found his ball perched on the right half of the green with a massive ridge between him and the hole. While Toms was not threatening to force a half, having left his approach short of the wickedly fast putting surface, two putts would give the Scot outright victory for his team. Not dissimilar to a chip he faced on the eighth green during his foursome match against Woods and Mickelson on Friday – and one he executed brilliantly – he took inordinate care and was rewarded. Rolling down to within five feet, it was greeted with huge cheers from both his teammates gathered by the side of the green and the now predominantly European supporters in the crowd. Even Toms brave par-saving putt could not spoil Monty's moment of glory. Stepping up to the treacherously fast putt as he had done so many times in his Ryder Cup career, he calmly slotted it home for a 1-up victory, and the celebrations could begin.

'When word came to me that Monty had won it, I was delighted', said Paul McGinley. 'It was almost his destiny to do it this time. No one is more deserving of holing a winning putt in the Ryder Cup than Monty. His contribution to the Ryder Cup down the years and again this week has been phenomenal.'

The final word was left to the European captain. 'Everyone's same goal was to win but we've achieved it much easier than I could have imagined', said Langer about the 18½–9½ margin of victory. 'We beat one of the strongest ever US teams on home soil. It all worked better than clockwork, beyond my wildest dreams.'

Captain Sutton must have wished he could join his friend, but back in the media centre the questioning was brusque and understandably critical. An empty chair on the stage where Tiger Woods was meant to sit remained empty as the rest of his team filed in behind Captain Sutton. For many it was a poignant reminder of just how disjointed the American team's efforts had

Below: 'Man of the moment' Colin Montgomerie drops his putter in disbelief that he managed to dig out a 1-up victory over David Toms of USA at the eighteenth.

Above: Irish supporters go mad as Paul McGinley beats Stewart Cink of the USA to clinch another valuable point for Europe during the final day's singles.

Right: Despite very negative press over his style of captaincy prior to the matches, Europe's captain-supreme Bernhard Langer showed everyone just how to execute sport's most demanding role.

been. Even when Woods joined them a short time later, it was hard not to conclude that this was a team made up of highly talented individuals who struggled to grasp the idea that the Ryder Cup is a team effort.

Defiant to the last, Sutton described how proud he was of his players and how they had played their hearts out and how he couldn't have asked for more. Indeed, he must have believed it, because he kept repeating it like a mantra every few minutes! Then came the half-hearted attempts to explain the US defeat. 'It's a lot tougher to be a captain than it is to be a player', he said, before admitting that his pairings had not borne fruit. 'I made mistakes and I take full responsibility for the mistakes that I made. I thought there was no bad way to pair our 12 guys. Obviously the pairings we sent out didn't create any charisma.'

As the microphone moved back and forth between the players like a perverse game of Russian roulette, it was left to Phil Mickelson to step into the firing line. After all, he had been the player to receive most criticism for his performances that week. 'When we get here we are under constant ridicule and scrutiny over our play', he said, trying to defend the indefensible. 'And not coming together as a team and all that stuff we know to be false. We want so badly to win this event that when we arrive on the first tee we don't play as though we have everything to gain and nothing to lose. We feel just the opposite almost.'

Far less forthcoming about the reasons behind the defeat, Tiger Woods preferred to answer questions about his own play that week. 'I thought we gelled', he said about his disastrous partnership with Phil Mickelson. 'We just didn't make enough putts.' The next question was hardly audible as the massed ranks of American journalists murmured to each other as they digested his inexplicable answer. The body language was the most visible clue to the abject disappointment of the team and their embattled captain. After all, these were world-class golf professionals used to success and the warm glow of the spotlight and here they were picking through the bones of defeat. It felt like an autopsy, and to make things worse, they could just about hear the European team celebrating victory and singing with their many supporters by the eighteenth green.

As the dust settles on Oakland Hills and moves to The K-Club in Ireland in 2006, perhaps they will remember what a bitter taste it was. Then imagine what a match we will have.

Records

1921
6 June

Gleneagles, Perthshire, Scotland
Captains: J.H. Taylor (GB & Ire.), E. French (US)

Great Britain & Ireland		United States	
Foursomes			
G. Duncan & A. Mitchell (halved)	½	W. Hagen & J. Hutchison (halved)	½
E. Ray & H. Vardon (5 & 4)	1	E. French & T. Kerrigan	0
J. Braid & J.H. Taylor (halved)	½	C. Hackney & F. McLeod (halved)	½
A.G. Havers & J. Ockendon (6 & 5)	1	W. Reid & G. McLean	0
J. Sherlock & Josh Taylor (1-up)	1	C. Hoffner and W. Mehlhorn	0
Singles			
G. Duncan (2 & 1)	1	J. Hutchison	0
A. Mitchell (halved)	½	W. Hagen (halved)	½
E. Ray	0	E. French (2 & 1)	1
J.H. Taylor	0	F. McLeod (1-up)	1
H. Vardon (3 & 1)	1	T. Kerrigan	0
J. Braid (5 & 4)	1	C. Hackney	0
A.G. Havers	0	W. Reid (2 & 1)	1
J. Ockendon (5 & 4)	1	G. McLean	0
J. Sherlock (3 & 2)	1	C. Hoffner	0
Josh Taylor (3 & 2)	1	W. Mehlhorn	0

GB & Ire. 10½	US 4½

1926
4–5 June

Wentworth Golf Club, Surrey, England
Captains: E. Ray (GB & Ire.), W. Hagen (US)

Great Britain & Ireland		United States	
Foursomes			
A. Mitchell & G. Duncan (9 & 8)	1	W. Hagen & J. Barnes	0
A. Boomer & A. Compston (3 & 2)	1	T. Armour & J. Kirkwood	0
A.G. Havers & G. Gadd (3 & 2)	1	W. Mehlhorn & A. Watrous	0
E. Ray & F. Robson (3 & 2)	1	C. Walker & F. McLeod	0
E.R. Whitcombe & H. Jolly (3 & 2)	1	E. French & J. Stein	0
Singles			
A. Mitchell (8 & 7)	1	J. Barnes	0
G. Duncan (6 & 5)	1	W. Hagen	0
A. Boomer (2 & 1)	1	T. Armour	0
A. Compston	0	W. Mehlhorn (1-up)	1
G. Gadd (8 & 7)	1	J. Kirkwood	0
E. Ray (6 & 5)	1	A. Watrous	0
F. Robson (5 & 4)	1	C. Walker	0
A.G. Havers (10 & 9)	1	F. McLeod	0
E.R. Whitcombe (halved)	½	E. French (halved)	½
H.J. Jolly (3 & 2)	1	J. Stein	0

GB & Ire. 13½	US 1½

1927
3–4 June

Worcester Country Club, Worcester, Massachusetts, USA
Captains: E. Ray (GB & Ire.), W. Hagen (US)

Great Britain & Ireland		United States	
Foursomes			
E. Ray & F. Robson	0	W. Hagen & J. Golden (2 & 1)	1
G. Duncan & A. Compston	0	J. Farrell & J. Turnesa (8 & 6)	1
A.G. Havers & H.J. Jolly	0	G. Sarazen & A. Watrous (3 & 2)	1
A. Boomer & C.A. Whitcombe (7 & 5)	1	L. Diegel & W. Mehlhorn	0
Singles			
A. Compston	0	W. Mehlhorn (1 hole)	1
A. Boomer	0	J. Farrell (5 & 4)	1
H.J. Jolly	0	J. Golden (8 & 7)	1
E. Ray	0	L. Diegel (7 & 5)	1
C.A. Whitcombe (halved)	½	G. Sarazen (halved)	½
A.G. Havers	0	W. Hagen (2 & 1)	1
F. Robson	0	A. Watrous (3 & 2)	1
G. Duncan (1 hole)	1	J. Turnesa	0

GB & Ire. 2½	US 9½

1929
26–27 April

Moortown Golf Club, Leeds, Yorkshire, England
Captains: G. Duncan (GB & Ire.), W. Hagen (US)

Great Britain & Ireland		United States	
Foursomes			
C.A. Whitcombe & A. Compston (halved)	½	J. Farrell & J. Turnesa (halved)	½
A. Boomer & G. Duncan	0	L. Diegel & A. Espinosa (7 & 5)	1
A. Mitchell & F. Robson (2 & 1)	1	G. Sarazen & E. Dudley	0
E.R. Whitcombe & T.H. Cotton	0	J. Golden & W. Hagen (2 holes)	1
Singles			
C.A. Whitcombe (8 & 6)	1	J. Farrell	0
G. Duncan (10 & 8)	1	W. Hagen	0
A. Mitchell	0	L. Diegel (8 & 6)	1
A. Compston (6 & 4)	1	G. Sarazen	0
A. Boomer (4 & 3)	1	J. Turnesa	0
F. Robson	0	H. Smith (4 & 2)	1
T.H. Cotton (4 & 3)	1	A. Watrous	0
E.R. Whitcombe (halved)	½	A. Espinosa (halved)	½

GB & Ire. 7	US 5

1931 26–27 June

Scioto Country Club, Columbus, Ohio, USA
Captains: C.A. Whitcombe (GB & Ire.), W. Hagen (US)

Great Britain & Ireland		United States	
Foursomes			
A. Compston & W.H. Davies	0	G. Sarazen & J. Farrell (8 & 7)	1
G. Duncan & A.G. Havers	0	W. Hagen & D. Shute (10 & 9)	1
A. Mitchell & F. Robson (3 & 1)	1	L. Diegel & A. Espinosa	0
S. Easterbrook & E.R. Whitcombe	0	W. Burke & W. Cox (3 & 2)	1
Singles			
A. Compston	0	W. Burke (7 & 6)	1
F. Robson	0	G. Sarazen (7 & 6)	1
W.H. Davies (4 & 3)	1	J. Farrell	0
A. Mitchell	0	W. Cox (3 & 1)	1
C.A. Whitcombe	0	W. Hagen (4 & 3)	1
B. Hodson	0	D. Shute (8 & 6)	1
E.R. Whitcombe	0	A. Espinosa (2 & 1)	1
A.G. Havers (4 & 3)	1	C. Wood	0
GB & Ire. 3		**US 9**	

1933 26–27 June

Southport & Ainsdale Golf Club, Southport, Lancashire, England
Captains: J.H. Taylor (GB & Ire.), W. Hagen (US)

Great Britain & Ireland		United States	
Foursomes			
P. Alliss & C.A. Whitcombe (halved)	½	G. Sarazen & W. Hagen (halved)	½
A. Mitchell & A.G. Havers (3 & 2)	1	O. Dutra & D. Shute	0
W.H. Davies & S. Easterbrook (1 hole)	1	C. Wood & P. Runyan	0
A.H. Padgham & A. Perry	0	E. Dudley & W. Burke (1 hole)	1
Singles			
A.H. Padgham	0	G. Sarazen (6 & 4)	1
A. Mitchell (9 & 8)	1	O. Dutra	0
A.J. Lacey	0	W. Hagen (2 & 1)	1
W.H. Davies	0	C. Wood (4 & 3)	1
P. Alliss (2 & 1)	1	P. Runyan	0
A.G. Havers (4 & 3)	1	L. Diegel	0
S. Easterbrook (1 hole)	1	D. Shute	0
C.A. Whitcombe	0	H. Smith (2 & 1)	1
GB & Ire. 6½		**US 5½**	

1935 28–29 September

Ridgewood Country Club, Ridgewood, New Jersey, USA
Captains: C.A. Whitcombe (GB & Ire.), W. Hagen (US)

Great Britain & Ireland		United States	
Foursomes			
A. Perry & J. Busson	0	G. Sarazen & W. Hagen (7 & 6)	1
A.H. Padgham & P. Alliss	0	H. Picard & J. Revolta (6 & 5)	1
W.J. Cox & E.W. Jarman	0	P. Runyan & H. Smith (9 & 8)	1
C.A. Whitcombe & E.R. Whitcombe (1 hole)	1	O. Dutra & K. Lafoon	0
Singles			
J. Busson	0	G. Sarazen (3 & 2)	1
R. Burton	0	P. Runyan (5 & 3)	1
R. Whitcombe	0	J. Revolta (2 & 1)	1
A.H. Padgham	0	O. Dutra (4 & 2)	1
P. Alliss (1 hole)	1	C. Wood	0
W.J. Cox (halved)	½	H. Smith (halved)	½
E.R. Whitcombe	0	H. Picard (3 & 2)	1
A. Perry (halved)	½	S. Parks (halved)	½
GB & Ire. 3		**US 9**	

1937 29–30 June

Southport & Ainsdale Golf Club, Southport, Lancashire, England
Captains: C.A. Whitcombe (GB & Ire.), W. Hagen (US)

Great Britain & Ireland		United States	
Foursomes			
A.H. Padgham & T.H. Cotton (4 & 2)	0	E. Dudley & B. Nelson	1
A.J. Lacey & W.J. Cox	0	R. Guldahl & T. Manero (2 & 1)	1
C.A. Whitcombe & D.J. Rees (halved)	½	G. Sarazen & D. Shute (halved)	½
P. Alliss & R. Burton (2 & 1)	1	H. Picard & J. Revolta	0
Singles			
A.H. Padgham & T.H. Cotton	0	E. Dudley & B. Nelson	1
A.H. Padgham	0	R. Guldahl (8 & 7)	1
S.L. King (halved)	½	D. Shute (halved)	½
D.J. Rees (3 & 1)	1	B. Nelson	0
T.H. Cotton (5 & 3)	1	T. Manero	0
P. Alliss	0	G. Sarazen (1 hole)	1
R. Burton	0	S. Snead (5 & 4)	1
A. Perry	0	E. Dudley (2 & 1)	1
A.J. Lacey	0	H. Picard (2 & 1)	1
GB & Ire. 4		**US 8**	

1947 — 1–2 November

Portland Golf Club, Portland, Oregon, USA
Captains: T.H. Cotton (GB & Ire.), B. Hogan (US)

Great Britain & Ireland		United States	
Foursomes			
T.H. Cotton & A. Lees	0	E. Oliver & L. Worsham (10 & 8)	1
F. Daly & C.H. Ward	0	S. Snead & L. Mangrum (6 & 5)	1
J. Adams & M. Faulkner	0	B. Hogan & J. Demaret (2 holes)	1
D.J. Rees & S.L. King	0	B. Nelson & H. Barron (2 & 1)	1
Singles			
F. Daly	0	E.J. Harrison (5 & 4)	1
J. Adams	0	L. Worsham (3 & 2)	1
M. Faulkner	0	L. Mangrum (6 & 5)	1
C.H. Ward	0	E. Oliver (4 & 3)	1
A. Lees	0	B. Nelson (2 & 1)	1
T.H. Cotton	0	S. Snead (5 & 4)	1
D.J. Rees	0	J. Demaret (3 & 2)	1
S.L. King (4 & 3)	1	H. Keiser	0
GB & Ire. 1		**US 11**	

1949 — 16–17 September

Ganton Golf Club, Scarborough, Yorkshire, England
Captains: C.A. Whitcombe (GB & Ire.), B. Hogan (US)

Great Britain & Ireland		United States	
Foursomes			
M. Faulkner & J. Adams (2 & 1)	1	E.J. Harrison & J. Palmer	0
F. Daly & K. Bousfield (4 & 2)	1	R. Hamilton & S. Alexander	0
C.H. Ward & S.L. King	0	J. Demaret & C. Heafner (4 & 3)	1
R. Burton & A. Lees (1 hole)	1	S. Snead & L. Mangrum	0
Singles			
M. Faulkner	0	E.J. Harrison (8 & 7)	1
J. Adams (2 & 1)	1	J. Palmer	0
C.H. Ward	0	S. Snead (6 & 5)	1
D.J. Rees (6 & 4)	1	R. Hamilton	0
R. Burton	0	C. Heafner (3 & 2)	1
S.L. King	0	C. Harbert (4 & 3)	1
A. Lees	0	J. Demaret (7 & 6)	1
F. Daly	0	L. Mangrum (4 & 3)	1
GB & Ire. 5		**US 7**	

1951 — 2–4 November

Pinehurst Country Club, Pinehurst, North Carolina, USA
Captains: A.J. Lacey (GB & Ire.), S. Snead (US)

Great Britain & Ireland		United States	
Foursomes			
M. Faulkner & D.J. Rees	0	C. Heafner & J. Burke (5 & 3)	1
C.H. Ward & A. Lees (2 & 1)	1	E. Oliver & H. Ransom	0
J. Adams & J. Panton	0	S. Snead & L. Mangrum (5 & 4)	1
F. Daly & K. Bousfield	0	B. Hogan & J. Demaret (5 & 4)	1
Singles			
J. Adams	0	J. Burke (4 & 3)	1
D.J. Rees	0	J. Demaret (2 holes)	1
F. Daly (halved)	½	C. Heafner (halved)	½
H. Weetman	0	L. Mangrum (6 & 5)	1
A. Lees (2 & 1)	1	E. Oliver	0
C.H. Ward	0	B. Hogan (3 & 2)	1
J. Panton	0	S. Alexander (8 & 7)	1
M. Faulkner	0	S. Snead (4 & 3)	1
GB & Ire. 2½		**US 9½**	

1953 — 2–3 October

Wentworth Club, Virginia Water, Surrey, England
Captains: T.H. Cotton (GB & Ire.), L. Mangrum (US)

Great Britain & Ireland		United States	
Foursomes			
H. Weetman & P. Alliss	0	D. Douglas & E. Oliver (2 & 1)	1
E.C. Brown & J. Panton	0	L. Mangrum & S. Snead (8 & 7)	1
J. Adams & B.J. Hunt	0	T. Kroll & J. Burke (7 & 5)	1
F. Daly & H. Bradshaw (1 hole)	1	W. Burkemo & C. Middlecoff	0
Singles			
D.J. Rees	0	J. Burke (2 & 1)	1
F. Daly (9 & 7)	1	T. Kroll	0
E.C. Brown (2 holes)	1	L. Mangrum	0
H. Weetman (1 hole)	1	S. Snead	0
M. Faulkner	0	C. Middlecoff (3 & 1)	1
P. Alliss	0	J. Turnesa (1 hole)	1
B.J. Hunt (halved)	½	D. Douglas (halved)	½
H. Bradshaw (3 & 2)	1	F. Haas	0
GB & Ire. 5½		**US 6½**	

1955 — 5–6 November

Thunderbird Ranch & Country Club, Palm Springs, California, USA
Captains: D.J. Rees (GB & Ire.), C. Harbert (US)

Great Britain & Ireland		United States	
Foursomes			
J. Fallon & J.R.M. Jacobs (1 hole)	1	C. Harper & J. Barber	0
E.C. Brown & S. Scott	0	D. Ford & T. Kroll (5 & 4)	1
A. Lees & H. Weetman	0	J. Burke & T. Bolt (1 hole)	1
H. Bradshaw & D.J. Rees	0	S. Snead & C. Middlecoff (3 & 2)	1
Singles			
C. O'Connor	0	T. Bolt (4 & 2)	1
S. Scott	0	C. Harbert (3 & 2)	1
J.R.M. Jacobs (1 hole)	1	C. Middlecoff	0
D.J. Rees	0	S. Snead (3 & 1)	1
A. Lees (3 & 2)	1	M. Furgol	0
E.C. Brown (3 & 2)	1	J. Barber	0
H. Bradshaw	0	J. Burke (3 & 2)	1
H. Weetman	0	D. Ford (3 & 2)	1
GB & Ire. 4		**US 8**	

1957 — 4–5 October

Lindrick Golf Club, Sheffield, Yorkshire, England
Captains: D.J. Rees (GB & Ire.), J. Burke (USA)

Great Britain & Ireland		United States	
Foursomes			
P. Alliss & B.J. Hunt	0	D. Ford & D. Finsterwald (2 & 1)	1
K. Bousfield & D.J. Rees (3 & 2)	1	A. Wall & F. Hawkins	0
M. Faulkner & H. Weetman	0	T. Kroll & J. Burke (4 & 3)	1
C. O'Connor & E.C. Brown	0	R. Mayer & T. Bolt (7 & 5)	1
Singles			
E.C. Brown (4 & 3)	1	T. Bolt	0
R.P. Mills (5 & 3)	1	J. Burke	0
P. Alliss	0	F. Hawkins (2 & 1)	1
K. Bousfield (4 & 3)	1	L. Hebert	0
D.J. Rees (7 & 6)	1	E. Furgol	0
B.J. Hunt (6 & 5)	1	D. Ford	0
C. O'Connor (7 & 6)	1	D. Finsterwald	0
H. Bradshaw (halved)	½	R. Mayer (halved)	½
GB & Ire. 7½		**US 4½**	

1959 — 6–7 November

Eldorado Country Club, Palm Desert, California, USA
Captains: D.J. Rees (GB & Ire.), S. Snead (US)

Great Britain & Ireland		United States	
Foursomes			
B.J. Hunt & E.C. Brown	0	R. Rosburg & M. Souchak (5 & 4)	1
D.J. Rees & K. Bousfield	0	J. Boros & D. Finsterwald (2 holes)	1
C. O'Connor & P. Alliss (3 & 2)	1	A. Wall & D. Ford	0
H. Weetman & D.C. Thomas (halved)	½	S. Snead & C. Middlecoff (halved)	½
Singles			
N.V. Drew (halved)	½	D. Ford (halved)	½
K. Bousfield	0	M. Souchak (3 & 2)	1
H. Weetman	0	R. Rosburg (6 & 5)	1
D.C. Thomas	0	S. Snead (6 & 5)	1
C. O'Connor	0	A. Wall (7 & 6)	1
D.J. Rees	0	D. Finsterwald (1 hole)	1
P. Alliss (halved)	½	J. Hebert (halved)	½
E.C. Brown (4 & 3)	1	C. Middlecoff	0
GB & Ire. 3½		**US 8½**	

1961
13–14 October

Royal Lytham & St Annes, St Annes, Lancashire, England
Captains: D.J. Rees (GB & Ire.), J. Barber (US)

Great Britain & Ireland		United States	
Foursomes: Morning			
C. O'Connor & P. Alliss (4 & 3)	1	D. Ford & G. Littler	0
J. Panton & B.J. Hunt	0	A. Wall & J. Hebert (4 & 3)	1
D.J. Rees & K. Bousfield	0	W. Casper & A. Palmer (2 & 1)	1
T.B. Haliburton & N.C. Coles	0	W. Collins & M. Souchak (1 hole)	1
Foursomes: Afternoon			
C. O'Connor & P. Alliss	0	A. Wall & J. Hebert (1 hole)	1
J. Panton & B.J. Hunt	0	W. Casper & A. Palmer (5 & 4)	1
D.J. Rees & K. Bousfield (2 & 1)	1	W. Collins & M. Souchak	0
T.B. Haliburton & N.C. Coles	0	J. Barber & D. Finsterwald (1 hole)	1
Singles: Morning			
H. Weetman	0	D. Ford (1 hole)	1
R.L. Moffitt	0	M. Souchak (5 & 4)	1
P. Alliss (halved)	½	A. Palmer (halved)	½
K. Bousfield	0	W. Casper (5 & 3)	1
D.J. Rees (2 & 1)	1	J. Hebert	0
N.C. Coles (halved)	½	G. Littler (halved)	½
B.J. Hunt (5 & 4)	1	J. Barber	0
C. O'Connor	0	D. Finsterwald (2 & 1)	1
Singles: Afternoon			
H. Weetman	0	A. Wall (1 hole)	1
P. Alliss (3 & 2)	1	W. Collins	0
B.J. Hunt	0	M. Souchak (2 & 1)	1
T.B. Haliburton	0	A. Palmer (2 & 1)	1
D.J. Rees (4 & 3)	1	D. Ford	0
K. Bousfield (1 hole)	1	J. Barber	0
N.C. Coles (1 hole)	1	D. Finsterwald	0
C. O'Connor (halved)	½	G. Littler (halved)	½
GB & Ire. 9½		**US 14½**	

1963
11–13 October

East Lake Country Club, Atlanta, Georgia, USA
Captains: J. Fallon (GB & Ire.), A. Palmer (US)

Great Britain & Ireland		United States	
Foursomes: Morning			
B. Huggett & G. Will (3 & 2)	1	A. Palmer & J. Pott	0
P. Alliss & C. O'Connor	0	W. Casper & D. Ragan (1 hole)	1
N.C. Coles & B.J. Hunt (halved)	½	J. Boros & A. Lema (halved)	½
D. Thomas & H. Weetman (halved)	½	G. Littler & D. Finsterwald (halved)	½
Foursomes: Afternoon			
D. Thomas & H. Weetman	0	W. Maxwell & R. Goalby (4 & 3)	1
B. Huggett & G. Will	0	A. Palmer & W. Casper (5 & 4)	1
N.C. Coles & G.M. Hunt (2 & 1)	1	G. Littler & D. Finsterwald	0
T.B. Haliburton & B.J. Hunt	0	J. Boros & A. Lema (1 hole)	1
Fourballs: Morning			
B. Huggett & D. Thomas	0	A. Palmer & D. Finsterwald (5 & 4)	1
P. Alliss & B.J. Hunt (halved)	½	G. Littler & J. Boros (halved)	½
H. Weetman & G. Will	0	W. Casper & W. Maxwell (3 & 2)	1
N.C. Coles & C. O'Connor	0	R. Goalby & D. Ragan (1 hole)	1
Fourballs: Afternoon			
N.C. Coles & C. O'Connor	0	A. Palmer & D. Finsterwald (3 & 2)	1
P. Alliss & B.J. Hunt	0	A. Lema & J. Pott (1 hole)	1
T.B. Haliburton & G.M. Hunt	0	W. Casper & W. Maxwell (2 & 1)	1
B. Huggett & D. Thomas (halved)	½	R. Goalby & D. Ragan (halved)	½
Singles: Morning			
G.M. Hunt	0	A. Lema (5 & 3)	1
B. Huggett (3 & 1)	1	J. Pott	0
P. Alliss (1 hole)	1	A. Palmer	0
N.C. Coles (halved)	½	W. Casper (halved)	½
D. Thomas	0	R. Goalby (3 & 2)	1
C. O'Connor	0	G. Littler (1 hole)	1
H. Weetman (1 hole)	1	J. Boros	0
B.J. Hunt (2 holes)	1	D. Finsterwald	0
Singles: Afternoon			
G. Will	0	A. Palmer (3 & 2)	1
N.C. Coles	0	D. Ragan (2 & 1)	1
P. Alliss (halved)	½	A. Lema (halved)	½
T.B. Haliburton	0	G. Littler (6 & 5)	1
H. Weetman	0	J. Boros (2 & 1)	1
C. O'Connor	0	W. Maxwell (2 & 1)	1
D. Thomas	0	D. Finsterwald (4 & 3)	1
B.J. Hunt	0	R. Goalby (2 & 1)	1
GB & Ire. 9		**US 23**	

1965   7–9 October

Royal Birkdale Golf Club, Southport, Lancashire, England
Captains: H. Weetman (GB & Ire.), B. Nelson (US)

Great Britain & Ireland		United States	
Foursomes: Morning			
L. Platts & P.J. Butler	0	J. Boros & A. Lema (1 hole)	1
D.C. Thomas & G. Will (6 & 5)	1	A. Palmer & D. Marr	0
B.J. Hunt & N.C. Coles	0	W. Casper & G. Littler (2 & 1)	1
P. Alliss & C. O'Connor (5 & 4)	1	K. Venturi & D. January	0
Foursomes: Afternoon			
D.C. Thomas & G. Will	0	A. Palmer & D. Marr (6 & 5)	1
P. Alliss & C. O'Connor (2 & 1)	1	W. Casper & G. Littler	0
J. Martin & J. Hitchcock	0	J. Boros & A. Lema (5 & 4)	1
B.J. Hunt & N.C. Coles (3 & 2)	1	K. Venturi & D. January	0
Fourballs: Morning			
D.C. Thomas & G. Will	0	D. January & T. Jacobs (1 hole)	1
L. Platts & P. Butler (halved)	½	W. Casper & G. Littler (halved)	½
P. Alliss & C. O'Connor	0	A. Palmer & D. Marr (6 & 4)	1
B.J. Hunt & N.C. Coles (1 hole)	1	J. Boros & A. Lema	0
Fourballs: Afternoon			
P. Alliss & C. O'Connor (2 holes)	1	A. Palmer & D. Marr	0
D.C. Thomas & G. Will	0	D. January & T. Jacobs (1 hole)	1
L. Platts & P.J. Butler (halved)	½	W. Casper & G. Littler (halved)	½
B.J. Hunt & N.C. Coles	0	K. Venturi & A. Lema (1 hole)	1
Singles: Morning			
J. Hitchcock	0	A. Palmer (3 & 2)	1
L. Platts	0	J. Boros (4 & 2)	1
P.J. Butler	0	A. Lema (1 hole)	1
N.C. Coles	0	D. Marr (2 holes)	1
B.J. Hunt (2 holes)	1	G. Littler	0
D.C. Thomas	0	T. Jacobs (2 & 1)	1
P. Alliss (1 hole)	1	W. Casper	0
G. Will (halved)	½	D. January (halved)	½
Singles: Afternoon			
C. O'Connor	0	A. Lema (6 & 4)	1
J. Hitchcock	0	J. Boros (2 & 1)	1
P.J. Butler	0	A. Palmer (2 holes)	1
P. Alliss (3 & 1)	1	K. Venturi	0
N.C. Coles (3 & 2)	1	W. Casper	0
G. Will	0	G. Littler (2 & 1)	1
B.J. Hunt	0	D. Marr (1 hole)	1
L. Platts (1 hole)	1	T. Jacobs	0
GB & Ire. 12½		**US 19½**	

1967   20–22 October

Champions Golf Club, Houston, Texas, USA
Captains: D.J. Rees (GB & Ire.), B. Hogan (US)

Great Britain & Ireland		United States	
Foursomes: Morning			
B. Huggett & G. Will (halved)	½	W. Casper & J. Boros (halved)	½
P. Alliss & C. O'Connor	0	A. Palmer & G. Dickinson (2 & 1)	1
A. Jacklin & D.C. Thomas (4 & 3)	1	D. Sanders & G. Brewer	0
B.J. Hunt & N.C. Coles	0	R. Nichols & J. Pott (6 & 5)	1
Foursomes: Afternoon			
B. Huggett & G. Will	0	W. Casper & J. Boros (1 hole)	1
M. Gregson & H. Boyle	0	G. Dickinson & A. Palmer (5 & 4)	1
A. Jacklin & D.C. Thomas (3 & 2)	1	G. Littler & A. Geiberger	0
P. Alliss & C. O'Connor	0	R. Nichols & J. Pott (2 & 1)	1
Fourballs: Morning			
P. Alliss & C. O'Connor	0	W. Casper & G. Brewer (3 & 2)	1
B.J. Hunt & N.C. Coles	0	R. Nichols & J. Pott (1 hole)	1
A. Jacklin & D.C. Thomas	0	G. Littler & A. Geiberger (1 hole)	1
B. Huggett & G. Will	0	G. Dickinson & D. Sanders (3 & 2)	1
Fourballs: Afternoon			
B.J. Hunt & N.C. Coles	0	W. Casper & G. Brewer (5 & 3)	1
P. Alliss & M. Gregson	0	G. Dickinson & D. Sanders (3 & 2)	1
G. Will & H. Boyle	0	A. Palmer & J. Boros (1 hole)	1
A. Jacklin & D.C. Thomas (halved)	½	G. Littler & A. Geiberger (halved)	½
Singles: Morning			
H. Boyle	0	G. Brewer (4 & 3)	1
P. Alliss	0	W. Casper (2 & 1)	1
A. Jacklin	0	A. Palmer (3 & 2)	1
B. Huggett (1 hole)	1	J. Boros	0
N.C. Coles (2 & 1)	1	D. Sanders	0
M. Gregson	0	A. Geiberger (4 & 2)	1
D.C. Thomas (halved)	½	G. Littler (halved)	½
B.J. Hunt (halved)	½	R. Nichols (halved)	½
Singles: Afternoon			
B. Huggett	0	A. Palmer (5 & 3)	1
P. Alliss (2 & 1)	1	G. Brewer	0
A. Jacklin	0	G. Dickinson (3 & 2)	1
C. O'Connor	0	R. Nichols (3 & 2)	1
G. Will	0	J. Pott (3 & 1)	1
M. Gregson	0	A. Geiberger (2 & 1)	1
B.J. Hunt (halved)	½	J. Boros (halved)	½
N.C. Coles (2 & 1)	1	D. Sanders	0
GB & Ire. 8½		**US 23½**	

1969   18–20 September

Royal Birkdale Golf Club, Southport, Lancashire, England
Captains: E.C. Brown (GB & Ire.), S. Snead (US)

Great Britain & Ireland		United States	
Foursomes: Morning			
N.C. Coles & B. Huggett (3 & 2)	1	M. Barber & R. Floyd	0
B. Gallacher & M. Bembridge (2 & 1)	1	L. Trevino & K. Still	0
A. Jacklin & P. Townsend (3 & 1)	1	D. Hill & T. Aaron	0
C. O'Connor & P. Alliss (halved)	½	W. Casper & F. Beard (halved)	½
Foursomes: Afternoon			
N.C. Coles & B. Huggett	0	D. Hill & T. Aaron (1 hole)	1
B. Gallacher & M. Bembridge	0	L. Trevino & G. Littler (1 hole)	1
A. Jacklin & P. Townsend (1 hole)	1	W. Casper & F. Beard	0
P.J. Butler & B.J. Hunt	0	J. Nicklaus & D. Sikes (1 hole)	1
Fourballs: Morning			
C. O'Connor & P. Townsend (1 hole)	1	D. Hill & D. Douglass	0
B. Huggett & G.A. Caygill (halved)	½	R. Floyd & M. Barber (halved)	½
B. Barnes & P. Alliss	0	L. Trevino & G. Littler (1 hole)	1
A. Jacklin & N.C. Coles (1 hole)	1	J. Nicklaus & D. Sikes	0
Fourballs: Afternoon			
P.J. Butler & P. Townsend	0	W. Casper & F. Beard (2 holes)	1
B. Huggett & B. Gallacher	0	D. Hill & K. Still (2 & 1)	1
M. Bembridge & B.J. Hunt (halved)	½	T. Aaron & R. Floyd (halved)	½
A. Jacklin & N.C. Coles (halved)	½	L. Trevino & M. Barber (halved)	½
Singles: Morning			
P. Alliss	0	L. Trevino (2 & 1)	1
P. Townsend	0	D. Hill (5 & 4)	1
N.C. Coles (1 hole)	1	T. Aaron	0
B. Barnes	0	W. Casper (1 hole)	1
C. O'Connor (5 & 4)	1	F. Beard	0
M. Bembridge (1 hole)	1	K. Still	0
P.J. Butler (1 hole)	1	R. Floyd	0
A. Jacklin (4 & 3)	1	J. Nicklaus	0
Singles: Afternoon			
B. Barnes	0	D. Hill (4 & 2)	1
B. Gallacher (4 & 3)	1	L. Trevino	0
M. Bembridge	0	M. Barber (7 & 6)	1
P.J. Butler (3 & 2)	1	D. Douglass	0
N.C. Coles	0	D. Sikes (4 & 3)	1
C. O'Connor	0	G. Littler (2 & 1)	1
B. Huggett (halved)	½	W. Casper (halved)	½
A. Jacklin (halved)	½	J. Nicklaus (halved)	½
GB & Ire. 16		**US 16**	

1971   16–18 September

Old Warson Country Club, St Louis, Missouri, USA
Captains: E.C. Brown (GB & Ire.), J. Hebert (US)

Great Britain & Ireland		United States	
Foursomes: Morning			
N.C. Coles & C. O'Connor (2 & 1)	1	W. Casper & M. Barber	0
P. Townsend & P. Oosterhuis	0	A. Palmer & G. Dickinson (1 hole)	1
B. Huggett & A. Jacklin (3 & 2)	1	J. Nicklaus & D. Stockton	0
M. Bembridge & P.J. Butler (1 hole)	1	C. Coody & F. Beard	0
Foursomes: Afternoon			
H. Bannerman & B. Gallacher (2 & 1)	1	W. Casper & M. Barber	0
P. Townsend & P. Oosterhuis	0	A. Palmer & G. Dickinson (1 hole)	1
B. Huggett & A. Jacklin (halved)	½	L. Trevino & M. Rudolph (halved)	½
M. Bembridge & P.J. Butler	0	J. Nicklaus & J.C. Snead (5 & 3)	1
Fourballs: Morning			
C. O'Connor & B. Barnes	0	L. Trevino & M. Rudolph (2 & 1)	1
N.C. Coles & J. Garner	0	F. Beard & J.C. Snead (2 & 1)	1
P. Oosterhuis & B. Gallacher	0	A. Palmer & G. Dickinson (5 & 4)	1
P. Townsend & H. Bannerman	0	J. Nicklaus & G. Littler (2 & 1)	1
Fourballs: Afternoon			
B. Gallacher & P. Oosterhuis (1 hole)	1	L. Trevino & W. Casper	0
A. Jacklin & B. Huggett	0	G. Littler & J.C. Snead (2 & 1)	1
P. Townsend & H. Bannerman	0	A. Palmer & J. Nicklaus (1 hole)	1
N.C. Coles & C. O'Connor (halved)	½	C. Coody & F. Beard (halved)	½
Singles: Morning			
A. Jacklin	0	L. Trevino (1 hole)	1
B. Gallacher (halved)	½	D. Stockton (halved)	½
B. Barnes (1 hole)	1	M. Rudolph	0
P. Oosterhuis (4 & 3)	1	G. Littler	0
P. Townsend	0	J. Nicklaus (3 & 2)	1
C. O'Connor	0	G. Dickinson (5 & 4)	1
H. Bannerman (halved)	½	A. Palmer (halved)	½
N.C. Coles (halved)	½	F. Beard (halved)	½
Singles: Afternoon			
B. Huggett	0	L. Trevino (7 & 6)	1
A. Jacklin	0	J.C. Snead (1 hole)	1
B. Barnes (2 & 1)	1	M. Barber	0
P. Townsend	0	D. Stockton (1 hole)	1
B. Gallacher (2 & 1)	1	C. Coody	0
N.C. Coles	0	J. Nicklaus (5 & 3)	1
P. Oosterhuis (3 & 2)	1	A. Palmer	0
H. Bannerman (2 & 1)	1	G. Dickinson	0
GB & Ire. 13½		**US 18½**	

1973

20–22 September

Muirfield, Gullane, Scotland
Captains: B.J. Hunt (GB & Ire.), J. Burke (US)

GB & Ireland		United States	
Foursomes: Morning			
B. Barnes & B. Gallacher (1 hole)	1	L. Trevino & W. J. Casper	0
C. O'Connor & N.C. Coles (3 & 2)	1	T. Weiskopf & J.C. Snead	0
A. Jacklin & P. Oosterhuis (halved)	½	J. Rodriguez & L. Graham (halved)	½
M. Bembridge & E. Polland	0	J. Nicklaus & A. Palmer (6 & 5)	1
Fourballs: Afternoon			
B. Barnes & B. Gallacher (5 & 4)	1	T. Aaron & G. Brewer	0
M. Bembridge & B. Huggett (3 & 1)	1	A. Palmer & J. Nicklaus	0
A. Jacklin & P. Oosterhuis (3 & 1)	1	T. Weiskopf & W. Casper	0
C. O'Connor & N.C. Coles	0	L. Trevino & H. Blancas (2 & 1)	1
Foursomes: Morning			
B. Barnes & P.J. Butler	0	J. Nicklaus & T. Weiskopf (1 hole)	1
P. Oosterhuis & A. Jacklin (2 holes)	1	A. Palmer & D. Hill	0
M. Bembridge & B. Huggett (5 & 4)	1	J. Rodriguez & L. Graham	0
N.C. Coles & C. O'Connor	0	L. Trevino & W. Casper (2 & 1)	1
Fourballs: Afternoon			
B. Barnes & P.J. Butler	0	J.C. Snead & A. Palmer (2 holes)	1
A. Jacklin & P. Oosterhuis	0	G. Brewer & W. Casper (3 & 2)	1
C. Clark & E. Polland	0	J. Nicklaus & T. Weiskopf (3 & 2)	1
M. Bembridge & B. Huggett (halved)	½	L. Trevino & H. Blancas (halved)	½
Singles: Morning			
B. Barnes	0	W. Casper (2 & 1)	1
B. Gallacher	0	T. Weiskopf (3 & 1)	1
P.J. Butler	0	H. Blancas (5 & 4)	1
A. Jacklin (3 & 1)	1	T. Aaron	0
N.C. Coles (halved)	½	G. Brewer (halved)	½
C. O'Connor	0	J.C. Snead (1 hole)	1
M. Bembridge (halved)	½	J. Nicklaus (halved)	½
P. Oosterhuis (halved)	½	L. Trevino (halved)	½
Singles: Afternoon			
B. Huggett (4 & 2)	1	H. Blancas	0
B. Barnes	0	J.C. Snead (3 & 1)	1
B. Gallacher	0	G. Brewer (6 & 5)	1
A. Jacklin	0	W. Casper (2 & 1)	1
N.C. Coles	0	L. Trevino (6 & 5)	1
C. O'Connor (halved)	½	T. Weiskopf (halved)	½
M. Bembridge	0	J. Nicklaus (2 holes)	1
P. Oosterhuis (4 & 2)	1	A. Palmer	0
GB & Ire. 13		**US 19**	

1975

19–21 September

Laurel Valley Golf Club, Ligonier, Pennsylvania, USA
Captains: B.J. Hunt (GB & Ire.), A. Palmer (US)

GB & Ireland		United States	
Foursomes: Morning			
B. Barnes & B. Gallacher	0	J. Nicklaus & T. Weiskopf (5 & 4)	1
N. Wood & M. Bembridge	0	G. Littler & H. Irwin (4 & 3)	1
A. Jacklin & P. Oosterhuis	0	A. Geiberger & J. Miller (3 & 1)	1
T. Horton & J. O'Leary	0	L. Trevino & J.C. Snead (2 & 1)	1
Fourballs: Afternoon			
P. Oosterhuis & A. Jacklin (2 & 1)	1	W. Casper & R. Floyd	0
E. Darcy & C. O'Connor, Jr.	0	T. Weiskopf & L. Graham (3 & 2)	1
B. Barnes & B. Gallacher (halved)	½	J. Nicklaus & R. Murphy (halved)	½
T. Horton & J. O'Leary	0	L. Trevino & H. Irwin (2 & 1)	1
Fourballs: Morning			
P. Oosterhuis & A. Jacklin (halved)	½	W. Casper & J. Miller (halved)	½
T. Horton & N. Wood	0	J. Nicklaus & J.C. Snead (4 & 2)	1
B. Barnes & B. Gallacher	0	G. Littler & L. Graham (5 & 3)	1
E. Darcy & G.L. Hunt (halved)	½	A. Geiberger & R. Floyd (halved)	½
Foursomes: Afternoon			
A. Jacklin & B. Barnes (3 & 2)	1	L. Trevino & R. Murphy	0
C. O'Connor, Jr. & J. O'Leary	0	T. Weiskopf & J. Miller (5 & 3)	1
P. Oosterhuis & M. Bembridge	0	H. Irwin & W. Casper (3 & 2)	1
E. Darcy & G.L. Hunt	0	A. Geiberger & L. Graham (3 & 2)	1
Singles: Morning			
A. Jacklin	0	R. Murphy (2 & 1)	1
P. Oosterhuis (2 holes)	1	J. Miller	0
B. Gallacher (halved)	½	L. Trevino (halved)	½
T. Horton (halved)	½	H. Irwin (halved)	½
B. Huggett	0	G. Littler (4 & 2)	1
E. Darcy	0	W. Casper (3 & 2)	1
G.L. Hunt	0	T. Weiskopf (5 & 3)	1
B. Barnes (4 & 2)	1	J. Nicklaus	0
Singles: Afternoon			
A. Jacklin	0	R. Floyd (1 hole)	1
P. Oosterhuis (3 & 2)	1	C. Snead	0
B. Gallacher (halved)	½	A. Geiberger (halved)	½
T. Horton (2 & 1)	1	L. Graham	0
J. O'Leary	0	H. Irwin (2 & 1)	1
M. Bembridge	0	R. Murphy (2 & 1)	1
N. Wood (2 & 1)	1	L. Trevino	0
B. Barnes (2 & 1)	1	J. Nicklaus	0
GB & Ire. 11		**US 21**	

1977

15–17 September

Royal Lytham & St Annes, St Annes, Lancashire, England
Captains: B. Huggett (GB & Ire.), D. Finsterwald (US)

GB & Ireland		United States	
Foursomes			
B. Gallacher & B. Barnes	0	L. Wadkins & H. Irwin (3 & 1)	1
N.C. Coles & P. Dawson	0	D. Stockton & M. McGee (1 hole)	1
N. Faldo & P. Oosterhuis (2 & 1)	1	R. Floyd & L. Graham	0
E. Darcy & A. Jacklin (halved)	½	E. Sneed & D. January (halved)	½
T. Horton & M. James	0	J. Nicklaus & T. Watson (5 & 4)	1
Fourballs			
B. Barnes & T. Horton	0	T. Watson & H. Green (5 & 4)	1
N.C. Coles & P. Dawson	0	E. Sneed & L. Wadkins (5 & 3)	1
N. Faldo & P. Oosterhuis (3 & 1)	1	J. Nicklaus & R. Floyd	0
A. Jacklin & E. Darcy	0	D. Hill & D. Stockton (5 & 3)	1
M. James & K. Brown	0	H. Irwin & L. Graham (1 hole)	1
Singles			
H. Clark	0	L. Wadkins (4 & 3)	1
N.C. Coles	0	L. Graham (5 & 3)	1
P. Dawson (5 & 4)	1	D. January	0
B. Barnes (1 hole)	1	H. Irwin	0
T. Horton	0	D. Hill (5 & 4)	1
B. Gallacher (1 hole)	1	J. Nicklaus	0
E. Darcy	0	H. Green (1 hole)	1
M. James	0	R. Floyd (2 & 1)	1
N. Faldo (1 hole)	1	T. Watson	0
P. Oosterhuis (2 holes)	1	J. McGee	0

| GB & Ire. 7½ | | US 12½ | |

1979

14–16 September

The Greenbrier, White Sulphur Springs, West Virginia, USA
Captains: J. Jacobs (Europe), W. Casper (US)

Europe		United States	
Foursomes: Morning			
A. Garrido & S. Ballesteros	0	L. Wadkins & L. Nelson (2 & 1)	1
K. Brown & M. James	0	L. Trevino & F. Zoeller (3 & 2)	1
P. Oosterhuis & N. Faldo	0	A. Bean & L. Elder (2 & 1)	1
B. Gallacher & B. Barnes (2 & 1)	1	H. Irwin & J. Mahaffey	0
Foursomes: Afternoon			
K. Brown & D. Smyth	0	H. Irwin & T. Kite (7 & 6)	1
S. Ballesteros & A. Garrido (3 & 2)	1	F. Zoeller & H. Green	0
A. Lyle & A. Jacklin (halved)	½	L. Trevino & G. Morgan (halved)	½
B. Gallacher & B. Barnes	0	L. Wadkins & L. Nelson (4 & 3)	1
Foursomes: Morning			
A. Jacklin & A. Lyle (5 & 4)	1	L. Elder & J. Mahaffey	0
N. Faldo & P. Oosterhuis (6 & 5)	1	A. Bean & T. Kite	0
B. Gallacher & B. Barnes (2 & 1)	1	F. Zoeller & M. Hayes	0
S. Ballesteros & A. Garrido	0	L. Wadkins & L. Nelson (3 & 2)	1
Fourballs: Afternoon			
S. Ballesteros & A. Garrido	0	L. Wadkins & L. Nelson (5 & 4)	1
A. Jacklin & A. Lyle	0	H. Irwin & T. Kite (1 hole)	1
B. Gallacher & B. Barnes (3 & 2)	1	L. Trevino & F. Zoeller	0
N. Faldo & P. Oosterhuis (1 hole)	1	L. Elder & M. Hayes	0
Singles: Morning			
B. Gallacher (3 & 2)	1	L. Wadkins	0
S. Ballesteros	0	L. Nelson (3 & 2)	1
A. Jacklin	0	T. Kite (1 hole)	1
A. Garrido	0	M. Hayes (1 hole)	1
M. King	0	A. Bean (4 & 3)	1
B. Barnes	0	J. Mahaffey (1 hole)	1
Singles: Afternoon			
N. Faldo (3 & 2)	1	L. Elder	0
D. Smyth	0	H. Irwin (5 & 3)	1
P. Oosterhuis	0	H. Green (2 holes)	1
K. Brown (1 hole)	1	F. Zoeller	0
A. Lyle	0	L. Trevino (2 & 1)	1
M. James (injured, halved)	½	G. Morgan (halved, match not played)	½

| Europe 11 | | US 17 | |

1981   18–20 September

Walton Heath Golf Club, Surrey, England
Captains: J. Jacobs (Europe), D. Marr (US)

Europe		United States	
Foursomes: Morning			
B. Langer & M. Pinero	0	L. Trevino & L. Nelson (1 hole)	1
A. Lyle & M. James (2 & 1)	1	B. Rogers & B. Lietzke	0
B. Gallacher & D. Smyth (3 and 2)	1	H. Irwin & R. Floyd	0
P. Oosterhuis & N. Faldo	0	T. Watson & J. Nicklaus (4 & 3)	1
Fourballs: Afternoon			
S. Torrance & H. Clark (halved)	½	T. Kite & J. Miller (halved)	½
A. Lyle & M. James (3 & 2)	1	B. Crenshaw & J. Pate	0
D. Smyth & J.M. Cañizares (6 & 5)	1	B. Rogers & B. Lietzke	0
B. Gallacher & E. Darcy	0	H. Irwin & R. Floyd (2 & 1)	1
Fourballs: Morning			
N. Faldo & S. Torrance	0	L. Trevino & J. Pate (7 & 5)	1
A. Lyle & M. James	0	L. Nelson & T. Kite (1 hole)	1
B. Langer & M. Pinero (2 & 1)	1	R. Floyd & H. Irwin	0
J.M. Cañizares & D. Smyth	0	J. Nicklaus & T. Watson (3 & 2)	1
Foursomes: Afternoon			
P. Oosterhuis & S. Torrance	0	L. Trevino & J. Pate (2 & 1)	1
B. Langer & M. Pinero	0	J. Nicklaus & T. Watson (3 & 2)	1
A. Lyle & M. James	0	B. Rogers & R. Floyd (3 & 2)	1
D. Smyth & B. Gallacher	0	T. Kite & L. Nelson (3 & 2)	1
Singles			
S. Torrance	0	L. Trevino (5 & 3)	1
A. Lyle	0	T. Kite (3 & 2)	1
B. Gallacher (halved)	½	B. Rogers (halved)	½
M. James	0	L. Nelson (2 holes)	1
D. Smyth	0	B. Crenshaw (6 & 4)	1
B. Langer (halved)	½	B. Lietzke (halved)	½
M. Pinero (4 & 2)	1	J. Pate	0
J.M. Cañizares	0	H. Irwin (1 hole)	1
N. Faldo (2 & 1)	1	J. Miller	0
H. Clark (4 & 3)	1	T. Watson	0
P. Oosterhuis	0	R. Floyd (1 hole)	1
E. Darcy	0	J. Nicklaus (5 & 3)	1
Europe 9½		**US 18½**	

1983   14–16 October

PGA National Golf Club, Palm Beach Gardens, Florida, USA
Captains: A. Jacklin (Europe), J. Nicklaus (US)

Europe		United States	
Foursomes: Morning			
B. Gallacher & A. Lyle	0	T. Watson & B. Crenshaw (5 & 4)	1
N. Faldo & B. Langer (4 & 2)	1	L. Wadkins & C. Stadler	0
J.M. Cañizares & S. Torrance (4 & 3)	1	R. Floyd & B. Gilder	0
S. Ballesteros & P. Way	0	T. Kite & C. Peete (2 & 1)	1
Fourballs: Afternoon			
B. Waites & K. Brown (2 & 1)	1	G. Morgan & F. Zoeller	0
N. Faldo & B. Langer	0	T. Watson & J. Haas (2 & 1)	1
S. Ballesteros & P. Way (1 hole)	1	R. Floyd & C. Strange	0
S. Torrance & I. Woosnam (halved)	½	B. Crenshaw & C. Peete (halved)	½
Fourballs: Morning			
B. Waites & K. Brown	0	L Wadkins & C. Stadler (1 hole)	1
N. Faldo & B. Langer (4 & 2)	1	B. Crenshaw & C. Peete	0
S. Ballesteros & P. Way (halved)	½	G. Morgan & J. Haas (halved)	½
S. Torrance & I. Woosnam	0	T. Watson & B. Gilder (5 & 4)	1
Foursomes: Afternoon			
N. Faldo & B. Langer (3 & 2)	1	T. Kite & R. Floyd	0
S. Torrance & J.M. Cañizares	0	G. Morgan & L. Wadkins (7 & 5)	1
S. Ballesteros & P. Way (2 & 1)	1	T. Watson & B. Gilder	0
B. Waites & K. Brown	0	J. Haas & C. Strange (3 & 2)	1
Singles:			
S. Ballesteros (halved)	½	F. Zoeller (halved)	½
N. Faldo (2 & 1)	1	J. Haas	0
B. Langer (2 holes)	1	G. Morgan	0
G. J. Brand	0	B. Gilder (2 holes)	1
A. Lyle	0	B. Crenshaw (3 & 1)	1
B. Waites	0	C. Peete (1 hole)	1
P. Way (2 & 1)	1	C. Strange	0
S. Torrance (halved)	½	T. Kite (halved)	½
I. Woosnam	0	C. Stadler (3 & 2)	1
J.M. Cañizares (halved)	½	L. Wadkins (halved)	½
K. Brown (4 & 3)	1	R. Floyd	0
B. Gallacher	0	T. Watson (2 & 1)	1
Europe 13½		**US 14½**	

1985

13–15 September

The Belfry Golf & Country Club, Sutton Coldfield, West Midlands, England
Captains, A. Jacklin (Europe), L. Trevino (US)

Europe		United States	
Foursomes: Morning			
S. Ballesteros & M. Pinero (2 & 1)	1	C. Strange & M. O'Meara	0
B. Langer & N. Faldo	0	C. Peete & T. Kite (3 & 2)	1
A. Lyle & K. Brown	0	L. Wadkins & R. Floyd (4 & 3)	1
H. Clark & S. Torrance	0	C. Stadler & H. Sutton (3 & 2)	1
Fourballs: Afternoon			
P. Way & I. Woosnam (1 hole)	1	F. Zoeller & H. Green	0
S. Ballesteros & M. Pinero (2 & 1)	1	A. North & P. Jacobsen	0
B. Langer & J.M. Cañizares (halved)	½	C. Stadler & H. Sutton (halved)	½
S. Torrance & H. Clark	0	R. Floyd & L. Wadkins (1 hole)	1
Fourballs: Morning			
S. Torrance & H. Clark (2 & 1)	1	T. Kite & A. North	0
P. Way & I. Woosnam (4 & 3)	1	H. Green & F. Zoeller	0
S. Ballesteros & M. Pinero	0	M. O'Meara & L. Wadkins (3 & 2)	1
B. Langer & A. Lyle (halved)	½	C. Stadler & C. Strange (halved)	½
Foursomes: Afternoon			
J.M. Cañizares & J. Rivero (4 & 3)	1	T. Kite & C. Peete	0
S. Ballesteros & M. Pinero (5 & 4)	1	C. Stadler & H. Sutton	0
P. Way & I. Woosnam	0	C. Strange & P. Jacobsen (4 & 2)	1
B. Langer & K. Brown (3 & 2)	1	R. Floyd & L. Wadkins	0
Singles:			
M. Pinero (3 & 1)	1	L. Wadkins	0
I. Woosnam	0	C. Stadler (2 & 1)	1
P. Way (2 holes)	1	R. Floyd	0
S. Ballesteros (halved)	½	T. Kite (halved)	½
A. Lyle (3 & 2)	1	P. Jacobsen	0
B. Langer (5 & 4)	1	H. Sutton	0
S. Torrance (1 hole)	1	A. North	0
H. Clark (1 hole)	1	M. O'Meara	0
J. Rivero	0	C. Peete (1 hole)	1
N. Faldo	0	H. Green (3 & 1)	1
J.M. Cañizares (2 holes)	1	F. Zoeller	0
K. Brown	0	C. Strange (4 & 2)	1
Europe 16½		**US 11½**	

1987

25–27 September

Muirfield Village, Columbus, Ohio, USA
Captains: A. Jacklin (Europe), J. Nicklaus (US)

Europe		United States	
Foursomes: Morning			
S. Torrance & H. Clark	0	C. Strange & T. Kite (4 & 2)	1
K. Brown & B. Langer	0	H. Sutton & D. Pohl (2 & 1)	1
N. Faldo & I. Woosnam (2 holes)	1	L. Wadkins & L. Mize	0
S. Ballesteros & J.M. Olazábal (1 hole)	1	L. Nelson & P. Stewart	0
Fourballs: Afternoon			
G. Brand, Jr. & J. Rivero (3 & 2)	1	B. Crenshaw & S. Simpson	0
A. Lyle & B. Langer (1 hole)	1	A. Bean & M. Calcavecchia	0
N. Faldo & I. Woosnam (2 & 1)	1	H. Sutton & D. Pohl	0
S. Ballesteros & J.M. Olazábal (2 & 1)	1	C. Strange & T. Kite	0
Foursomes: Morning			
J. Rivero & G. Brand, Jr.	0	C. Strange & T. Kite (3 & 1)	1
N. Faldo & I. Woosnam (halved)	½	H. Sutton & L Mize (halved)	½
A. Lyle & B. Langer (2 & 1)	1	L. Wadkins & L. Nelson	0
S. Ballesteros & J.M. Olazábal (1 hole)	1	B. Crenshaw & P. Stewart	0
Fourballs: Afternoon			
N. Faldo & I. Woosnam (5 & 4)	1	C. Strange & T. Kite	0
E. Darcy & G. Brand, Jr.	0	A. Bean & P. Stewart (3 & 2)	1
S. Ballesteros & J.M. Olazábal	0	H. Sutton & L. Mize (2 & 1)	1
S. Lyle & B. Langer (1 hole)	1	L. Wadkins & L. Nelson	0
Singles			
I. Woosnam	0	A. Bean (1 hole)	1
H. Clark (1 hole)	1	D. Pohl	0
S. Torrance (halved)	½	L. Mize (halved)	½
N. Faldo	0	M. Calcavecchia (1 hole)	1
J.M. Olazábal	0	P. Stewart (2 holes)	1
J. Rivero	0	S. Simpson (2 & 1)	1
A. Lyle	0	T. Kite (3 & 2)	1
E. Darcy (1 hole)	1	B. Crenshaw	0
B. Langer (halved)	½	L. Nelson (halved)	½
S. Ballesteros (2 & 1)	1	C. Strange	0
K. Brown	0	L. Wadkins (3 & 2)	1
G. Brand, Jr. (halved)	½	H. Sutton (halved)	½
Europe 15		**US 13**	

1989

22–24 September

The Belfry Golf & Country Club, Sutton Coldfield, West Midlands, England
Captains: A. Jacklin (Europe), D. Stockton (US)

Europe		United States	
Foursomes: Morning			
N. Faldo & I. Woosnam (halved)	½	T. Kite & C. Strange (halved)	½
H. Clark & M. James	0	L. Wadkins & P. Stewart (1 hole)	1
S. Ballesteros & J.M. Olazábal (halved)	½	T. Watson & C. Beck (halved)	½
B. Langer & R. Rafferty	0	M. Calcavecchia & K. Green (2 & 1)	1
Fourballs: Afternoon			
S. Torrance & G. Brand, Jr. (1 hole)	1	C. Strange & P. Azinger	0
H. Clark & M. James (3 & 2)	1	F. Couples & L. Wadkins	0
N. Faldo & I. Woosnam (2 holes)	1	M. Calcavecchia & M. McCumber	0
S. Ballesteros & J.M. Olazábal (6 & 5)	1	T. Watson & M. O'Meara	0
Foursomes: Morning			
I. Woosnam & N. Faldo (3 & 2)	1	L. Wadkins & P. Stewart	0
G. Brand, Jr. & S. Torrance	0	C. Beck & P. Azinger (4 & 3)	1
C. O'Connor, Jr. & R. Rafferty	0	M. Calcavecchia & K. Green (3 & 2)	1
S. Ballesteros & J.M. Olazábal (1 hole)	1	T. Kite & C. Strange	0
Fourballs: Afternoon			
N. Faldo & I. Woosnam	0	C. Beck & P. Azinger (2 & 1)	1
B. Langer & J.M. Cañizares	0	T. Kite & M. McCumber (2 & 1)	1
H. Clark & M. James (1 hole)	1	P. Stewart & C. Strange	0
S. Ballesteros & J.M. Olazábal (4 & 2)	1	M. Calcavecchia & K. Green	0
Singles			
S. Ballesteros	0	P. Azinger (1 hole)	1
B. Langer	0	C. Beck (3 & 2)	1
J.M. Olazábal (1 hole)	1	P. Stewart	0
R. Rafferty (1 hole)	1	M. Calcavecchia	0
H. Clark	0	T. Kite (8 & 7)	1
M. James (3 & 2)	1	M. O'Meara	0
C. O'Connor, Jr. (1 hole)	1	F. Couples	0
J.M. Cañizares (1 hole)	1	K. Green	0
G. Brand, Jr.	0	M. McCumber (1 hole)	1
S. Torrance	0	T. Watson (3 & 1)	1
N. Faldo	0	L. Wadkins (1 hole)	1
I. Woosnam	0	C. Strange (2 holes)	1

Europe 14	**US 14**

1991

13–15 September

The Ocean Course, Kiawah Island, South Carolina, USA
Captains: B. Gallacher (Europe), D. Stockton (US)

Europe		United States	
Foursomes: Morning			
S. Ballesteros & J.M. Olazábal (2 & 1)	1	P. Azinger & C. Beck	0
B. Langer & M. James	0	R. Floyd & F. Couples (2 & 1)	1
D. Gilford & C. Montgomerie	0	L. Wadkins & H. Irwin (4 & 2)	1
N. Faldo & I. Woosnam	0	P. Stewart & M. Calcavecchia (1 hole)	1
Fourballs: Afternoon			
S. Torrance & D. Feherty (halved)	½	L. Wadkins & M. O'Meara (halved)	½
S. Ballesteros & J.M. Olazábal (2 & 1)	1	P. Azinger & C. Beck	0
S. Richardson & M. James (5 & 4)	1	C. Pavin & M. Calcavecchia	0
N. Faldo & I. Woosnam	0	R. Floyd & F. Couples (5 & 3)	1
Foursomes: Morning			
D. Feherty & S. Torrance	0	H. Irwin & L. Wadkins (4 & 2)	1
M. James & S. Richardson	0	M. Calcavecchia & P. Stewart (1 hole)	1
N. Faldo & D. Gilford	0	P. Azinger & M. O'Meara (7 & 6)	1
S. Ballesteros & J.M. Olazábal (3 & 2)	1	F. Couples & R. Floyd	0
Fourballs: Afternoon			
I. Woosnam & P. Broadhurst (2 & 1)	1	P. Azinger & H. Irwin	0
B. Langer & C. Montgomerie (2 & 1)	1	C. Pavin & S. Pate	0
M. James & S. Richardson (3 & 1)	1	L. Wadkins & W. Levi	0
S. Ballesteros & J.M. Olazábal (halved)	½	P. Stewart & F. Couples (halved)	½
Singles			
N. Faldo (2 holes)	1	R. Floyd	0
D. Feherty (2 & 1)	1	P. Stewart	0
C. Montgomerie (halved)	½	M. Calcavecchia (halved)	½
J.M. Olazábal	0	P. Azinger (2 holes)	1
S.R. Richardson	0	C. Pavin (2 & 1)	1
S. Ballesteros (3 & 2)	1	W. Levi	0
I. Woosnam	0	C. Beck (3 & 1)	1
P. Broadhurst (3 & 1)	1	M. O'Meara	0
S. Torrance	0	F. Couples (3 & 2)	1
M. James	0	L. Wadkins (3 & 2)	1
B. Langer (halved)	½	H. Irvin (halved)	½
D. Gilford (halved)	½	S. Pate (halved)	½
		(Pate withdrew through injury)	

Europe 13½	**US 14½**

1993

26–28 September

The Belfry Golf & Country Club, Sutton Coldfield, West Midlands, England
Captains: B. Gallacher (Europe), T. Watson (US)

Europe		United States	
Foursomes: Morning			
S. Torrance & M. James	0	L. Wadkins & C. Pavin (4 & 3)	1
I. Woosnam & B. Langer (7 & 5)	1	P. Azinger & P. Stewart	0
S. Ballesteros & J.M. Olazábal	0	T. Kite & D. Love III (2 & 1)	1
N. Faldo & C. Montgomerie (4 & 3)	1	R. Floyd & F. Couples	0
Fourballs: Afternoon			
I. Woosnam & P. Baker (1 hole)	1	J. Gallagher, Jr. & L. Janzen	0
B. Langer & B. Lane	0	L. Wadkins & C. Pavin (4 & 2)	1
N. Faldo & C. Montgomerie (halved)	½	P. Azinger & F. Couples (halved)	½
S. Ballesteros & J.M. Olazábal (4 & 3)	1	D. Love III & T. Kite	0
Foursomes: Morning			
N. Faldo & C. Montgomerie (3 & 2)	1	L. Wadkins & C. Pavin	0
B. Langer & I. Woosnam (2 & 1)	1	F. Couples & P. Azinger	0
P. Baker & B. Lane	0	R. Floyd & P. Stewart (3 & 2)	1
S. Ballesteros & J.M. Olazábal (2 & 1)	1	D. Love III & T. Kite	0
Fourballs: Afternoon			
N. Faldo & C. Montgomerie	0	J. Cook & C. Beck (1 hole)	1
M. James & C. Rocca	0	C. Pavin & J. Gallagher, Jr. (5 & 4)	1
I. Woosnam & P. Baker (6 & 5)	1	F. Couples & P. Azinger	0
J.M. Olazábal & J. Haeggman	0	R. Floyd & P. Stewart (2 & 1)	1
Singles			
I. Woosnam (halved)	½	F. Couples (halved)	½
B. Lane	0	C. Beck (1 hole)	1
C. Montgomerie (1 hole)	1	L. Janzen	0
P. Baker (2 holes)	1	C. Pavin	0
J. Haeggman (1 hole)	1	J. Cook	0
M. James	0	P. Stewart (3 & 2)	1
C. Rocca	0	D. Love III (1 hole)	1
S. Ballesteros	0	J. Gallagher, Jr. (3 & 2)	1
J.M. Olazábal	0	R. Floyd (2 holes)	1
B. Langer	0	T. Kite (5 & 3)	1
N. Faldo (halved)	½	P. Azinger (halved)	½
S. Torrance*	½	L. Wadkins	½
(*S. Torrance retired due to injury; match halved)			

Europe 13	**US 15**

1995

22–24 September

Oak Hill Country Club, Rochester, New York, USA
Captains: B. Gallacher (Europe), L. Wadkins (US)

Europe		United States	
Foursomes: Morning			
N. Faldo & C. Montgomerie	0	C. Pavin & T. Lehman (1 hole)	1
S. Torrance & C. Rocca (3 & 2)	1	J. Haas & F. Couples	0
H. Clark & M. James	0	D. Love III & J. Maggert (4 & 3)	1
B. Langer & P.U. Johansson (1 hole)	1	B. Crenshaw & C. Strange	0
Fourballs: Afternoon			
D. Gilford & S. Ballesteros (4 & 3)	1	B. Faxon & P. Jacobsen	0
S. Torrance & C. Rocca	0	J. Maggert & L. Roberts (6 & 5)	1
N. Faldo & C. Montgomerie	0	F. Couples & D. Love III (3 & 2)	1
B. Langer & P.U. Johansson	0	C. Pavin & P. Mickelson (6 & 4)	1
Foursomes: Morning			
N. Faldo & C. Montgomerie (4 & 2)	1	C. Strange & J. Haas	0
S. Torrance & C. Rocca (6 & 5)	1	D. Love III & J. Maggert	0
I. Woosnam & P. Walton	0	L. Roberts & P. Jacobsen (1 hole)	1
B. Langer & D. Gilford (4 & 3)	1	C. Pavin & T. Lehman	0
Fourballs: Afternoon			
S. Torrance & C. Montgomerie	0	B. Faxon & F. Couples (4 & 2)	1
I. Woosnam & C. Rocca (3 & 2)	1	D. Love III & B. Crenshaw	0
S. Ballesteros & D. Gilford	0	J. Haas & P. Mickelson (3 & 2)	1
N. Faldo & B. Langer	0	C. Pavin & L. Roberts (1 hole)	1
Singles			
S. Ballesteros	0	T. Lehman (4 & 3)	1
H. Clark (1 hole)	1	P. Jacobsen	0
M. James (4 & 3)	1	J. Maggert	0
I. Woosnam (halved)	½	F. Couples (halved)	½
C. Rocca	0	D. Love III (3 & 2)	1
D. Gilford (1 hole)	1	B. Faxon	0
C. Montgomerie (3 & 1)	1	B. Crenshaw	0
N. Faldo (1 hole)	1	C. Strange	0
S. Torrance (2 & 1)	1	L. Roberts	0
B. Langer	0	C. Pavin (3 & 2)	1
P. Walton (1 hole)	1	J. Haas	0
P.U. Johansson	0	P. Mickelson (2 & 1)	1

Europe 14½	**US 13½**

1997 — 26–28 September

Valderrama Golf Club, Sotogrande, Spain
Captains: S. Ballesteros (Europe), T. Kite (US)

Europe		United States	
Fourballs: Morning			
J.M. Olazábal & C. Rocca (1-up)	1	D. Love III & P. Mickelson	0
N. Faldo & L. Westwood	0	F. Couples & B. Faxon (1-up)	1
J. Parnevik & P.U. Johansson (1-up)	1	T. Lehman & J. Furyk	0
B. Langer & C. Montgomerie		T. Woods & O'Meara (3 & 2)	1
Foursomes: Afternoon			
J.M. Olazábal & C. Rocca	0	S. Hoch & L. Janzen (1-up)	1
B. Langer & C. Montgomerie (5 & 3)	1	T. Woods & M. O'Meara	0
N. Faldo & L. Westwood (3 & 2)	1	J. Leonard & J. Maggert	0
I. Garrido & J. Parnevik (halved)	½	T. Lehman & P. Mickelson (halved)	½
Fourballs: Morning			
C. Montgomerie & D. Clarke (1-up)	1	F. Couples & D. Love III	0
I. Woosnam & T. Björn (2 & 1)	1	J. Leonard & B. Faxon	0
N. Faldo & L. Westwood (2 & 1)	1	T. Woods & M. O'Meara	0
J.M. Olazábal & I. Garrido (halved)	½	P. Mickelson & T. Lehman (halved)	½
Foursomes: Afternoon			
C. Montgomerie & B. Langer (1-up)	1	L. Janzen & J. Furyk	0
N. Faldo & L. Westwood	0	S. Hoch & J. Maggert (2 & 1)	1
J. Parnevik & I. Garrido (halved)	½	J. Leonard & T. Woods (halved)	½
J.M. Olazábal & C. Rocca (5 & 4)	1	D. Love III & F. Couples	0
Singles			
I. Woosnam	0	F. Couples (8 & 7)	1
P.U. Johansson (3 & 2)	1	D. Love III	0
C. Rocca (4 & 2)	1	T. Woods	0
T. Björn (halved)	½	J. Leonard (halved)	½
D. Clarke	0	P. Mickelson (2 & 1)	1
J. Parnevik	0	M. O'Meara (5 & 4)	1
J.M. Olazábal	0	L. Janzen (1-up)	1
B. Langer (2 & 1)	1	B. Faxon	0
L. Westwood	0	J. Maggert (3 & 2)	1
C. Montgomerie (halved)	½	S. Hoch (halved)	½
N. Faldo	0	J. Furyk (3 & 2)	1
I. Garrido	0	T. Lehman (7 & 6)	1
Europe 14½		**US 13½**	

1999 — 24–26 September

The Country Club, Brookline, Boston, Massachusetts, USA
Captains: M. James (Europe), B. Crenshaw (US)

Europe		United States	
Foursomes: Morning			
C. Montgomerie & P. Lawrie (1-up)	1	D. Duval & P. Mickelson	0
J. Parnevik & S. Garcia (2 & 1)	1	T. Lehman & T. Woods	0
M.A. Jiménez & P. Harrington (halved)	½	D. Love III & Stewart (halved)	½
D. Clarke & L. Westwood	0	H. Sutton & J. Maggert (3 & 2)	1
Fourballs: Afternoon			
C. Montgomerie & P. Lawrie (halved)	½	D. Love III & J. Leonard (halved)	½
J. Parnevik & S. Garcia (1-up)	1	P. Mickelson & J. Furyk	0
M.A. Jiménez & J.M. Olazábal (2 & 1)	1	H. Sutton & J. Maggert	0
D. Clarke & L. Westwood (1-up)	1	D. Duval & T. Woods	0
Foursomes: Morning			
C. Montgomerie & P. Lawrie	0	H. Sutton & J. Maggert (1-up)	1
D. Clarke & L. Westwood (3 & 2)	1	J. Furyk & M. O'Meara	0
M.A. Jiménez & P. Harrington	0	S. Pate & T. Woods (1-up)	1
J. Parnevik & S. Garcia (3 & 2)	1	P. Stewart & J. Leonard	0
Fourballs: Afternoon			
D. Clarke & L. Westwood	0	P. Mickelson & T. Lehman (2 & 1)	1
J. Parnevik & S. Garcia (halved)	½	D. Love III & D. Duval (halved)	½
M.A. Jiménez & J.M. Olazábal (halved)	½	J. Leonard & H. Sutton (halved)	½
C. Montgomerie & P. Lawrie (2 & 1)	1	S. Pate & T. Woods	0
Singles			
L. Westwood	0	T. Lehman (3 & 2)	1
D. Clarke	0	H. Sutton (4 & 2)	1
J. Sandelin	0	P. Mickelson (4 & 3)	1
J. Van de Velde	0	D. Love III (6 & 5)	1
A. Coltart	0	T. Woods (3 & 2)	1
J. Parnevik	0	D. Duval (5 & 4)	1
P. Harrington (1-up)	1	M. O'Meara	0
M.A. Jiménez	0	S. Pate (2 & 1)	1
J.M. Olazábal (halved)	½	J. Leonard (halved)	½
C. Montgomerie (1-up)	1	P. Stewart	0
S. Garcia	0	J. Furyk (4 & 3)	1
P. Lawrie (4 & 3)	1	J. Maggert	0
Europe 13½		**US 14½**	

2002

The Belfry Golf & Country Club, Sutton Coldfield, West Midlands, England
Captains: S. Torrance (Europe), C. Strange (US)

Europe		United States	
Foursomes: Morning			
D. Clarke & T. Bjorn (1-up)	1	T. Woods & P. Azinger	0
S. Garcia & L. Westwood (4 & 3)	1	D. Duval & D. Love III	0
C. Montgomerie & B. Langer (4 & 3)	1	S. Hoch & J. Furyk	0
P. Harrington & N. Fasth	0	P. Mickelson & D. Toms (1-up)	1
Fourballs: Afternoon			
D. Clarke & T. Bjorn	0	H. Sutton & S. Verplank (2 & 1)	1
S. Garcia & L. Westwood (2 & 1)	1	T. Woods & M. Calcavecchia	0
C. Montgomerie & B. Langer (halved)	½	P. Mickelson & D. Toms (halved)	½
P. Harrington & P. McGinley	0	S. Cink & J. Furyk (3 & 2)	1
Foursomes: Morning			
P. Fulke & P. Price	0	P. Mickelson & D. Toms (2 & 1)	1
L. Westwood & S. Garcia (2 & 1)	1	S. Cink & J. Furyk	0
C. Montgomerie & B. Langer (1-up)	1	S. Verplank & S. Hoch	0
D. Clarke & T. Bjorn	0	T. Woods & D. Love III (4 & 3)	1
Fourballs: Afternoon			
N. Fasth & J. Parnevik	0	M. Calcavecchia & D. Duval (1-up)	1
C. Montgomerie & P. Harrington (2 & 1)	1	P. Mickelson & D. Toms	0
S. Garcia & L. Westwood	0	T. Woods & D. Love III (1-up)	1
D. Clarke & P. McGinley (halved)	½	S. Hoch & J. Furyk (halved)	½
Singles			
C. Montgomerie (5 &4)	1	S. Hoch	0
S. Garcia	0	D. Toms (1-up)	1
D. Clarke (halved)	½	D. Duval (halved)	½
B. Langer (4 & 3)	1	H. Sutton	0
P. Harrington (5 & 4)	1	M. Calcavecchia	0
T. Bjorn (2 & 1)	1	S. Cink	0
L. Westwood	0	S. Verplank (2 & 1)	1
N. Fasth (halved)	½	P. Azinger (halved)	½
P. McGinley (halved)	½	J. Furyk (halved)	½
P. Fulke (halved)	½	D. Love III (halved)	½
P. Price (3 & 2)	1	P. Mickelson	0
J. Parnevik (halved)	½	T. Woods (halved)	½
Europe 15½		**US 12½**	

2004

Oakland Hills Country Club, Bloomfield Township, Michigan, USA
Captains: B. Langer (Europe), H. Sutton (US)

Europe		United States	
Fourballs: Morning			
C. Montgomerie & P. Harrington (2 & 1)	1	T. Woods & P. Mickelson	0
D. Clarke & M.A. Jimenéz (5 & 4)	1	C. Campbell & D. Love III	0
P. McGinley & Luke Donald (halved)	½	C. Riley & S. Cink (halved)	½
S. Garcia & L. Westwood (5 & 3)	1	D. Toms & J. Furyk	0
Foursomes: Afternoon			
M.A. Jimenéz & T. Levet	0	C. DiMarco & J. Haas (3 & 2)	1
C. Montgomerie & P. Harrington (4 & 2)	1	D. Love III & F. Funk	0
D. Clarke & L. Westwood (1-up)	1	P. Mickelson & T. Woods	0
S. Garcia & L. Donald (2 & 1)	1	K. Perry & S. Cink	0
Fourballs: Morning			
S. Garcia & L. Westwood (halved)	½	C. DiMarco & J. Haas (halved)	½
D. Clarke & I. Poulter	0	T. Woods & C. Riley (4 & 3)	1
P. Casey & D. Howell (1-up)	1	J. Furyk & C. Campbell	0
C. Montgomerie & P. Harrington	0	S. Cink & Davis Love III (3 & 2)	1
Foursomes: Afternoon			
D. Clarke & L. Westwood (5 & 4)	1	J. Haas & C. DiMarco	0
M.A. Jimenéz & T. Levet	0	P. Mickelson & D. Toms (4 & 3)	1
S. Garcia & L. Donald (1-up)	1	J. Furyk & F. Funk	0
P. Harrington & P. McGinley (4 & 3)	1	Davis Love III & T. Woods	0
Singles			
P. Casey	0	T. Woods (3 & 2)	1
S. Garcia (3 & 2)	1	P. Mickelson	0
D. Clarke (halved)	½	D. Love III (halved)	½
D. Howell	0	J. Furyk (6 & 4)	1
L. Westwood (1-up)	1	K. Perry	0
C. Montgomerie (1-up)	1	D. Toms	0
L. Donald	0	C. Campbell (5 & 3)	1
M.A. Jimenéz	0	C. DiMarco (1-up)	1
T. Levet (1-up)	1	F. Funk	0
I. Poulter (3 & 2)	1	C. Riley	0
P. Harrington (1-up)	1	J. Haas	0
P. McGinley (3 & 2)	1	S. Cink	0
Europe 18½		**US 9½**	

Index

Note: page references in *italics* indicate
illustrations.

Aaron, Tommy 102, *104*, 104
ABC Television 128
Adams, Jimmy *44*, *45*, 45, 46, 49, 50, 52, 56, 57, 58
Aldington, Lord 116
Alexander, Skip 49
Alliss, Percy 22, 23, 26, *26*, 27, 32, 33, 36, 37, 40, 56
Alliss, Peter 56–7, 59, 61, 65, 66, 67–8, 73, *76*, 77, 78, 83, *83*, 88, 90, 91, 92, 96, 116
Andrew, Prince, Duke of York *175*
appearance money 116–17, 121
Archer, George 95
Armour, Tommy 15, 27, 41
autographs 153, 197
Azinger, Paul 136, 138, 139, 144–5, 153, 155, 156, 161, 187, 188, 192

Baker, Peter *149*, 150, 155, 156, 157, *157*
ball size 83, 90, 93, 94–5
Ballantine, Jock 48
Ballesteros, Severiano 112, 113, 115, 116–17, 120, 121, 121, *122*, 122–3, 124, 125, 126, 132, 134, 137, *137*, 138, 139, *143*, 143, 144, 145, 146, 147, 150, 155, 157, 162, 163, 169, 170–1, *171*, 174, 175, 176, *177*, 178
Bannerman, Harry 98
Barber, Jerry 61, 62, 63, 72, 73, 76, 77, *79*
Barber, Miller 95, 99
Barnes, Brian 95, 102, 103, 104, 105–6, 107, 109, 115, 116
Barnes, Jim 14, 15, 27
Barron, Herb 45–6
Bean, Andy 113, 131, 132, 133

Beard, Frank 99
Beck, Chip 136, 137, 138, 140, 142, *144*, 144, 146, 153, 155–6, 157
Belfry, The 116, 124–7, 136–41, 148–61, 186–93
Bell's (Scotch whisky company) 121
Bembridge, Maurice 95, 96, 99, 100, 102
Berkemo, Walter 55, *55*, 57
Binnie-Clark, R. 85
Björn, Thomas 176, 188, 189, 191, 195
Blancas, Homero 102, 104
Bollanack, Michael 147, 185
Bolt, Tommy 61, 62–3, 66, 67, 69
Boomer, Aubrey 20, 22, 24, 25, 26, 27, 30, 35
Boros, Julius 65, 72, 83, 87, 88, 89, 91, *91*
Bousfield, Ken 49, 52, 61, 66, 68–9, *76*, 77
Boyle, Hugh 91, 92
Brabazon, Lord, of Tara 63, 74
Bradshaw, Harry 57, 59, 67, 70
Braid, James 12, 14, 30, 116
Brand, Gordon J. 121
Brand, Gordon, Jr. 131, 132, 138
Brewer, Gay 91, 102
Broadhurst, Paul 143, 145, 146
Brookline (The Country Club course) 178–85
Brown, Eric 57, 58, 62, 63, 66, 67, *67*, 73, 95, 96, 98, 99, 100
Brown, Ken 109, 113, *114*, 114–15, 121, 122, 123, 124, 129
Burke, Billy 28, 30
Burke, Jack 51, 52, 57, 58, 62–3, 65, 66, 67, 102, 103, 118
Burns, Stewart 22, 23
Burton, Dick 38, 40, 42, 47, 49, 50
Bush, George, Sr. 175, *175*, 189
Bush, George W. 179
Busson, Jack 36

Butler, Brian 112
Butler, Peter 86, 88, 99, 103

caddies 121
Calcavecchia, Mark 129, 131, 133, 137, *138*, 139, 140, 146, 147, 188, 190, 191
Caldwell, Robert 45, 46
Campbell, Chad 198, 200
Campbell, Guy 33
Cañizares, José-Maria 118, 119, 122, 123, 127, *135*, 139, 140
captains, non-playing 80
Carr, Joe 86
Casey, Paul 199, 200
Casper, Billy 72, 76, 88, 91, 96–7, 99, 102, 104, 113, 115
Caygill, Alex 95
Champions Golf Club 90–3
Charles, Bob 73
Cink, Stewart 191, 195, 200
Clark, Clive 102, 103
Clark, Howard 109, 117, 127, 129, *130–1*, 133, 136, 139, 140, *163*
Clarke, Darren 179, 188, *188*, 189, 190, 191, 198, 199, 200
Clinton, Bill 152–3
clothing 129
clubs (equipment)
  legality questioned 45, 47–8
  metal shafts 23–4
clubs (organisations)
  early players' dependence on 16
Coles, Neil *76*, 77, 78, 80, 82, 88, 92, 95, 96, 99, 100, 102, 103, 109, *109*, 117
Collins, Bill 76, 77
Coltart, Andrew 179, 182
commercialization 129
Commonwealth players 73, 74, 111
Compston, Archie 20, 22, 24, *24*, 25

Coody, Charles 99
Cook, John 152, 153, 155–6
Cotton, Henry 22–3, 25, 26–7, 30, 34, 35, 38, 39, *39*, 40, 43, 45, 46, 48, 52, 55–6, *56*, 57–8, *59*, 61, 83, 95
Cotton, Toots 45, 58
Country Life 28–9
Couples, Fred 136, 140, 144, 145, *146*, 146, 155, 156, 157, 163, 169, 171, 174, 175
Cox, Whiffy 28
Crawley, Leonard 48, 51, 73
Crenshaw, Ben 123, 131, 132, 133–4, *134*, 150, 179, 180, 184–5, 191

Daily Mail 79
Daily Telegraph 44, 185, 188
Dalmahoy golf course 85
Daly, Fred 43, 45, 46, 49, 50, 52, 53, 57, 58, 64
Daly, John 142, 151
Darcy, Eamonn 105, 109, 129, 132, 133–4
Darwin, Bernard 11, 21, 30, 33, 39, 47–8
Davies, W.H. 28
Dawson, Peter 109
Demaret, Jimmy *45*, 45, 46, *46*, 49, 50, 52–3
Derby, Lord 96, 111–12
Dickinson, Gardner 91, 92, 100
Diegel, Leo 24–5, 28
DiMarco, Chris 196
Donald, Luke 195–6, *196*
Douglas, Dale 56–7, 59
Drew, Norman 70, 73
Drobny, Jaraslov 54
Dudley, Ed 25, 39, 40
Duncan, George 11, 12, 14, 15, 20, 22, 23, 24, 25, *25*, 27, 28
Dunlop Masters tournament 65, 91
Dutra, Olin 30, 32–3, 36
Duval, David 179, 190, 191

East Lake Country Club 80–3
Easterbrook, Syd 28, 33
Edward, Prince of Wales 32, 33, *33*
Edwards, Bruce *151*, 158
Elder, Lee 113, 115
Eldorado Country Club 70–3

Espinosa, Al 24–5
European players
    decision to include in Ryder Cup 111–13
European Tournament Players Division 116
Exclusive Press Features Ltd 85
exhibitions, trade 85

Faldo, Nick 109–10, *110*, 115, 118, 119, 122, 123, 124, 129, 131, 133, *133*, 137, 138, 139, 140, 143, 144–5, 146, 148, 150, *154*, 155–6, 159, 161, 162, 163, 164, 165–8, *166*, *167*, 169, 170, 174, 179, 185, 185, 195
Fallon, Johnny 61–2, 80, 82, 83
Farrell, Johnny 24, *24*, 25, 28
Fasth, Niclas 189, 190, 192
Faulkner, Max *45*, 45, *48*, 49–50, 52, *53*, 57, 58, 66, *66*, 69, 70
Faxon, Brad 163, 169, 174, 176
Feherty, David 143, 146
financing 10, 16–18, 23, 43, 60, 64, 84–5, 116, 121
Finsterwald, Dow 65, 66, 68, *72*, 73, 109, 110, 150
Floyd, Raymond 95, 109–10, 122, 123, 126, 129, 136–7, 139, 141, 142, 144, 145, 146, *146*, 150, 152, 156, 161
Forbes, Charles 56
Ford, Doug 61, 66, 68, 72, 73, 77, 78
fourball matches 20, 60, 74, 80, 82, 92, 100
Fraser, Leo 94
Freedman, Lou 72
French, Emmett 11
Fulke, Pierre 189, 192
Furgol, Ed 65, 67, 68
Furgol, Marty 61, 63
Furyk, Jim 190, 192, 195, 198, 200

Gadd, George 19, 20
Gallacher, Bernard 95, 96, 100, 102, 103, 104, 106, 109, 110, 115, 121, 122, 123, 140, 141, 143, 144, 145–6, 150–1, 154–5, 156, 157, 162–4, 165, *168*, 168–9, *169*
Gallagher, Jim, Jr. 152, *152*, 169
Ganton Golf Club 47–50

Garcia, Sergio 179, *182*, 187, 188, *189*, 191, 192, 196, 197, 198, *198*, 200
Garner, John 98, 100
Garrido, Antonio *112*, 113, 115
Geiberger, Al 91, 92
General Strike 14
Gibson, George 80
Gilder, Bob 121, 122, 123
Gilford, David 143, 144–5, 146, 163
Glasgow Herald 37
Glasgow Herald 1000 Guineas 11
Gleneagles (Kings Course) 10–11
Glenmuir (company) 129
Golden, Johnny 19, 25
Golf Illustrated 14, 21, 26, 37, 48, 52, 74, 78, 83
    contributes to cost of trophy 15
    tries to raise finances 16–18, 23
Golf Monthly 14, 20, 39
Goodman, Johnny 30
Goodwin, Stuart 64, 84
Graham, Lou 102, 106, 109
Green, Eric 46
Green, Hubert 109, 115, 124, 125
Green, Ken 136, 137, 139, 140
Greenbrier, The 111–15
greens 93
Greenwood, George 13–14
Gregson, Malcolm 91, 92
Guldahl, Ralph 39, 40

Haas, Fred 59
Haas, Jay 121, 122–3, 163, 164, 168, 169, 195
Haeger, Ronald 70–1
Haeggman, Joakim 150–1
Hagen, Walter 10, 11, 12, 13, *14*, 14, 19, *19*, 20, 22, 23, 24, 25, *27*, 28, *28*, *29*, 30–2, 33, 35, 38, 39, 40–1, 41, 46
Haliburton, Tom *76*, 77, 78
Hamilton, Bob 49, 50
Harbert, Chick 61, *63*
Harnett, James 10
Harper, Chandler 61, 62
Harrington, Padraig 179, *182*, 189, 190, 191, 198
Harrison, E.J. ('Dutch') 46, 49–50, 55
Havers, Arthur 12, 14, 19, *27*, 28
Hawkins, Fred 65, 66, 67–8
Hayes, Mark 113

Heafner, Clayton 49, 50, 51, 52, 53
Heath and Heather Company 12, 13
Hebert, Jay 72, 73, 99
Hebert, Lionel 65, 68–9
Herd, Alex 14
Hill, Dave 96
Hill, John 12
Hilton, Harold 20
Hines, Jimmy 61
Hitchcock, Jimmy 86, 89
Hoch, Scott 176–7, 190, 191
Hodson, Bert 28
Hoffman, Harold 37
Hogan, Ben 42, 44, *44*, 45, *45*, 46, 47, *47*, 48, *48*, 49, 51, 52, 54–5, 65, 66, 90–1, 195
Horne, Reg 46
Horton, Tommy 102, 105
Houston *see* Champions Golf Club
Howell, David 199, 200
Hudson, Robert A. 43, 47, 60, *63*, 84
Huggett, Brian 80, 91, 92, 95, 96–7, 99, *99*, 100, 104, 106, 109, 110
Hunt, Bernard 57, 59, 61, 65, 66, 68, *68*, 72, *76*, 88, 92, 102, 103, 104, 105, 106, 112
Hunt, Geoffrey 80
Hunt, Guy 105, 107

International Management Group 129
Irwin, Hale 107, 109, 115, 145, 146–7, 148

Jacklin, Tony 90, 91, 92, 94, 95, 96, 97, *97*, 98, 99, 100, 101, 102, 104, 105, 106, 109, 110, 116, 117, 120–1, *121*, 122, 123, 124, 125, 126, *127*, 128–9, 132, 133, 134, 136, 138–9, 140, 141, 150
Jacobs, John 61, 62, 63, 113–15, 117, 118
Jacobs, Tommy 88, 89
Jacobson, Fredrik 195
Jacobson, Peter 124, 125, 126–7
James, Mark 109, 113, *114*, 114–15, 117, 139, 178, 179, *179*, 182, 183, 185
January, Don 88, 109
Janzen, Lee 152, 169, 171
Jermain, S.P. 10

Jiménez, Miguel-Angel 179, 196, 198, 200
Johansson, Per-Ulrik 151, 162, 175–6
Jolly, Herbert 19, 28
Jones, Bobby 13, 80
journeys 70–2, 80, 120–1

Keiser, Herman 46
Kiawah Island *see* Ocean Course
King, Sam 38, 40, 43, 45–6, 48, 49, 50
Kirkaldy, Andrew 11
Kirkwood, Joe 15
Kite, Tom 113, 115, 119, 122, 123, 126, 128, 129, *130–1*, 131, 137, 138–9, *139*, 140, 155, 171, 175, *176*, 177
Kroll, Ted *55*, 57, 58, 66, 67

Lacey, Arthur 52
Lafoon, Ky 36
Lamour, Dorothy 43
Lane, Barry 151, 157
Langer, Bernhard 117, 118, 119, 122, 123, 124, 125, 127, 129, 131, 132, *132*, 134, 136, 137, 139, 145, 146–7, *147*, 163, *165*, 176, 179, 189, 191, *191*, 192, 194, *195*, 195–6, 197, 199, 200, 201, *203*
Laurel Valley Golf Club 105–7
Lawrie, Paul 179, 182
Leadbetter, David 163
Lees, Arthur 45, 46, 48, *48*, 49, 50, 52, 53, 61, 62, 63
Lehman, Tom 163, 164, 171, 174, 179–80
Lema, Tony 81, *86*, 86, 88, 89
Leonard, Justin 171, 175, 176, 182–3, *183*, 187
Letters, John 72
Levet, Thomas 196, 200
Levi, Wayne 143, 146
Lietzke, Bruce 118
Lindrick Golf Club 64–9
Littler, Gene 76, 77, 78, *79*, 88, 92, 96, 106
Locke, Bobby 73
Longhurst, Henry 37, 51, 52, 59, 74, 77–8, 81, 89
Love, Davis, III 152, 155, 156, 157–61, *159*, 171, 175–6, 179, 189, 190, 192, 195, 198, 200

Love, Robin 155, 160
Lucas, P.B. ('Laddie') 93, 115
Lyle, Sandy 119, 121, 122, 124, 125, 126–7, 129, 131, *132*, 132, 136

McCormack, Mark 91, 129
McCumber, Mark 136, 139
MacFarlane, C.B. 37
McGee, Jerry 109
McGinley, Paul 190, 192, *193*, 201
Mackie, John 10
McLeod, Fred 15
Maggert, Jeff 163, 169, 182
Mahaffey, John 113, 115
Manero, Tony 39, 40
Mangrum, Lloyd 45, 49, 50, *50*, 52, 55, *55*, 57, 58, 59, *59*
Marr, Dave 87–8, 117, 118
Martin, Jimmy 86
Martin, Miguel Angel 170–1
Matthews, Stanley 54
Maxwell, Billy 81
Mayer, Dick 65, 66
media 85–6, *98*, 136
Melville, David 96
memorabilia *88*, *118*
   see also programmes
Mickelson, Amy *184*
Mickelson, Phil 163, 174, 189, 190, 191, 192, *192*, 194–5, 196, 197–8, 199, 200, 202
Middlecoff, Cary 49, 57, 58, 63, 65, 73
Miller, Johnny 107, 119
Mills, Peter 65, 67, 72
Mitchell, Abe *12*, 12, 13, 14, *15*, *17*, 18, 19, 22, 25, 30, *31*, 32–3
Mize, Larry 129, 131
Moffitt, Harry 69
Moffitt, Ralph *76*, 77, 78
Montgomerie, Colin 143, 145, 146, *154*, 155–6, 164, 174, 176–7, 179, 182, 185, 189, 190, 191, 192, 196, *197*, 197–8, 200–1, *201*
Moody, Orville 95
Moortown Golf Club 22–5
Morgan, Gil 113, 122–3
Morris, 'Old' Tom 101
Muirfield, Scotland 101–4
Muirfield Village, Ohio 128–35

Nagle, Kel 73
Nelson, Byron 39, 40, 44, 45–6, 86, 89
Nelson, Larry 113, 118, 124, 132, 134
Nichols, Bobby 91, 92
Nicklaus, Jack 86, 91, 94, 95, *95*, 96, 97, *97*, 99, 101, 102, 103, *105*, 106, 107, 109–10, 111–12, 118, 119, *119*, 120, 121, 123, 128, *128*, 129, 131, 132–3, *134*, 134, 151
North, Andy 124, 125, 127
North and South tournament 51

Oak Hill Country Club 162–9
Oakland Hills Country Club 194–203
Ocean Course 142–7, 148
O'Connor, Christy 61, 63, 66, 67, 68, 73, *76*, 77, 86, 88, 89, 91, 92, 96, 99, 100, 102, 103, 104
O'Connor, Christy, Jr. 105, 136, 140, *140*
Olazábal, José-Maria 129, 132, *135*, 137, 138, 139, 140, *143*, 144, *144*, 145, 150, 155, 161, 163, 170–1, 179, 182–3, 195
Old Warson Country Club 98–100
O'Leary, John 105
Oliver, Ed ('Porky') 45, 46, 52, 53, *55*, 56–7, *57*, 76
O'Meara, Mark 124, 125, 127, 145, 146, 182
Oosterhuis, Peter 98, 100, 106, 107, 109–10, *110*, 117, 118
Open Championship, British 12, 13, 34, 36, 42, 60, 85, 86, 101
Open Championship, US 20, 39, 42
Operation Desert Storm 142, 143
Order of Merit 120, 124

Padgett, Don 111
Padgham, Alf 32, 34, 38, 39, 40
Palm Beach Gardens *see* PGA National Golf Club
Palmer, Arnold 72, *75*, 76–7, 78, *79*, 81, *82*, 83, *83*, 87–8, *90*, 90, 91, 92, 99, 100, 102, *105*, 106, 107, 111
Palmer, Johnny 49, 50
Panton, John 52, 57, 58, 72, *76*, 78
Park, Brian 84–5, 90
Parks, Sam 36

Parnevik, Jesper 151, 170, 179, *180*, 187, 190, 191, 192
Pate, Jerry 119
Pate, Steve 142, 143, 145
Pavin, Corey 143, 145, *145*, 146, *152*, *154*, *157*, 164, 165
Peete, Calvin 121, 122, 123
Pennink, Frank 72
Perrins, Percy 19, 27
Perry, Alf 34, 36, 38
PGA *see* Professional Golfers' Association, British; Professional Golfers' Association, US
PGA Championship (US) 39
PGA National Golf Club 120–3
PGA Tour (European) 112, 113
PGA Tour (US) 169
Philpot, George 16–18, 20, 21, 23, 27
Pinehurst Country Club 51–3
Pinero, Manuel 118, 119, 125, 126
Platts, Lionel 86, 88
Player, Gary 73, 111
Pohl, Dan 129, 133
points system 108–9, 113
Polland, Eddie 102, 103
Portland Golf Club 42–6
Pott, Johnny 81, 86, 92
Poulter, Ian 187, 199
press *see* media
Price, Phillip 187, 189, 191, *192*, 192
Professional Golfers' Association, British
  and beginnings of Ryder Cup 13, 15, 16, 19
  and changeover to European team 111–13
  and changes in format 60, 74, 80, 108–9, 110, 111, 129
  Cotton's dispute with 26–7, 30
  elects first non-playing captain 30
  financial difficulties 23
  and illegal clubs controversy 47–8
  official delegations 80
  post-war difficulties 43
  selection procedures 49, 52, 55, 60–1, 65, 77, 105
  and US summer matches 29
Professional Golfers' Association, US
  and beginnings of Ryder Cup 10, 15, 19

  and changeover to European team 110, 111
  and changes in format 20, 108
  gifts to players 37
  penalizes Snead 75–6
  post-war fund-raising 43
  probationary rule 91
  proposes extension to four days 128–9
  selection procedures 39, 44, 49, 124
  wish to include fourball matches 20, 74, 80
professional status 17
programmes *49*, *52*, *64*, *85*, *85*, *93*, *100*
putting 21

Rafferty, Ronan 136, 137, *138*, 140, *140*
Ragan, Dave 81
Ransom, Henry 51, 52
Ray, Edward 10, *14*, 14, 19, *19*, 20–1
Rees, Dai 38, 40, 43, 45–6, *46*, 47, 48, 50, 52–3, *57*, 57, 58, 61, 63, 64, *63*, 65, 66–7, 68, *69*, 70, 72, 73, *76*, 77–8, 80, 90, 92, 93
Revolta, Johnny 36, *37*, 38, 40
Richardson, Steven 143, 146
Ridgewood Country Club 34–7
Riley, Chris 200
Rivero, José 124, 129–31, 132
Roberts, Loren 163
Robson, Fred *19*, 22, 25
Rocca, Costantino 151, 157–61, *158*, *164*, 176
Rodriguez, Chi Chi 102
Roe, R.C.T. 35, 41, 64, 72, *74*, 80
Rogers, Bill 118
Roosevelt, Franklin D. 40
Roosevelt, Theodore 161
Rosburg, Bob 72
Rose, Justin 187
Ross, Donald 51
Ross, Walter 10
Rotella, Bob 160
Royal and Ancient Golf Club of St Andrews 13, 15, 23, 42, 47
Royal Birkdale Golf Club 84–9, 94–7
Royal Lytham and St Annes 74–9, 108–11
Runyan, Paul 30
Ryder, James 11–12, 13–14

Ryder, Samuel A.
  background and instigation of Ryder
    Cup 11–12, *12*, *13*, 13–14, 15
  and finances of Ryder Cup 17, 84
  and first official Ryder Cup match
    17, *17*, 18
  and qualifications for playing in
    Ryder Cup 22, 27
  quoted 185
  as spectator at British matches 13, 25
Ryder Cup trophy 13, 15
Ryder Cup Trust Deed 27, 30, 80, 113
'resident' clause 25, 26, 30
Ryder-Scarfe, Joan 15, 113

St Andrews *see* Royal and Ancient Golf
  Club
St George's Hill Golf Club 14
St John, Lauren 145
Sandelin, Jarmo 179, 182
Sanders, Doug 91, *92*, 92
Sarazen, Gene 25, *32*, 32, 36, 39, 40, 49
Schneiter, George 44
Schofield, Ken 112, 117, 120
Scioto Country Club 26–9
Scott, Syd 61, 62, 63
Scott, Tom 78
selection procedures
  British 49, 52, 55, 60–1, 65, 77, 105
  European 120
  US 44, 49, 124
Senior Service tournament (1962) 85
September 11th terrorist attacks (2001)
  186
Shute, Densmore *27*, 28, 30, 33, 38, 40
Sikes, Dan 96
Simms, George 85
Simpson, Scott 129, 131
Smith, Horton 23–4, 32, 33, *36*, 39
Smyth, Des 115, 118, 119
Snape, Colin 128
Snead, Jesse 99, 100, 102, 104
Snead, Sam 39, 40, 45, 46, 49, 50, 51, 52,
  57, *57*, 58–9, 60, 61, 63, 65, 66,
  75–6, 95, 96
Sneed, Ed 109
Souchak, Mike 72, 77, *77*, 78
Southport and Ainsdale Golf Club
  30–3, 38–41
spectators 73, 85, 148, 169

sponsorship 116, 121
  see also Goodwin, Stuart; Hudson,
    Robert A.
Stadler, Craig 121, 122, 123, 125, *125*,
  126
Stain, Joe 15
Stark, Alick 30
stewards 85
Stewart, Payne 129, 132, 137, 138, 139,
  140, 145, 146, 147, *180–1*
Still, Ken 96
Stockton, Dave 99, 142, 143
Strange, Curtis 121, 123, 125, 126, 128,
  129, *130–1*, 131, 134, 137, 138, 139,
  139, 140–1, 163, 164, 165–8, 169,
  187, 188, 189, 190–1, 192–3
Sun Alliance 116
Sunningdale Golf Club 13
Sutton, Hal 124, 127, 131, 179, 182, *184*,
  191, 194–5, *195*, 196, 197, 198, 199,
  200, 201–2
Swedish players 151

'target' golf 128
Taylor, John Henry *11*, 12, 14, 30–2, 33,
  33, 56
team size 95
'Texan wedge' shot 58
Thomas, Dave 70, 87–8, 89, 91, 92, 116
Thompson, Peter 73, 111
Thunderbird Ranch and Country Club
  60–3
Toms, David 189, 190, 191, 195, 198,
  200–1
Torrance, Sam 118, 119, 122, 123, 126,
  127, 129, *130–1*, 138, 146, 153, 154,
  156, 185, 188, 190–1, 192
Townsend, Peter 95
Trevino, Lee 95, 96, 99, 100, 101–2, 106,
  106, 113, *114*, 115, 118, 119, 124,
  128
Turnesa, Jim *55*, 59
Turnesa, Willie 24, *24*

Valderrama Golf Club 170–7
Van de Velde, Jan 179, 182
Vardon, Harry 10, 11, *11*, 12, 14, 30
Venturi, Ken 86
Verplank, Scott 191

Verulum Golf Club 12, 14, 18

Wadkins, Lanny 109, 113, 115, 122,
  123, 125, 126, 128, 132, 135, 136,
  138, 140, *151*, 152, *154*, 156, 157,
  160, *160*, 163–4, 165, 166, 169
Waites, Brian 121, 122, 123
Walker Cup (1965) 86
Wall, Art 65, 66, 73, 78
Walton, Philip 168, *168*
Walton Heath Golf Club 116–19
Ward, Charlie 42, 45, 46, 49, 50, 52
Watson, Linda 155
Watson, Tom 6, 105, 109, 113, 116, *117*,
  118, 119, *119*, 123, 124, 129, 136–7,
  148, 150, 151–4, 155, 156, 157, 158,
  160, 161, *161*
Way, Paul 121, *122*, 122–3, 125, 126
weather, US 29
Weetman, Harry 52, *53*, 56–7, 58–9,
  62, *66*, 66–7, *76*, 78, 83, 86, 90
Weiskopf, Tom 102, 103, 104, 106, 107
Wentworth Golf Club 13–15, 54–9
Westwood, Lee 174, 179–80, 187, 188,
  189, 190, 191, 197, 198, *198*, 199
Whitcombe, Charlie 20, 22, 24, *24*, 25,
  28, *29*, 30, 32, 33, 34, 36, 38, 39, *39*,
  40, 48, 49
Whitcombe, Ernest 22, 25, 34, 36
Whitcombe, Reg 34, *37*
Will, George 80, 83, 87–8, 91
Williams, Roy 151
Wilson, Brownlow 37
Wilson, Harold 89
Wood, Craig 28, 30, 33
Wood, Norman 105
Woods, Tiger 170, 171, 174, *174*, 175,
  176, 179, *184*, 187, *187*, 188–9,
  190–1, 192, 194, 195, 196, *197*,
  197–8, 199, *199*, 200, 201–2
Woosnam, Ian 121, 123, 125, 126, 129,
  131, 132, 133, 137, 138, 139, 140–1,
  144, 145, 146, *149*, 156, 157, 162,
  163, *164*, 165, 168, 169, 175, 179, 195
Worcester Country Club 16–21
World War II 41, 42
Worsham, Lew 45, 46

Zoeller, Fuzzy 113, *114*, 114–15, 122,
  125, 127

ACKNOWLEDGEMENTS

The author would like to extend his sincere and grateful thanks to the following people: Rosemary Anstey; Robert Aziz; Gaston Barras, Canon European Masters; Peter Butler; Simon Caney, Editor, *Golf Weekly*; Rich Carr; Phoebe Clapham, Managing Editor, Aurum Press; Ian Connelly; Graham Coster, Editorial Director, Aurum Press; Scott Crockett, Golden Bear Inc.; David Cronin; Max Faulkner; Peter Fry; Bert Gadd; Matthew Harris; Michael Hobbs; Jock Howard, *Golf World*; John Huggan; Warren Humphreys; Bernard Hunt; John Jacobs; Michael King; Sam King; Renton Laidlaw; Bernhard Langer; Pete Masters, *Golf World*; Bill McCreadie, Managing Director, Aurum Press; Anne McDowall; Linda Milton, *Golf Weekly*; Mizuno; Ralph Moffatt; Peter Oosterhuis; PGA European Tour Media Department, especially Frances Jennings, Gordon Simpson, Vanessa Brannetti, Valerie Steele and Julie Medlock; Phil Pilley; Andy Prodger; Graham Rowley; Gill of the Phil Sheldon Golf Picture Library; John Sinnott; Sam Snead; Christina Steinmann; Charles H. Ward; Tim Ward; Bob Warters; Paul Way.

PICTURE CREDITS

The majority of the photographs in this book have been supplied by Concannon Golf History Collection at oldgolfimages.com: pages 10–117 (except as detailed below) and Matthew Harris/The Golf Picture Library at www.golfpicturelibrary.com: pages 1–9, 89, 101, 103, 109, 116, 121 and 125–218 (except as detailed below).

Other pictures have been supplied by Colorsport: page 97; Graham Rowley, offers4golf.com: early golf programmes on pages 49, 52, 58, 64, 85, 93, 98, 100, 105, 107 and 118; Phil Sheldon Golf Picture Library: pages 110, 112, 114, 119, 122, 126, 144, 147, 158, 167, 175 and 183; the Wentworth Club: page 15.

While every effort has been made to credit all of the images in this book, it has not always been possible to find the original copyright owner. The publisher will be happy to correct any omissions in future editions.